THE ILLUSTRATED STORY OF

JAZZ

KEITH SHADWICK

For Jay Coltrane and Louis Jerome who will one day laugh and say they were sure he never knew the half of it.

Editor Jenny Mulherin
Designer Simon Wilder
Picture Research Jackum Brown
Production Craig Chubb

This 1991 edition published by CRESCENT BOOKS distributed by Outlet Book Company, Inc.,
a Random House Company, 225 Park Avenue South, New York, New York 10003

Concept, design and production by Marshall Cavendish Books Limited,
119 Wardour Street, London W1V 3TD

First printing 1991

© Marshall Cavendish Limited 1991

Printed in Hong Kong

ISBN 0-517-06125-2

87654321

THE ILLUSTRATED STORY OF

KEITH SHADWICK

CRESCENT BOOKS
New York

foreword

Jazz could only have been invented in America. The cultural potpourri created there by mixing together slaves who had originated in different parts of Africa made a musical form of communication a necessity of survival. The new music's two main ingredients were the Christian hymnal forms of the masters and the slaves' African tribal rhythmic approach to them. Its main compositional devices, used by every jazzmen no matter his style, are the call and united response of the 'field hollers' chanted by slave workers as they toiled.

From these humble beginnings, jazz has grown to become an international art form, with great players from everywhere in the world. I know. I once had a European quartet who were as good a group of players as ever heard anywhere in the US.

Jazz continues to be the music most representative of freedom: it survived and even thrived in Poland, Yugoslavia, Czechoslovakia and other former Iron Curtain countries. Today, the US State Department has even recognized jazz as a goodwill ambassador (although it receives pitiably small amounts of grant money in recognition of this new status). It is now so popular that jazz education can be found at every school level. You can even major in jazz at most US universities; unfortunately, when you graduate you areunlikely to play it for a living – you have to teach it instead in order to survive.

No other segment of society has more heroic ideals than does the fraternity of jazz musicians. Generally, individuals are consumed with the irrepressible desire to play music from an early age – jazz is not usually meant for those who feel they have a choice in the matter. So if a student tell me he would like to be a jazzman, but is also toying with the possibility of becoming a brain surgeon, I usually advise him to opt for the latter occupation.

As an occupation, it is more dangerous than bomb demolition work, but not as steady, and the average lifespan of jazz musicians is a mere 42 years. In spite of this, jazz and its practitioners have changed the world of music as surely and as seriously as Bach and Beethoven ever did. An important consideration here is the number and quality of those musicians who have survived the rigours of the road *and* the indifference of their countrymen.

If anyone qualifies as the father of jazz it has to be Louis Armstrong. The art form as we know it today is relatively young, under one hundred years old, and 'Pops' was there at the beginning. He remained active and famous well into his seventies. Duke Ellington, too, was working, playing and writing right up to the coda. And although Bird's demise at 35 was a tragic loss, the still active Mr Benny Carter, in his ninth decade, is a big warm consolation. Anyone looking for a real life role model and a definition of dedication to music would do well to look here. Dizzy Gillespie, in his seventies, remains constantly at 35,000 feet above the ground and accumulates more bonus flight miles than many large-corporation executives.

The jazz community resembles a tribe and as such as evolved a wonderful oral tradition and expressiveness that has permeated the English language. 'Cool', 'hip', and 'hot' all come from the jazz world. I once asked Porter Kilbert, my alto sax man in Quincy Jones' band, how he felt: 'Phil, I feel so good, I could kick ass with a lion in a phone booth with a toothpick!' Man, that is feeling good!

A great deal of humour pervades the jazz scene, best represented perhaps by the legendary jazz violinist Joe Venuti, who sent Wingy Manone, the one-armed trumpet player, one cufflink for a Christmas present. Or by Al Cohn, the distinguished tenor man, who when asked if he had tried Elephant Beer, replied: 'No, man, I drink to forget!'

In spite of its proclaimed demise every seven years, jazz continues to excite the world. 'Jazz isn't dead. It just smells funny,' Frank Zappa once declared one one of these occasions when jazz appeared to be in the doldrums.

A poll of my countrymen once revealed the astonishing information that 98 per cent of Americans have no heroes. Well, the pollsters would have got a completly different result if they had questioned jazz fans. We have plenty of heroes, and most of them are featured in this book. Welcomes to the *Ilustrated Story of Jazz*, and to my heroes.

Phil Woods

Juke joint outside Clarksdale, Missouri 1939

contents

Jelly Roll Blues 1915

Dizzy Gillespie, Jimmy Rushing and Buck Clayton 1959

Bessie Smith

Joe Harriot with trumpeter Shake
Keane and drummer Tommy Jones

Ray Charles

Steve Williamson 1989

Donald and Albert
Ayler 1966

introduction

Although jazz is a relatively young musical form, its influence on this century's musical and cultural life has been so pervasive that there is very little popular music which does not trace its stylistic roots back to this unique American invention. In jazz and its close relation, blues, we have a perfect expression of the modern sensibility, and a music as complete in its emotional and intellectual range as humanity itself. That is the secret of its universal appeal.

This new telling of the music's story primarily depicts its stylistic evolution, but also attempts to place it against the social background from which it emerged. The music's origins and early history are as dominated by legend as they are by fact, but it will be my purpose in this book to get as close to the truth as current research and opinion allows: after all, the truth is colourful enough on its own! It is a cliché to talk of people as being 'larger than life', but there is no other phrase which so readily describes such early greats as Jelly Roll Morton, Buddy Bolden, Sidney Bechet and Louis Armstrong.

A word about the inevitable selectivity involved in any history of a music which has restrictions of space and time: this book was not written for experts, who will already know this story. It was written for people new to the music, or jazz-lovers with a new interest in unexplored areas of jazz and blues. There is always more to learn about the music, and I am sure I will continue to learn about it for the rest of my life. Consequently, some rather painful decisions had to be made on who to write about in detail, who to mention in passing, and who to silently pass by. Such decisions are in no way intended to be a dismissive comment on any of the musicians concerned: there are personal favourites of mine who go unnoticed here, but I had to keep to my criterion of inclusion: people who moved the music on, or had a wide influence on the mainstream of the music, or became written about. Others suffered the small indignity of my neglect.

I have a few special people to thank. Firstly, my father, Leonard Shadwick, who got me started, and my brother Ian, who never gave up on me, indirectly made this book possible. I also take pleasure in thanking my wife, Alison, whose perspicacity and exactness at every turn has made this history a far better thing than it began life as.

Jazz has often been talked of as a freedom music. This is true in many ways: certainly it is a style of music which gives its practitioners great expressive freedom as well as unique responsibilities. Jazz was born out of oppression and the spirit to survive and triumph over bitter adversity. It is the creation of black Americans, and has been at every stage a celebration of the lives of its creators. This musical language is one now spoken the world over, and in a real sense jazz is America's gift to world culture. This book will have achieved its aim if it inspires the reader to seek out the music itself, either to renew an old acquaintanceship, or to embrace it for the first time.

first flowering

'Basin Street is the street
where all the dark & the light folks meet
down in New Orleans – the land of dreams –
you'll never know how nice it seems
or just how much it really means'

W. C. Handy – *Basin Street Blues*

IMAGINE NEW Orleans on a hot summer evening in 1905: you're sitting on your verandah, or standing around on some street corner outside of the bar 'cause it's too hot to be inside. You're taking in the cooler night breeze, sipping a drink, jiving perhaps with friends. Then the music begins: sounds waft across the Mississippi water in that hot, close air: sounds from outdoor celebrations. There's a new music around, and your ear is catching it. Somebody says 'Buddy's playing at Johnson Park tonight', and you all crane in that direction, towards the far shore of the mighty river, as the heavy air and the smooth water amplify the sound. The excitement grows as the music starts to get through to you: you finish your drinks and set off to catch the streetcar out to the park on the other side of town, to have a 'funky' time with Buddy Bolden, King of New Orleans trumpeters . . .

Right: The New Orleans bands often evoked the steamboats in their stage act. This photograph from August 1915 shows Roy Palmer, Sugar Johnny and Lawrence Dewey fronting their band onstage against a backdrop of a venerable riverboat.

The black musical tradition in New Orleans was a very old one even in the days when jazz was first being conceived. Since the early 18th century, slave dancing, accompanied by African music, was a regular feature of huge negro gatherings in Congo Square (then known as Place Congo, echoing the city's French origins) on Sundays after late morning church services.

More than 500 blacks, descended from a whole range of African tribes, would meet up and dance from mid-afternoon till the late evening. Those who dropped out through sheer exhaustion would have their place taken by eager youngsters from the 2000 or so onlookers gathered to share the ritual celebrations. Drums, stringed instruments of African ancestry, and singing were all interwoven and heightened until a state of trance or ecstacy had been reached by the majority of the participants: then people would begin to fall, fainting, to the ground.

This practice was officially terminated in 1843 by city authorities, but the tradition was merely taken inside the church and sanctified. Independent of this, white-influenced musicians were playing and performing to large crowds of black people. The cross-fertilization of white and black cultures which was to eventually bring forth jazz had already begun.

It is fascinating to consider just how quickly jazz came into existence as a distinct musical form. In the last decade of the 19th century, most of the elements considered essential to an authentic jazz style existed in the music played by the blacks of New Orleans and its surrounding areas. However, the fusion of these elements was still some time away, and it was only through the innovative efforts of a few, select musicians that the

unique mix of rhythm, melody, harmony and instrumental expressiveness gelled in a musical alchemy during the first decade of the new century. Within a handful of years jazz would become a distinct music, and the word 'jazz' become descriptive of that music's vibrant message.

NEW ORLEANS – THE FIRST CITY OF JAZZ

So, what was so special about New Orleans? To understand this, one must look at the position of the majority of blacks in the southern states of the US who, until the American Civil War and its carthartic aftermath were slaves in lifetime bondage to white farmers and plantation owners. Under such conditions, the rich musical heritage from their African past remained remarkably complete.

This in itself is not surprising, considering the artificially closed and isolated communities these people inhabited. During the 40 or so years between Emancipation and the end of the century, there was a gradual quickening of pace in the assimilation of outside musical influences, and different streams of black music evolved, often directly related to geography and social position or utility. So it was that blues, the closest cousin of jazz, was probably in all major aspects fully formed in the rural South by around 1880, some 30 years before jazz came on the scene. It was the musical language of the poor and dispossessed country negro, mostly performed either for the player's own fulfilment, or for the local community, friends and family.

Music for another type of community was the work song, which has direct stylistic links with Africa. Used in thousands of work settings by groups of people

NEGRO PLANTATION WORKERS: **The conditions for negro plantation workers in the 1860s were harsh and oppressive. Often caught between the desire for a new life and the need to keep body and soul together, they had little choice but to accept their bitter lot. Although, as a result of the American Civil War (1860-1865), slavery officially came to an end in the US, the real chances for negroes to better themselves were very limited.**

often forced unwillingly to serve imposed masters, this rhythmically complex and sophisticated music was almost entirely functional. It was used by the work gangs, either convict or 'free', which were a permanent feature of 19th-century American life.

The radical changes in values and customs which occurred after the Civil War were especially significant for the newly-liberated

Shore work was one of the few job opportunities available to black men outside of the cotton fields. Below: a group of labourers stand and pose for the camera near their levee on the James River, Virginia.

negro population of the southern states. Although the majority remained inextricably bound to their white masters, whether the new 'carpetbaggers' from the north or the remnants of the old southern gentry, they were technically a free people, and a significant minority throughout the south took advantage of their newfound freedom to strike out for themselves.

One of the few trades which was open to the southern black in this period, apart from farming and the railway, was that of musician and entertainer. Naturally, the people being entertained

were black, and so it was from the pre-war black tradition that these new entertainers largely drew their styles and repertoires.

Along with the work songs and field hollers, the blues and spirituals, came the invigorating thrust of negro dance rhythms, often directly traceable back to West African ritual and work music, although often in greatly simplified form. And so the people of the outside world gradually became aware of such dance rhythms as the cakewalk, the jig or the buck-and-wing.

They were brought into contact with this exciting new develop-

ment through the minstrel shows and the brass bands, as well as the popular black song composers such as James Bland and the anonymous pianists in low-life dives and whorehouses. In fact, Bland and his fellow musician – composer – entertainer Samuel Lucas were to anticipate the curious acceptance which their jazz-playing descendants were to enjoy generations later when they toured Europe, and especially England. Bland found that there, for the first time in his career, he could dispense with the blackface makeup essential to his stage appearance in the US, and

he became a hugely popular singer-banjoist elegantly dressed onstage in evening wear. Lucas, meanwhile, was a tremendous hit in musical comedy, receiving a diamond cluster as a token of appreciation from none other than Queen Victoria herself.

These are two instances of the recognition and popularity accorded black musical forms in Europe in the 20 years either side of 1900. Another is the use of ragtime syncopation by classical composers such as Debussy in his *Golliwog's Cakewalk*, written in 1905, and by Stravinsky in three separate works composed

between 1918 and 1920. This was an appreciation unparalleled in American outside of Tin Pan Alley itself, which took a commercially-led interest in the music in the 20th century's first decade and then proceeded to take it over for its own ends.

By far the most popular black style of music in America prior to the development of jazz was ragtime. This was a style which in part reflected the upwards social thrust and aspirations of a better-educated new generation of negro musicians, while paradoxically also being looked down upon by the new black middle class as being forever associated with gin-joints, red-light districts and a dissolute way of life.

A piano-based music, it developed as a direct result of the urban and town-dwelling negro's absorption of both the African and the European traditions of music. Freely available to educated blacks through published sheet music, the popular white music of the time, such as Sousa marches, waltzes and polkas by Strauss and Lanner, and the more homegrown compositions of Stephen Foster, were widely played. These combined with the aural black tradition in vaudeville and dance music to create a new style which was adopted by musicians and composers throughout the southern states.

The key to ragtime's special identity, and consequently its eventual popular success throughout the world, was its constant use of syncopation. This newly-sprung rhythm, combined with the easy melodicism of popular European music and an uncomplicated harmonic approach, enabled this fresh, optimistic black creation to take the US (and, as we have seen, Europe as well) by storm. Within 12 months of the first publication of a ragtime song in 1897, it was a certified craze which had crossed over from the urban negro communities in the larger cities to the white population at large.

Ragtime was helped in its rapid dissemination by the dominance in every parlour of the family piano, on which the average middle-class child had to take at least a handful of lessons. Sheet music sales of this new, infectious style were phenomenal, with over one million copies of Scott Joplin's *Maple Leaf Rag* being sold in America alone. Joplin, incidentally, remained a composer true to ragtime for the whole of his career, and was an outstandingly brilliant man who not only wrote songs and instrumental pieces in the ragtime style, but also composed ragtime operas which, after many years of critical dismissal, have now been performed and recorded by first-rate classical music and opera companies.

Ragtime betrayed its European origins in the virtually complete absence of improvisation. This ran counter to the direction being taken by other contemporary negro music. Based on dance rhythms such as the jig, cakewalk and quadrille, with clear overtones of the military march, it happily embraced the disciplines of those forms, while unaccom-panied blues, work songs and percussion pieces allowed for a great deal more embellishment and interpretative licence.

Still, despite its popularity, ragtime was, with good reason, often associated in the minds of respectable, middle-class people with bordellos, bars, fast women and loose living. Somewhat less questionable was the music played by the black marching bands, partly because its social function was seen to be more useful to the community. Again a combination of African and European traditions, this music followed much more closely the ritualistic usages of its African parentage, combining the effect of the music with its social function within a simple ceremony, most often the funeral ceremony.

At its most basic level, a New Orleans funeral, for example, was not only a solemn wake on the journey to the graveyard and during the religious rites, but also, by contrast, a celebration of the deceased's life on the way back into town. These funerals, and the entertainments which followed, were not in any way casual affairs: they were planned meticulously, often by the funeral parlour itself in league with the deceased's relatives and personal club or association.

Jelly Roll Morton, one of jazz's first great pianists, composers and bandleaders, remembered these occasions vividly: 'You see, New Orleans was very organization-minded, which I guess the world knows, and a dead man always belonged to several organizations – secret orders and so forth and so on. So when anybody died, there was always a big band turned out on the day he was supposed to be buried. Never buried at night, always in the day ... Now those parades were really tremendous things ... [they all had] the second line, armed with sticks and bottles and baseball bats and all forms of ammunition ready to fight the foe when they reached the dividing line [between city districts]. It's a funny thing that the second line marched at the

PRIDE OF THE SOUTH: New Orleans was unique in US history as a city with an English, French, Spanish and African heritage. In the 19th century, it was one of the wealthiest cities in America, as the centre of the lucrative cotton trade (which, of course, was dependent on negro labour). It also had the mighty Mississippi at its heart (the paddle steamer, left, is making its way upstream in 1900) and a decidedly cosmopolitan urban architecture (right). After the Civil War, it dropped from third to twelfth place in the national rank. However, during the 20th century, it steadily prospered and is now a thriving, vibrant city with a flourishing tourist trade. It is renowned as one of the restaurant capitals of America and for its celebrated Mardi Gras annual street festival of music and theatre.

head of the parade, but that's the way it had to be in New Orleans. They were our protection. You see, whenever a parade would get to another district the enemy would be waiting at the dividing line. If the parade crossed that line it would mean a fight, a terrible fight.

'Well, if they had ten fights one Sunday, they didn't have many. Sometimes it would require a couple of ambulances to come around and pick up the people that was maybe cut or shot occasionally. This didn't happen all the time, but very seldom it didn't. The fact of it is, there was no parade at no time you couldn't find a knot on somebody's head where somebody had got hit with a stick or something. And always plenty to eat and drink, especially for the men in the band, and with bands like Happy Galloway's, Manuel Perez's and Buddy Bolden's we had the best ragtime music in the world.'

The parades alone could last all day, after which there would often be a hall hired for dancing until the early hours of the next morning. With the amount of festivals, the Club Parades and the funerals, there was plenty of work, for musicians although it was tremendously demanding on their energy and stamina. And at Mardi Gras time, few of them got to sleep before dawn.

In the last two decades of the 19th century, the music played on these occasions was a selection of 'light' classical music, marches, anthems and church hymns, mixed with folk material that could be adequately handled by the marching band instrumentation. This would all be played without any embellishment and with no attempt at syncopation. At the scene of the burial itself, the minister would read the funeral rites, there would be lamentations, then the band would start with the dead march, leading the mourners back to town. After a while, the tempo would pick up and the celebrations would begin. The music played on the way back from the ceremony would, at this stage, contain no improvisa-

Scott Joplin (right) *was not simply a Ragtime pianist and songwriter, with hits such as* The Entertainer. *He also composed an opera,* Treemonisha, *which has been successfully staged and recorded in the past two decades.*

tion, but would be a collection of vaudeville numbers, jigs, marches and dance steps, and would almost certainly have included syncopation. Certainly, by the close of the century, ragtime rhythm was widely used, and certain ragtime melodies became stock marching band numbers. Jelly Roll remembers a particular song always sung by the second line as soon as things picked up: in fact he later made it into a jazz piece –

> *Didn't he ramble?*
> *He rambled*
> *Rambled all around*
> *In and out of the town.*
> *Didn't he ramble?*
> *He rambled.*
> *He rambled till the butchers cut him down.*

As Jelly recalled, 'the snare drummer would make a hot roll on the drums and the boys in the band would just tear loose . . .'

Some of the main brass and concert band leaders in this pre-jazz period – because the bands which played at the funerals were also the ones which gave concerts and 'entertainments' – were people such as Sylvester Decker,

concert master of the Excelsior Band, Charlie Jaeger and Louis Martin. And by the late 1890s, amidst strong competition from such as John Robichaux and Manuel Perez, there emerged Buddy Bolden.

BUDDY BOLDEN, THE FIRST JAZZ LEGEND

It has been hotly debated for years as to whether the music Bolden and his band played was jazz. One thing, however, is certain: by the beginning of the new century, Bolden's low-down, 'gut-bucket' musical style and his charismatic personality had made such a deep impression on his audience that he was being hailed as the 'King' of the New Orleans music circuit. Many younger contemporaries of Bolden give him credit for being the first to combine previously disparate elements, notably blues and dance forms, and convincingly create something later recognized by all as the earliest strains of jazz.

This is, in fact, rather difficult to reconcile with the chronology of

jazz's emergence, as it is pretty well certain that even the word 'jazz' was not in use until about 1910-1911 as a means of describing a style of music, and by then Bolden had not played a note in public for at least four years. W.C. Handy, famous as the composer of *St Louis Blues* and many others, never referred to himself as anything but a novelty or minstrel musician in these early years, and in fact had never heard of New Orleans musicians such as Bolden. Still, the sheer vitality of Bolden's life and his music radiates through the anecdotes, and he deserves his place at the beginning of it all.

Buddy Bolden (1877-1931) has had so many colourful stories attached to him in the absence of generally accepted facts that people have written whole books exploding the myths and legends and trying to substantiate the precious few facts known about him. What has never been in dispute, however, is that his was an overpowering musical and personal presence in turn-of-the-century New Orleans. The sole surviving picture of him, taken with his band, shows a large,

well-built man with a full face and magnetic eyes. That he was a tremendously powerful player is attested by many of his contemporaries, with stories of him blowing the tuning slide out of his trumpet by the force of his playing, or literally beckoning revellers away from rival dances through the volume and vitality of his sound.

And when he was at one of his favourite places such as the Odd Fellows Hall, things got pretty wild, as clarinettist George Baquet recalls:

'Nobody took their hats off [always a sure sign of low life at this time] . . . You paid fifteen cents and walked in. The band, six of them was sitting on a low stand. They had their hats on and were resting, pretty sleepy. All of a sudden, Buddy stomps, knocks on the floor with his trumpet to give the beat and they all sit up straight. They played *Make Me A Pallet*. Everybody rose and yelled out "Oh, Mr Bolden, play it for us, Buddy, play it!" I'd never heard anything like that before. I'd played legitimate stuff. But this, it was something that pulled me in.'

Buddy had an open, friendly personality and was also quite a ladies' man, happy to have girls holding his handkerchief, coat or hat while he was busy with other things. At gigs, he would have more than one girlfriend hanging around the bandstand, and he was running around town with three or four women at once.

More than one contemporary remembers women giving him clothes, money and liquor. That in itself is enough to make him a memorable figure among his peers, although there is no actual evidence that he was a pimp at any stage. What makes the Bolden story doubly intriguing is that he was one of those gifted beings who burned out early.

By early 1906, when he was still only 28, he began to experience the onset of dementia, probably exacerbated by a lifestyle which was based on alcohol, the punishing routines of the professional musician working out of hotels, street parades, whorehouses and bars, and the stresses of trying to support a more-or-less legitimate family while living such a dissolute life. In the months prior to his breakdown, he had experienced such anguish every time he played that he developed searing headaches: shortly after this, he had a form of mental collapse involving violent

delusions of persecution, and was arrested for insanity. Released within a couple of days, he spent the next few months trying to maintain his normal routine, but there was a steady deterioration. By the spring of 1907 it was clear that he was beyond help, and his family had him committed. He lived on in the State Insane Asylum in Jackson, Louisiana, for another 24 years, well into the era of 78rpm records. Yet not a single note of his music survives.

Bolden was a vital element in the development of one stream of New Orleans music and, before his withdrawal from the scene, managed to establish himself as King of black music. However, there was another stream which fed the live music scene and against which Bolden vigorously competed, and that was the music of the downtown Creoles.

The Creoles were a racial group showing mixed negro and French, or negro and Spanish, ancestry.

They were an important substratum of 19th-century Louisiana life, and by the middle of the century there were a great many prosperous Creole families – that of Sidney Bechet's was one – in and around New Orleans. As musician Danny Barker pointed out, 'The city was split by Canal Street, with one part of the people uptown and the Creoles downtown. When people would come into New Orleans, like gamblers and workers from Memphis, and they'd say "Let's go down to Frenchtown", that meant you went below Canal Street.'

FRENCHTOWN CREOLES

However, with worsening conditions in the South as it dragged itself out of the economic and social catastrophe of the Civil War, there was a string of racist legislation which, by the 1890s,

forced the people of mixed race into social and occupational areas previously only considered fit for blacks. While Creoles considered this an unmitigated disaster, in fact it had a galvanizing effect on the musical community. Creole musicians were generally well-schooled, able to read music fluently, and excellent technicians. They naturally tended to look askance at the mostly self-taught, full-blood blacks, and their professional associations were generally with Creole-led bands. As the 19th century ended, the intermingling of Creole and black musical styles was gathering apace as younger black players were being schooled by Creoles and the two sets of musicians were appearing on the same bill or at rival halls. Even at that late time, however, Creole contemporaries of Bolden such as clarinettist Alphonse Picou could say of New Orleans' trumpet King: 'He was the best at ragtime. Perez, Oliver and Keelin were better musicians. The ability to read and write music and accuracy and finesse that went with it, was highly valued by the old musicians.' Yet Bolden could, and did, read music; the simple fact was that he and his band played from memory, as do many classical soloists and chamber groups.

The more traditional Creole band music had two outstanding exponents in Bolden's day: John Robichaux and Manuel Perez. Robichaux, born in 1866, played the grand New Orleans venues with his orchestra before the 1894 Black Code amendment barred Creoles from working in such places: after that date he established himself with great determination in the Uptown areas. Perez, a near-contemporary of Bolden, was born in 1879 and led two bands, the Onward Brass Band from 1903 until 1930 and the Imperial Orchestra from 1901

to 1908, with the band specializing in funerals and the like, and the orchestra in indoor events.

Perez was universally regarded as a fine cornettist, with a marvellous big sound and a highly professional approach to the marches and popular music his bands played. He was also one of the first Creole musicians to be directly influenced by Buddy Bolden, thereby providing a valuable bridge between the city's two previously disparate musical communities. Perez himself was a quiet, modest man who avoided the excesses of Bolden's lifestyle. Perhaps not surprisingly, he lived a long and happy life, dying in 1946, and kept a parallel career

W.C. Handy himself played in marching band and also toured on the vaudeville circuit before going into publishing and delving into the rich blues material of the Delta and beyond.

going by working as a cigar maker in the daytime. Late in life he made a series of 78rpm sides with Sidney Bechet where they reminisced about New Orleans, and the warmth of his personality shines through as he talks, welcoming Bechet with: 'I'm certainly glad to see you. Glad that you're here among your friends.'

One of Buddy Bolden's most popular routines in the low-life dives was the slow blues, in a roughouse manner. Bolden him-

self would supply both the vocals and vocal exhortations to the audience and musicians, starting a number with: 'way down, way down low/so I can hear those whores/drag their feet across the floor ... oh you bitches, shake your asses!' This was no casual invocation: whores and street-walkers were an integral part of New Orleans musical life, and in fact in Bolden's day there was a recognized district of the city, Storyville, where the main industry was prostitution of all types and practised at every level.

STORYVILLE

For many years in the post-war period, New Orleans was a wide-open town, openly acknowledged as corrupt and a haven for every form of low life. However, towards the end of the 19th century a large US Navy base was established in New Orleans, a city with few legal controls (a statute passed in 1857 had made prostitution, if not entirely legal, at least not illegal throughout the city, and the prostitutes themselves were licensed and paid fees for the privilege). Naturally, as in Saigon 70 years

later, there was a terrific demand for sexual services of every description. In 1897, in an attempt to contain the problem and palliate the city's more morally upright inhabitants, Alderman Charles Story sponsored an ordnance which limited prostitution to a specific area of the city, later dubbed Storyville in ironic tribute to its creator. This area, an uptown district bordered on one side by the Mississippi and by Perdido and Basin Streets on the other, had within it a black sub-group which serviced, and was serviced by, the honky-tonks, gin-houses, cat-houses and street-walkers of the black community.

Storyville, for a relatively brief time was America's first experiment with legalized prostitution, and it is no accident that it happened in the then most cosmopolitan of US cities, with roots in French, British, Spanish and African cultures. The district's brothels became legendary, with some of the more high-class resembling nothing so much as mansions. Up and down Basin Street, each house competed for passing trade by offering enticing delicacies of flesh and entertainment. The titles of some of the best-known early jazz compositions are filled with the names of

Trumpeter Freddie Keppard (pictured here in band uniform in 1912) was the successor to Buddy Bolden after Buddy's withdrawal from the music scene.

the streets where these sex-palaces stood, or where more mundane streetwalkers earned their keep: Basin St, Perdido St, South Rampart St, Lafayette, Bourbon St and Canal St.

Legend and folklore has it that jazz developed in the Storyville whorehouses and honky-tonks in the long evenings of entertainment offered by the musicians to the paying guests. In fact, this was simply not the case, at least

as far as the bands went. Though the musicians used to hang out in the bars and low dives in the black section of Storyville, and there were a small number of bars specializing in live music, this amounted to nothing more than usually a pianist playing on a beat-up old piano to keep the atmosphere 'lively'. Another thing to bear in mind was that a lot of the musicians did their drinking and playing in barber's shops, friends' houses and anywhere that they congregated during the day or night. Although Bolden's successor as trumpet 'King' of New Orleans, Joe Oliver, played a steady gig at Pete Lala's in the District, he was one of the few, and his main musical employment was still at balls, parades and outdoor events.

What really came out of Storyville were the piano players. The entertainment called for in the mansions and other establish-

ments was in the way of accompaniment to the main action. It was punishing work, with long hours and no great amount of money, but with only one mouth to feed, it was a viable way of scratching a living for the better pianists. Jelly Roll Morton described it vividly: 'They had everything in the District from the highest class to the lowest-creep joints where they'd put the feelers on the guy's clothes, cribs that rented for about five dollars a day and had just about room enough for a bed, small-time houses where the price was fifty cents to a dollar and they put on naked dances, circuses and jive.'

Within this world, some of the best pianists in New Orleans earned a living. At world-famous Lulu White's, for instance, Kid Ross was resident 'professor'. Down the street at Gypsy Schaeffer's, Jelly's pal Tony Jackson held sway. As Morton said, 'Walk

Joe 'King' Oliver with his Creole Band, Chicago 1923, l to r: Baby Dodds, Kid Ory, Joe Oliver, Bill Johnson, Louis Armstrong, Johnny Dodds and Lil Hardin.

into Gypsy Schaeffer's and, right away, the bell would ring upstairs and all the girls would walk into the parlour, dressed in their fine evening gowns and ask the customer if he would care for wine. They would call for the professor and, while champagne was being served, Tony would play a couple of numbers. If the Naked Dance was desired, Tony would dig up one of his fast speed tunes and one of the girls would dance on a little narrow stage, completely nude.'

Apart from the popular melodies of the day, the main style of music played in the Storyville bordellos up to The Great War was ragtime: not surprisingly, considering that ragtime was at this point essentially a keyboard-based adaptation of brass band and orchestral music, and that most establishments usually had a piano already in them. There was also a more basic reason, as pianist and composer Clarence Williams remembered: 'Most of the pimps were gamblers and pianists. The reason so many of them were pianists was because whenever they were down on their luck, they could always get a job and be close to their girls – play while the girls worked.' Jelly Roll Morton himself claimed to have played at being the 'professor' in any number of high-class 'establishments' all across the cities of the South in these formative years. But in the cheaper whorehouses, a few musicians developed more than the most basic talents, and there was little interaction between solo pianists and band players.

The grandest of the houses have passed into legend, immortalised by the infamous guide to the Tenderloin District, as Story-

Edward 'Kid' Ory had the liveliest band in New Orleans in the early teens. Here he is seen with cornettist Mutt Carey and pianist Buster Wilson.

ville was also known: The Blue Book. This was a comprehensive Baedecker of the underworld, listing alphabetically every prostitute in the area, divided into 'white' and 'coloured', and also listing the key Basin Street establishments. As mentioned by Jelly Roll, Lulu White's was probably the most impressive: a four-storey mansion with tower, marble facings inside and out, and furnishings so plush that only millionaires and royalty could outstrip its grandeur. And only the rich could afford to use it. The place eventually gained a permanent place in jazz history when Louis Armstrong named one of his evergreens, *Mahogany Hall Stomp*, after it. In Lulu's advertisement in The Blue Book at the turn of the century, she wrote: 'As an entertainer Miss Lulu stands foremost, having made a life-long study of music and literature. She is well read and one that can interest anybody and make a visit to her place a continued round of pleasure.'

Clarence Williams remembered the splendour of these grand establishments but also recognized the motive behind it all. 'Those places were really something to see – those sportin' houses. They had the most beautiful parlours, with cut glass, and draperies, and rugs and expensive furniture ... And the girls would come down dressed in the finest of evening gowns, just like they were going to the opera ... I'm telling you that Ziegfeld didn't have any more beautiful women than those ... Places like that were for rich people, mainly white ... Why, do you know that a bottle of beer was a dollar? ... When the piano player would get tired, there would be a player piano that you put a quarter in and we'd make money then too. Those houses hired nothing but the best, but only piano players, and maybe a

girl to sing. And there was no loud playin' either. It was sweet, just like a hotel.'

Armstrong also recalled the darker side of the area he knew as a teenager: 'Many nights ... I would make the rounds of the honky-tonks watching the people and laughing at the drunks. The bouncers left them alone if they fell asleep propped against the wall, but if they collapsed or started raising hell they were thrown out pronto. We would often dig that jive and watch the whores, who would often get into quarrels over the same pimp and fight like mad dogs ... We wanted to learn all we could about life, but mostly we were interested in music. We were always looking for a new piano player with something new on the ball like a rhythm that was all his own. These fellows with real talent often came from the levee camps. They'd sit on a piano stool and beat out some of the damnedest blues you ever heard in your life.'

Storyville was closed down in 1917 on the orders of the Department of Navy. The closure was rigorously acted upon by the city worthies and their police force. Within nine months, nothing remained of the old district, and most of the prostitutes, pimps, hustlers, gamblers, grifters, musicians and down-and-outs who had populated the area for a good 20 years or more were either rounded up and sent to jail, or they left the city for good. This dramatic crackdown, an action taken not so much because the US government had suddenly developed a conscience, but rather because it was entering The Great War and suddenly needed to drastically improve morale and discipline in its military forces, has often been cited as the catalyst for the spread of jazz to other cities. However, for a number of years prior to this, the

South had been experiencing a fierce depression which made work hard to get, and many blacks had begun moving to the North, where the new industrialization had created an abundance of jobs, often of a skilled and rewarding nature. The musicians simply followed this population shift, to entertain the new ghettos wherever they became established.

Thus the closing of Storyville was largely symbolic in its impact on jazz. But the history books were not wrong in pointing to a general exodus of talent from the Crescent City because, within a handful of years, all the leading musicians had left New Orleans for good.

Who were these leading musicians, the ones who had inherited Bolden's legacy and developed it into what the world would call Jazz? They were the new generation who had been pushing King Bolden hard in his last couple of years at the top of the heap, and who were to build on his innovations and fashion the new music in the process. Men like Bunk Johnson, who claimed to have played in Bolden's band, but who had to move his birthdate by about ten years to make the claim stick, yet whose style was uncannily close to the great man's decades later. Or Freddie Keppard, another trumpeter who by reputation kept his music-making very much within the tradition laid

down by Bolden.

Keppard was the first jazzman given the opportunity by the Victor company to make a record in 1916, the year before the Original Dixieland Jazz Band actually did it. He turned it down. He is claimed to have said at the time, 'Nothin' doin', boys. We won't put our stuff on records for everybody to steal', although an alternative tradition suggests that Keppard, a proud and suspicious man with a short temper, lost patience with the record company when they asked him to rehearse his band in the studio for no pay prior to making their recording debut. And so the sad history of the troubled relationship between jazz musicians and record com-

SIDNEY BECHET, 'ARTIST OF GENIUS': After hearing Bechet at a concert in London, the musicologist Ernest Ansermet wrote: 'There is ... an extraordinary clarinet virtuoso who [has] composed perfectly formed blues on the clarinet ... Extremely difficult, they are equally admirable for their richness of invention, force of accent, and daring in novelty and the unexpected. Already, they give the idea of a style and their form was gripping, abrupt, harsh with a brusque and pitiless ending ... I wish to set down the name of this artist of genius: ... I shall never forget it, it is Sidney Bechet.'

Sidney Bechet (left), *soprano saxophonist and clarinettist supreme, in the early fifties.*

Bechet as a much younger man, appearing in a revue shortly after the end of the Great War.

panies began, before ever a note was recorded!

Another musician with musical roots back in parade days, with quadrilles, two-steps, waltzes and other pre-jazz musical forms, but who succesfully stayed the course for the next 50 years, was Edward 'Kid' Ory. He was the Creole trombonist who virtually invented, and then championed, what was known as 'tailgate' style (generally, wide musical smears and glissandos, easily available technically to the slide trombonist) and who introduced to jazz an old French quadrille which he tarted up and called 'Tiger rag'.

LIFE AFTER BUDDY

By far the most important younger musician playing in the Bolden tradition was Joe Oliver. He emerged after the crucial period between 1906 and 1913, when the uptown and downtown styles somehow merged into each other, one becoming 'hotter' and picking up some of the blues inflexions of Bolden and his successors, with the other acquiring

some of the musicianship and smoothness of tone and technique associated with the Creole bands. For a decade, Oliver was to eclipse every other trumpeter or cornettist in the city, including people as respected by fellow-musicians as Mutt Carey and Buddy Petit. In the immediate aftermath of Bolden's departure, only Keppard could lay claim to any primacy in the music, but by around 1911, Oliver had challenged Keppard by standing in the street near the club where Keppard was playing with his band, putting his cornet to his lips and blowing such powerful music that his fans immediately acclaimed him 'King' of the New Orleans brass players. He has been known by that name ever since.

Joe 'King' Oliver (1885-1938) was a big, strongly built man with a dominating onstage personality and the physical power to lead his musicians through the sheer force of his playing. In the early days, on parades, Joe would stride on ahead of his band, wearing his trademark bowler hat tilted over one eye, his shirt open

to reveal a flaming red undershirt, his bearing tall and straight, his stride purposeful. After a spell in the Eagle Band, a group of mainly ex-Bolden musicians, learning his trade, he formed his own band and gradually became the prime musical attraction in Storyville with a 'residency' at Pete Lala's. It was here that the teenaged Louis Armstrong first saw his idol – 'What I appreciated most about being able to go into Storyville ... was Pete Lala's cabaret where Joe Oliver had his band and where he was blowing up a storm on his cornet. Nobody could touch him ... That was the hottest jazz band ever heard in New Orleans between the years 1910 and 1917'.

Oliver also knew how to put on a show, as had Bolden, and used to do routines with other brass players in the band, swinging around to play unison riffs to the audience, suddenly growling out surprising notes with one of his many mutes, and prowling the stage exhorting his musicians to greater heights. He and Kid Ory joined forces around 1914, and the band became unbeatable,

with Ory's uproarous slide trombone and Oliver's powerful, full-toned cornet and its unexpected wah-wah effects constantly surprising and delighting their fans. With Keppard's departure for Chicago, Oliver and Ory took over at all the best dance halls and functions, often playing as featured soloists with other bands.

Another key instrument in this early phase, and one that again came direct from the marching bands, was the clarinet. All the bands, from Perez, Robichaux and Bolden onwards, had a clarinettist, and in fact his role in the move from straight statement of themes and melodies, or by-rote unison and harmony playing, was crucial. The clarinettist was given the task of embellishment, and it was this embellishment which later grew into fully-fledged collective improvisation, as the other musicians got excited enough to join in with their own ideas.

Alphonse Picou, who started as a 17-year-old with the Manual Perez band, was the man who added the clarinet accompaniment to the main theme of the song *High Society* which is

played to this day in Trad Jazz bands worldwide. Picou commented '[Perez] bought that *High Society* for me. It was a march tune. I took the piccolo part and transposed it to my instrument ... Perez liked the way I played *High Society* ... and they let me play that solo by myself. I made a wonderful hit – Lord! They played *High Society* all night.' Other seminal figures such as George Baquet and Lorenzo Tio were to help set the style, both through their influential playing in public, and through their acknowledged role as teachers of the next generation. And it was this new group of young players who were to send shockwaves throughout the world of music in the following 20 years.

Easily the most gifted of the youngsters was Sidney Bechet. A Creole, and a child prodigy of even greater distinction than Louis Armstrong, Bechet was able to impress professional musicians and audiences by the age of nine. For his brother Leonard's 21st birthday, his mother had hired the young Freddie Keppard and his band, as recommended by Emanuel Perez. His clarinettist, George Baquet, was late arriving, so the nine-year-old Bechet, from the safety of an adjoining room, played along with Keppard's group. Hearing this strange, distended clarinet weaving in and out of the music, Keppard stopped and went to investigate, probably in the belief that Baquet was warming up. To his amazement he found the boy. When Baquet arrived and heard the story, he offered to teach young Sidney himself. Though Bechet accepted with alacrity, Baquet's lessons were only partially successful, since every attempt to get him to read music was doomed to failure. After all, the boy had perfect pitch, could follow the most congested of chord patterns unerringly, and could play note-for-note anything he heard just once: with that sort of ability, reading music charts seemed tiresome indeed.

A further series of lessons with Lorenzo Tio's brother Luis, a stickler for 'legitimate' techniques, was similarly undermined by Bechet's determination to be a free spirit: at one point, the older man was reduced to shouting, 'No! No! No! – we do not bark like a dog or meow like a cat!' Needless to say, that is what young Sidney kept right on doing.

After more sympathetic tutoring by Louis 'Big Eye' Nelson, Bechet soon began appearing with groups around New Orleans, and by the time he was about 14, around the year 1911, he joined Bunk Johnson's Eagle Band. Within a few years his unique combination of gifts was recognized by all the better musicians. Bechet, even as a teenager, had a photographic musical memory, an unfailing rhythmic drive, and unflagging enthusiasm. Aside from that, he was utterly dedicated to music, as only the greats are: at all times of the day and

night, he could be found playing, practising or thinking about his music or his clarinet. He was proud of his innate gift for melodic invention, and his ability to 'sing' the melody or counterpoint in a piece, but his pride never led to laziness.

Young Sidney's appetite for life rivalled his appetite for music. Even as a teenager, still living at home and under the nominal authority of his parents and older brothers, he was wild. He played with a glass of gin next to him and, as 'Big Eye' Nelson observed, was a 'regular little devil, always runnin' off down the alley after them little women.' He was also the type who, after a few drinks, became maudlin, and after a few more, if not insensible, would be looking for trouble, not caring where or with whom he found it. Every good and bad character trait of his was given an unlimited licence in the Storyville of his youth and he not infrequently ended up in jail. Bassist Pops Foster recalled a typical incident: 'One night we ended up in jail together. He was fooling around with a chick at a dance out at the lake. She pulled a knife and stabbed him. I grabbed a stick and started out after her. When the cops came we told them we were playing. They took us to jail and then let us go. When we got back to the dance she thanked us for not getting her into trouble. Sidney was always wanting to fight but they never came off.'

Always a restless soul, Bechet was one of the first to quit New Orleans and tour as a member of a variety of bands throughout the south. The reason he always gave was the poor pay available to the

Johnny Dodds (right) *was a clarinettist who played with most of the early jazz greats, including Joe Oliver. His style was very much involved in blues inflections, and he could be marvellously affecting.*

average New Orleans musician, and there is no reason to doubt this. Not that these tours were always a financial success: often they foundered halfway through and the surviving musicians had to make their own way back to Crescent City, sometimes riding the railroad hobo-style to do it.

One tour, however, was immeasurably more successful for Bechet in particular: Mrs Bruce's travelling vaudeville troupe needed a band to act and play, and Bechet was included. It had a particular hit in Chicago (although one critic noted that 'the clarinet player should have sense enough to play soft for soloists, so people can hear the words') and when the tour began to lose impetus a little later in the midwest, Bechet was happy to return to Chicago and play with other expatriates from New Orleans. Within a few months of his arrival, both King Oliver and Freddie Keppard were

also in town, playing the two best venues, the Royal Gardens and the Dreamland Cafe, as guest soloists. Always a resourceful fellow, Bechet was soon appearing at both venues with his two friends and colleagues.

In 1919 the famed black musician and orchestra leader Will Marion Cook was putting together a large group (including a choir and vocal soloists), and asked the clarinettist to join the tour. Bechet, game for anything, quickly accepted. This led to a prolonged absence from America for Bechet, plus at least one memorable watersheds in the music.

One afternoon, while strolling down Wardour Street in London's Soho, Bechet discovered a soprano saxophone in a music shop window and went in to investigate. This straight-bodied member of the saxophone family was probably the most neglected

member of a family of instruments which was still a musical stepchild, used mostly in brass bands to soften the impact of trumpet and trombone harmonies, or in vaudeville and circus acts as a freak and novelty noise-maker. However, the soprano was precisely what Bechet, frustrated with the sonic limitations of the clarinet, had been looking for. With this new instrument he could compete equally, in terms of sound level, with any other player. He could also get a whole lot closer to the sound of the human voice than before: he could really wail to his audience in a new and startling way.

After this discovery, playing with the Southern Syncopated Orchestra at Buckingham Palace by the personal invitation of the Prince of Wales came a distinct second-best, especially when, three years later, Bechet was arrested, imprisoned and then

deported from England after a late-night fracas at an all-nighter in Percy St, Fitzrovia. As he left Southampton for New York City by boat, he is said to have thrown all the English money he had with him overboard, in an attempt to exorcise the miserable experience.

LITTLE LOUIS

In 1913, the year Sidney Bechet was making a name for himself playing with Freddie Keppard and Bunk Johnson's Eagle Band, Louis Armstrong, then 12 years old, was arrested for firing a pistol in the air as part of the New Year's Day celebrations. As a result he was to spend over a year in the Coloured Waif's Home For Boys, where he learned the cornet from a strict but talented music master, Peter Davis. On his release, he kept up with the instrument, and within a short time was playing cornet as an underage musician in a variety of bands and venues. As he himself said, 'I was young and strong and had all the ambition in the world . . . After I got set at [clubowner] Henry Ponce's place, I got another job driving a coal cart during the day. After I had finished work at four in the morning I would run back home and grab a couple of hours' sleep. Then I would go to the C.A. Andrews Coal Company at Ferret and Perdido Streets two blocks away from the honky-tonk. From seven in the morning to five in the evening I would haul hard coal at fifteen cents per load. And I loved it. I was fifteen years old . . .'

At this point, his idol was Joe 'King' Oliver, and he spent so much time watching Oliver's band that Oliver took a paternal interest in the young cornet player, doing him a great many little favours in the following years. Armstrong never forgot this: 'I can never stop loving Joe Oliver. He was always ready to come to my rescue when

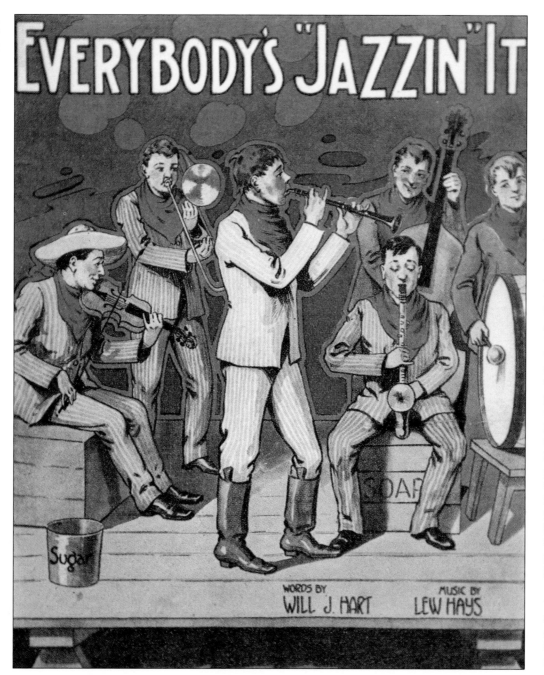

By the beginning of the twenties, the word 'jazz' had become fashionable in the world outside New Orleans, and stretched across the Atlantic to the Old World. Even Tin Pan Alley publishers (above) *started borrowing the word for its up-to-the-minute connotations.*

I needed someone to tell me about life and its little intricate things, and help me out of difficult situations . . . I often did errands for Stella Oliver, his wife, and Joe would give me lessons for my pay. I could not have asked for anything I wanted more. It was my ambition to play as he did.'

Oliver clearly recognized the burning talent in the youngster, and did all he could to foster it. When he left New Orleans for Chicago in 1918, like many before him, looking for better pay and a wider career, it was Armstrong – called 'Little Louis' at that point – who took the older man's place in Kid Ory's band, the top trumpet spot in New Orleans at that time.

Still short of his 19th birthday, he was now the best New Orleans had to offer. A few years later, in 1922, he received a summons from King Oliver to join him in Chicago at the prestigious Lincoln Gardens. After a train journey along to a strange big city, he finally met up with his mentor and, from the start, things went well both musically and personally. Oliver at this time had an outstanding band, with Lil Hardin, Armstrong's wife-to-be, on the piano, and the Dodds brothers, Johnny and Baby, on clarinet and drums respectively; Louis immediately felt at home. On their first night playing together he and Oliver chanced upon what was to be one of their most astounding and characterist musical effects: 'It was then that Joe and I developed a little system for the duet breaks. We did not have to write them down. I was so wrapped up in him and lived so closely to his music that I could follow his lead in a split second.' This system of playing, true to the old New Orleans ideas of collective playing and embellishment of themes, is very much the basis of the seminal recordings Louis was to make with King Oliver's creole Band in the following year, 1923. Within a year of this, Louis would be out on his own, making jazz history.

So New Orleans and the country around it had, by the second decade of this century, produced a new musical form called jazz. All it needed was for the world to sit up and pay attention. And, sure enough, the world did – in a most peculiar way.

classic jazz of the 20s

'Hello central, give me Dr Jazz;

he's got what I need – I'll say he has!'

Jelly Roll Morton – *Doctor Jazz*

THE MUSICIANS leaving New Orleans in increasing numbers by the closing years of The Great War had no clear idea of their destiny, and no notion that they were ambassadors of a new musical creed. For them, making their kind of music was a living, the only one thing they knew and one which utterly consumed them. Nevertheless, it was the itinerant musician, and the touring band, who took the jazz message to other parts of the US and began the dissemination of a vital, arresting music.

Historians often wonder why it took the fledgling recording industry 30 years to record the first jazz title, when classical music was getting intensive treatment from about 1904 onwards. Usually, pig-ignorance and racio-cultural bias are cited as prime reasons. But it seems more likely, on closer inspection, that the real causes lay in the areas of distance, population, communication and the relative development of modern industries. It is surely no coincidence that jazz and blues musicians were recorded with reasonable frequency by a range of companies soon after the musicians' abandonment of the Mississippi delta and neighbouring states as their main professional bases. After all, trumpeters, drummers, pianists and clarinettists were only reflecting

Left: *The first great jazz band on records: King Oliver's Creole Jazz Band, photographed in San Francisco in summer 1921, two years prior to their entry into the studio. L to r: Minor Hall, Honore Dutrey, Joe Oliver, Lil Hardin, Dave Jones, Johnny Dodds, Jimmy Palao, Ed Garland. Louis Armstrong joined one year later.*

The Original Dixieland Jazz Band, Chicago, 1917. L to r: *Henry Ragas, Larry Shields, Eddie Edwards, Nick LaRocca, Tony Spargo. With the ODJB, recorded jazz began. Ironically, a white, not a negro band was first in the studios.*

what others of their race were doing in tremendous numbers: deserting the economically depressed and socially repressive south for the labour-hungry northern states. The music followed the coloured population north, in a drive for work opportunity and escape from a socio-economic system which had allowed over 3,600 lynchings in the southern states and parts of the midwest since the Civil War.

THE FIRST RECORDINGS

It is an irony often bitterly resented by devotees of classic jazz and by later musicians exploited by less-than-scrupulous record companies that the first jazz recordings were made by a white band, The Original Dixieland Jazz Band. Some have passed it off as no more than a black musician could

expect, while others have found it a symbol of all that is socially unacceptable in the US. After all, no one could claim that white people had invented the musical style. Still, there is no changing the facts, and, in early 1917, a band led by trumpeter Nick LaRocca which specialized in a small-group ragtime variant along with a large degree of hokum and 'novelty' routines made the first jazz records.

Although the clarinettist Larry Shields confirmed in an interview many years later that the repertoire was very well rehearsed, the solos plotted beforehand and virtually no variations permitted from performance to performance, this was still the start of jazz recording. As such, it was a misleading reflection what was actually being played by the mainstream jazz musicians although, in fairness, improvisation within the jazz ensemble was still in its infancy, and only being practised by a small percentage

of the then-active New Orleans fraternity of players, let alone musicians scattered across the rest of the States. Within the white fraternity, improvisation was an unused concept.

Prior to the ODJB, there had been one major white New Orleans band: Jack Laine's Ragtime Band. Laine (1873-1966) had gathered a following for his ragtime effusions towards the end of the 19th century, and had been the first to popularize *Livery Stable Blues* (then known as *Meatball Blues*), which the ODJB later took and recorded, with a few 'novelty' animal noises thrown in, and sold over a million copies. So there was nothing particularly novel or revolutionary about the band. What they had

going for them – in a big way – was showmanship, a sense of the dramatic in music, and the knack of being in the right place when record companies began sniffing around.

They had moved to Chicago, along with various other white musicians and groups, and had caught the Victor Talking Company's eye and ear after the earlier abortive effort to record Freddie Keppard's band. Controversy seemed to be a staple part of their existence, and many contemporaries had axes to grind as they watched the ODJB, in the years between 1917 and 1923, conquer first the US and then Europe through their records and personal appearances. Chicago had become the new focus for the music, with white, Creole and black musicians playing a variety of gigs around town, all elbowing each other for space. Some felt they did not get their due. One such was drummer Johnny Stein, who organized and brought Stein's Original Dixieland Jazz Band to Chicago in March 1916. He claimed that he was ousted from this band which was then reorganized into The Original Dixieland Jazz Band. Others remember the incident as simply a swap of drummers before the band made its first jaunt to New York.

The cutting edge of jazz had left New Orleans by the time of the ODJB's records, with many musicians drifting north and others working their passage on the steamboats up the Mississippi. The music played on the steamboats was not jazz, but it was at least a relation of it, however distant. And the King of the riverboats was Fate Marable (1890-

1947). As drummer Zutty Singleton remembered: "You know, Fate had a white band on the riverboats before he had his coloured band . . . The way it worked on the boats was Monday night the dances were for coloured. Every night the boats would travel up and down the river for a while and then come back. The riverboats played dance music mostly. But Fate had things like Jelly Roll's tunes in the book. Numbers like *The Pearls* and *Jelly Roll Blues*. This is not surprising, considering that a pre-Great War novelty hit worldwide *Darktown Strutters' Ball* has a lyric which included the line 'when they play the *Jelly Roll Blues*' so Morton's published music had a wide appeal. Marable was an exacting musical director, and a tenure with his band meant a rise in prestige for the musician concerned. As Zutty Singleton

Wingy Manone with his San Sue Strutters, in Okeh's Chicago studios in November 1925. The primitive techniques of early recordings are well to the fore in this shot, with all the players at varying distances from the single studio horn. Wingy is on trumpet.

remarked, 'when some musician would get a job on the riverboats with Fate Marable, they'd say, "Well, you're going to the conservatory." . . . the men who worked with him had to be pretty good.'

One of the youngsters who was good enough to go to the conservatory was Louis Armstrong, prior to joining King Oliver in Chicago. He recalled, 'Fate had his own way of dealing with his musicians. If one of us made an error or played part of a piece wrong he wouldn't say a thing about it until everyone thought it'd been forgotten. When you came to work the next day with a bad hangover from the night before, he picked the music you'd failed with and asked you to play before the other members of the band. And believe me, brother, it was no fun to be shown up before all the others . . . we used to call this experience our Waterloo.'

With the arrival of this exciting new type of music came audiences from previously untapped social strata. Until then, jazz and its near-relatives had been enjoyed by crowds and dancers from the bottom strata, as well as from the very top. But in Chicago, middle-class people began to get curious. This greatly extended the music's earning power, which in turn fed the pool of musicians eager to cash in on their popularity. Nick LaRocca's group, and bands like the New Orleans Rhythm Kings or the Louisiana Five, captured the best white gigs, and so most of the white audience. But the blacks were listening to King Oliver, and with Armstrong's arrival as second trumpet in the group, Oliver's band was the hottest thing jazz had ever seen. To this day it remains one of the most significant and it is fortunate that the

King's band proved so popular that it was one of the very first black jazz bands to be recorded – in April 1923 by the Gennett Company, a tiny firm based in Richmond, Indiana, and owned by the Starr Piano Company from the same town.

A listener to these sides today unused to anything but digital sound would be hard put to hear anything but a weird, compressed, scratchy noise. They would probably wonder why anybody ever bothered to make such things, let alone listen to them for enjoyment. However, a word or two on recording techniques at this time may put things a little more in perspective.

For a start, magnetic tape for recording purposes was still 30 years away: even the primitive wire tape recorders were a good 15 years down the line. And the 78rpm lacquer or bakelite disc had only succeeded the even more primitive Edison Cylinder some 20 years previously. In fact, nobody had even figured out a way of using electricity for recording purposes: that was still three years in the future when Oliver's Creole Jazz Band cut their first discs. And the word 'cut' was in those days entirely accurate. The way music was then recorded was purely through acoustic waves tracked through diaphragms and traced by a steel needle cutting a concentric path into a wax disc, which was then called a wax 'master'. Now, this was a hit-and-miss process. Firstly, the wax could have an imperfection in it, and so, regardless of the quality of the band's performance, the master would be scrapped, the wax melted down, and then re-used. Secondly, there was absolutely no possibility of recording things in part, or different musicians separately: it all had to go off accurately, all the way through, or it did not go at all. Finally, the early 'microphones'

Above: *Jack Laine was important in the early century as the leader of a major white New Orleans band, playing ragtime. He was the first to popularize* **Livery Stable Blues,** *later a bestseller for The Original Dixieland Jazz Band.*

were actually horns which funnelled the sounds of the musicians down into the cutting instruments: no more, no less. The average studio had one giant horn mounted on a wall, which the musicians more or less played at or towards. In an effort to get a relatively balanced overall sound, the quietest instruments would play immediately adjacent to it, while the louder ones, such as brass and drums, would be at the furthest possible point. For the first ten years of jazz recording, even this was not enough: the

primitive cutting equipment simply could not handle the overwhelming bumps and surges demanded of it by a drummer thrashing away on his complete kit, and would jump wildly all over the wax master. So, in one of the most demeaning compromises ever endured by a professional musician, all drummers up until the early 1930s could only use woodblocks, small cymbals and other less sonically devastating parts of their kit when they were in the studio.

Things gradually got better as the twenties progressed, especially with the invention and utilization of electric recording techniques. However, a great deal of the important early jazz was recorded by tiny companies with the cheapest and worst equipment available. Only large companies, such as Victor and Columbia, could afford to use the best, and the difference is painfully clear. This was a cause of much bitterness and resentment later, when in retrospect it was clear that the bigger companies had a deliberate policy to record what they called 'race music' as cheaply and as quickly as they could, while lavishing their best equipment and studios on classical, semi-classical and variety music for white audiences. Yet it quickly became obvious that these large companies – and many of the smaller ones had made a basic miscalculation about their audience for jazz and blues records. They anticipated an almost totally black clientele – so much so that they did not even distribute, sell or advertise their 'race recordings outside ethnic areas or publications. But from the outset young white enthusiasts were hunting out and buying these records.

In recording for Gennett, the Oliver band had one last obstacle to overcome. The Gennett studio was in fact a converted wooden barn which backed onto a local goods railway line. With sound-proofing unheard of, and a cutter which would jump at the sound of drums, the rather more impressive disruptions made by a steam locomotive and a gaggle of trucks made recording impossible: all operations simply had to be suspended until the train went by! No doubt the engineers at Gennett had a copy of the local train timetable handy at all times!

Taking all this into consideration, it is miraculous what Oliver's Creole Jazz Band achieved. This band, and these recordings, were so seminal that it is worth noting who the musicians were. On cornets were Joe 'King' Oliver and Louis Armstrong; the trombonist was Honore Dutrey (1887-1935); the pianist was Lillian Hardin (1898-1971), a fine player and strong personality who married Armstrong the following year and encouraged him to go out on his own; the bassist was Bill Johnson (1872-1972), while the clarinet and drum roles were taken by the Dodds brothers. It was a truly remarkable collection of talent, with Oliver, Armstrong, Johnny and Baby Dodds universally regarded as the finest on their instruments in their own day, and each blazing influential musical paths in the decade that followed.

So what was their achievement in the Gennett, and later the Columbia/Okeh studios in 1923? The most immediate and perhaps most surprising discovery is that this is a band fully immersed in collective improvisation. Oliver takes the lead brass role, mirrored and commented upon by Armstrong's paraphrases and melodic variations. Meanwhile, Johnny Dodds is continually weaving counter-melodies and what they called 'obbligato' lines in and around what the two horn players are doing. This all leads to a startling polyphony which, joined with the exuberant, expressivity and unprecedentedly headlong rhythmic drive, can be an overwhelmingly exciting experience. What must this band have been like to listen to in the flesh!

Discs such as Snake Rag and Chimes Blues quickly bring it home to the listener that, up to and including these Oliver recordings, the classic style of New Orleans jazz did not embrace the idea of instrumental solos. As such, early New Orleans jazz reached its finest expression in these 1923 recordings, which simultaneously witnessed its swan-song. For, within two years of these sides, Louis Armstrong would begin recording for Okeh with his studio group the Hot Five (later, the Hot Seven) and, in the process, revolutionize jazz more profoundly than any other artist before or since. The reason? Louis had outgrown the strict New Orleans conventions, and in his burning desire to play as much trumpet as possible, created the role of improvisatory soloist and dominant 'voice' within a jazz band.

Armstrong made history with a select group of musicians, all of whom had previously played with Oliver. He had left the Creole Jazz Band in 1924 at the urging of his new wife Lil, and joined the New-York-based Fletcher Henderson Orchestra, which at that time was resident at New York's famous Roseland Ballroom, and which was pretty much a dance band, playing music strongly influenced by jazz, rather than jazz music. Henderson at that time saw his sound as a coloured people's version of the type of 'sophisticated' quasi-orchestral contemporary dance music that white bands such as Paul Whiteman and Ted Lewis were producing.

ARMSTRONG THE SOLOIST

That the band included such to-be-famous names as Coleman Hawkins (1904-1969), Buster Bailey (b.1925) and Don Redman (1900-1964) before Louis even joined only underlines the impact Armstrong had on the jazz world – because it was his playing, and

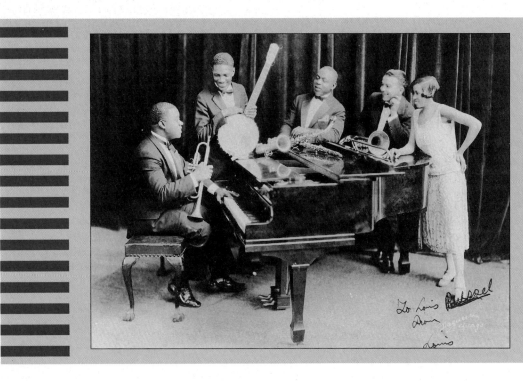

A FIRST CLASSIC: In 1926, Armstrong recorded Cornet Chop Suey (along with Heebie Jeebies), an extraordinary solo vehicle for his cornet playing. At the time there had never been anything like this in the music; Louis really was breaking new musical ground. In it he displayed his virtuosity, allied with his unfailing musicality. The daring and poise and the sense of excitement in discovery can still thrill listeners today. It became an instant jazz classic, and still remains one. Armstrong also possessed a flair for showmanship which allowed him to reach a far wider audience than devotees of pure jazz.

Louis Armstrong with his Hot Five, Chicago 1925. L to r: Louis, Johnny St Cyr, Johnny Dodds, Kid Ory, Lil Hardin. The Hot Five never performed outside the studio.

his entirely, which inspired these men to follow a similar stylistic path on their own instruments. Fletcher Henderson, in an interview decades after the event, was specific about Louis' impact: 'Needless to say, Louis was a big success right from the start. About three weeks after he joined us he asked me if he could sing a number ... He was great: the band loved it, the crowd just ate it up. I believe that was the first time he ever sang anywhere. He didn't sing with Oliver, I'm sure.'

To begin with, Armstrong was resented by the other band members. Henderson remembered the first rehearsal: 'The band at first was inclined to be a bit reserved ... and there seemed to be a little tension in the air. At rehearsal he was perplexed by the trumpet part I gave him ... Now those parts were well marked with all the dynamics of the music, and at one point the orchestration was marked as *fff* with a diminuendo down to *pp*. The band followed these notations and was playing very softly, while Louis still played

his part at full volume. I stopped the band and said ... "Louis, how about that *pp*?" and Louis broke us all up by replying "Oh, I thought that meant "pound plenty". There was no tension after that.'

Armstrong returned to Chicago to join his wife's band in 1925, and began the Hot Five recordings with a string of staggering achievements within the confines of the 78rpm record. Edward 'Kid' Ory, the trombonist on these dates, recalled the circumstances of their creation: 'We made our first records in Chicago at the Okeh studios ... Times were good, and people had money to buy records. One thing that helped the sale was the fact that for a while the Okeh people gave away a picture of Louis to everyone that bought one of the records.' In the studio, Ory continued, the band was nothing if not professional – a fact of which he was clearly proud. 'We would get to the studio at nine or ten in the morning. We didn't have to make records at night, with the lights out, or get drunk like some

Louis Armstrong (pictured below in 1925) spent most of his performing time in the twenties as a featured artist on the trumpet with orchestras led by other men, while he recorded what he wanted to play, with the players he preferred to work with, in the studio.

Right: *By the end of the 1920s, Louis (seen here in a publicity shot) was fronting his own big band. He had become such a major personality that the force of his singing and trumpet playing could carry the whole band through any song, however trite.*

Fletcher Henderson is credited with having formed and successfully led the most important early big band in jazz. His 1924 orchestra (below) *sports Coleman Hawkins and Louis Armstrong (second and third from left). Henderson is seated, fourth from left. The 1932 Henderson band* (bottom) *relaxes on the Atlantic City promenade. Coleman Hawkins is still there, now joined by Russell Procope, J.C. Higginbothan and Rex Stewart, among others.*

musicians think they have to before they can play . . . We were a very fast recording band. In fact, the records I made with the Hot Five were the easiest I ever made . . . I think one reason those records came out so well was that the Okeh people left us alone, and didn't try to expert us.'

Early in 1926, two sides were made which became instant classics – *Heebie Jeebies* and *Cornet Chop Suey.*

Heebie Jeebies is a lighthearted vehicle for Louis's unique vocal style, which at this early point was more rough-hewn and closer to an actual solo instrument than later. What was so special about this outing was the scat vocal, which was the first-ever improvised vocal. It came about, as do so many innovations, by sheer accident. According to legend, and to eyewitness Joe Glaser, later Armstrong's manager, Louis had a sheet of lyrics in his hand as the vocals started, but dropped them while clowning silently at the mike, waiting for the moment to sing. The colourful raconteur and sometime musician Mezz Mezzrow takes up the story: '. . . the music slipped out of Louis's hand. He wasn't stumped, not that cat, On he went, remembering a couple of phrases here and there, and then he forgot about the words entirely, making up syncopated scats that were copied right from his horn tones . . . Right then and there, when Louis dropped that sheet of paper and gave his improvising genius the floor, he started a musical craze that become as much part of America's cultural life as Superman . . .'

For the next two years, Armstrong continued to record with his studio-bound small groups, the Hot Five and Hot Seven, while appearing in person primarily as featured artist with the Carroll Dickerson Orchestra at the Sunset Café and other well-known Chicago haunts. In mid-1928, with a later edition of his Hot Five that included pianist Earl Hines (1903-1983) and drummer Zutty Singleton (1898-1975), Armstrong recorded a side written by his mentor and erstwhile employer, Joe Oliver, *West End Blues*, which has an unaccompanied trumpet introduction guaranteed to gobsmack even today's first-time hearer. For sheer audacity, rhythmic and melodic vitality, and breath-stopping excitement, that odd 15-seconds of music is hard to beat. It certainly floored every other trumpeter in jazz for the next ten years. As a rather sad

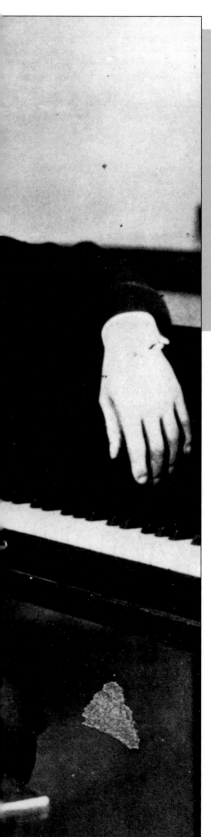

FERDINAND 'JELLY ROLL' MORTON (1890-1941): **The first great arranger – and, some would claim, composer as well – in classic jazz was also a self-confessed hustler, pool-shark, ladies' man, gambler and self-promoter. Jelly was playing New Orleans hotspots prior to the closure of Storyville in 1917, but cut his greatest records in Chicago in the mid-twenties, with his band Jelly Roll Morton's Red Hot Peppers. A harsh taskmaster, he drove musicians to a more flexible, inventive approach to jazz. The picture to the left shows him looking very dashing at the piano in 1923, while the one on the right is a 1926 Victor publicity shot.**

Jelly Roll Morton's Red Hot Peppers: Andrew Hilaire, Edward 'Kid' Ory, George Mitchell, John Lindsay, Jelly Roll Morton, Johnny St Cyr and Omer Simeon.

postscript, a jaded King Oliver went into the studio for Victor soon after to cut his version of his own song. The unaccompanied introduction, played by Oliver's lead trumpeter, and copied painstakingly from Armstrong's effortless invention, is a crude approximation of the original. Quite conclusively, the pupil was now his master's better.

bars and dives, and earning a living as a gambler, pool-hustler, sometime-pimp, smooth-talking self-promoter, and con-man. At various times in his diverse and colourful life, he settled on music long enough to compose and

arrange pieces as distinctive as any before or since in the jazz canon, and also became a remarkably fine pianist, with a style exhibiting deep ragtime roots. He spent many years travelling around the south, mid-

west and west, either as a solo act or as a leader of various pickup bands, and as a pianist had an unequalled reputation, as bandleader George Morrison pointed out: 'Oh, but he could stomp the blues out. When he got to pattin'

MISTER JELLY ROLL

In the mid-twenties, only one other man could compete with Louis Armstrong in terms of orginality, invention and wit. The man was Ferdinand 'Jelly Roll' Morton (1890-1941). A Creole and proud of it, he had been around in New Orleans long before Louis, playing piano in whorehouses, clubs,

The classic Joe 'King' Oliver's Creole Band in a posed 'action' shot, probably taken in late 1922. Armstrong is pictured here playing the rare slide trumpet, an instrument he never played in public. L to r: Honore Dutrey, Baby Dodds, Joe 'King' Oliver, Louis Armstrong, Lil Hardin, Bill Johnson and Johnny Dodds.

that foot, playing the piano and a cigar in his mouth, man, he was gone – he was gone!'

By 1923 he had arrived in Chicago, and put down sufficient roots to stay for five years. He made a number of piano rolls, and various poorly-recorded versions of his best-known pieces, before in 1926 signing an exclusive contract with Victor, negotiated for him by the Melrose Publishing Company. This break came after three years of loneliness and scuffling: Jelly had found it impossible to organize regular work for a band, and so turned his hand to solo work or publishing his songs to make a living. The stranglehold on Chicago entertainment by the mobsters who did

not appreciate forceful and articulate Creoles like Morton, plus his own pride and downright prejudice against full-blood negro musicians, kept him poor and isolated. However, when he finally did enter the studios for Victor, he did it on his terms, and with a handpicked selection of players who were Creole to the last man. He did not waste time playing cover versions of other peoples' hits: it was his music, and his concepts, strong and pure. Between September 1926 and June 1927, in a creative purple patch extraordinary in its diversity, depth and consistent quality, Morton created a body of recordings as definitive of one side of the New Orleans jazz legacy as

Armstrong's are of the other.

On these Red Hot Peppers sides, the meshing of ragtime blues and jazz as musical forms set within a composed framework reaches its zenith. Omer Simeon, the clarinettist with the Peppers at these sessions, remembered clearly Jelly's working method, quite at odds with the freewheeling Armstrong approach: 'I'll tell you how he was in rehearsing a band. He was exact with us. Very jolly, very full of life all the time, but serious. We used to spend maybe three hours rehearsing four sides and in that time he'd give us the effects he wanted, like the background behind a solo – he would run that over on the piano with one finger [for the guys

to] harmonise it.' Baby Dodds remembers a similar routine: 'Jelly Roll would work on each and every number until it satisifed him. Everybody had to do just what Jelly wanted him to do . . . We used his original numbers and he always explained what it was all about and played a synopsis of it on the piano . . . His own playing was remarkable and kept us in good spirits . . . I never saw him upset and he didn't raise his voice at any time.'

Simeon remembered Morton as a leader who liked to leave the individual solos and their content to the player, although he would give an indication of the general point the solo was trying to make in the song. Johnny St Cyr (1890-

1966), a banjoist who was also a member of Armstrong's Hot Five, remembers Morton deliberately giving solo space in parts of tunes when the players least expected it, so that their ideas would be fresh, and their minds stimulated. With this meticulous approach, it was essential for him to pick musicians who were generally sympathetic to his aims, and who could respond positively to the discipline of his methods. On one of his very earliest sessions for

Bix Beiderbecke and His Rhythm Jugglers at a Gennett recording session in Richmond, Indiana, January 1925, relaxing between takes. Full personnel, l to r: Howdy Quicksell, Tom Gargano, Paul Mertz, Don Murray, Bix Beiderbecke, Tommy Dorsey.

Okeh in 1923, Morton came across a trombonist who simply refused to play a melody in the particular style he wanted. After repeated, fruitless attempts to persuade the man verbally, Jelly took a large pistol which he always carried with him out of his pocket, and laid it on the top of the piano. He got his melody played, just the way he wanted.

In Morton's best recordings, the drama of the music resides in the constant interchange between a shifting intrumental backdrop and the lead voices. Jelly would ruthlessly push the lead melodies and solos from one player to another during the course of a single piece, with each new combination of sounds calling forth a new and striking harmonic and melodic blend. Added to this was a commitment to a strong rhythmic drive, probably resulting from half a lifetime spent accompanying himself at the piano and having of necessity to create a powerful pulse for this purpose. Firmly based in ragtime syncopation but without its strict, rather unflowing style, Morton's music had all the individual elements of what big-band jazz was to become in the following decade, except the even rhythmic accents of 'swing'. He had riffs, counter-melodies, orchestral colour, blues-filled melodic motifs, rhythmic drive, and a welter of arrangement devices to make each instrument play a clear role. Most of these devices can be found in *'Dead Man Blues'*, along with another key Morton element mostly dismissed as unworthy of the music it decorates: humour.

Nobody minded Louis Armstrong's sense of fun and hamming it up, both on record and in person, but Jelly's clowning got him a bad name. On *Dead Man Blues*, for example, the side opens with a conversation between two wise guys in a New Orleans street:

'What's that I hear 12 o'clock in the daytime – church bells ringing?'

'Man, you don't hear no church bells ringin' 12 o'clock in the day'

'Don't tell me – somebody must be dead!'

'There ain't nobody dead – somebody must be dead drunk!'

'No – I think there's a funeral ... I believe I hear that trombone phone.'

The music proceeds directly to a snatch of the famous Chopin *Funeral March*, then picks up tempo and walks the mourners back to town, as in the old days in the Crescent City funeral parades. A marvellously evocative opening, it adds piquancy to a beautifully worked-through composition where collective improvisation on the theme and chords gives way to a clarinet solo which tells the story almost like a relative's lamentation. A trumpet solo adding its own touches is supported by some colourful piano playing before the whole band segues into a wonderful, snaking long melody which is played in three-part harmony by the clarinets, anticipating similar work from Duke Ellington by half a decade. Gently, a swooping trombone delivers a 'feeling no pain' counter-melody on the recapitulation of this section, giving the piece another dimension entirely – almost as if an amiable drunk has joined in on the conversation. At the end, all the main instruments join together in recapitulation to wrap things up nicely.

Jelly could get a lot sillier than this as in, for example, the 'laughing policeman' vocal which runs right through the appropriately named *Hyena Stomp*, or the deliberately chronic beginning to the same song which stops with somebody yelling out, 'Jelly, that's terrible'. Another track, cut

the same June day in 1927, has a man imitating a billy-goat all the way through. But on the same day, Morton's Peppers produced *Jungle Blues*, a delicate and audacious piece of music, in its way as far ahead of its time as Armstrong's *West End Blues* was a year later. Based on the idea of playing a piece which is one long decrescendo prior to the closing ensemble, at one point it even features acoustic guitar as the main melody instrument.

Perhaps the easiest way to appreciate Jelly's special genius is to play, back-to-back, his composition *The Pearls*, first in the solo piano version, and then in the orchestral version. The brilliance of his arranging genius will then be demonstrated, bar by bar. With music like this, Morton's future should have been assured. But a combination of changing fashions, with the move to instru-

The first great boogie pianist, Jimmy Yancey, at the piano during the 1920s. Yancey was a key figure in the development of blues piano into what was in the 1930s to become a world-famous keyboard style. Although other more accomplished players would emerge later, he was the catalyst.

mental soloists dominating bands which were formed purely to give support to the star, and a reputation for being 'difficult' soon made him yesterday's man. Unable to keep a regular band employed and, after Victor terminated his contract in late 1930, unable to get inside a studio for another eight years, he slipped from sight. As the fine St Louis trumpeter Louis Metcalf (1905-1981) commented: 'Jelly resented the agencies beatin' bands out of money and wouldn't give in. And because he wouldn't give in, he was pushed aside.'

Morton's wife Mabel saw storm clouds coming from the other side, too: 'He began to have more and more trouble getting the co-operation of the coloured [negro] musicians. They wanted to play everything but what he had dotted down. They thought they could bring along a bottle of whisky to the job in their back pockets. All that hurt them . . . he used to say to the boys around the Rhythm Club "You can't play around, just because you think you're great. I'm telling you those white boys are not playing corny any more . . . They're getting the idea of how to play hot. Once they get it . . . they're gonna sell you for five cents a dozen" . . . and that's what happened, just the way he told them.'

BIX BEIDERBECKE: YOUNG, GIFTED AND WHITE

Mabel was reflecting the typical Creole prejudices of the day, fully shared by her husband, against full-blood negroes. But, in fact, there was a whole new generation of white musicians, based in and around Chicago, who by the late 1920s had digested the exciting lessons from men like Oliver, Morton, Bechet, Armstrong and

others, and had something of their own to say. Significantly younger than the members of the ODJB or Papa Laine, they and their southern, white contemporaries, the New Orleans Rhythm Kings, set about proving Jelly Roll right. The best of them, and a man destined to become a legend in the music, was Bix Beiderbecke (1903-1931). His was a natural talent, which manifested itself quickly after a comparatively late start at the age of 15, when he began learning the cornet. A quiet boy from a middle-class home, he was excited by the recordings of the ODJB and taught himself to play by practising along with their records. Growing up in Davenport, Iowa, he heard the music played on the riverboats, and it is likely that he first heard the young Louis Armstrong in this way, as well as another early influence, the white player Emmet Hardy

(1903-1925). Hardy himself was Bix's junior by a few months, but had begun playing earlier. He never recorded, but those who heard him claimed he had the same approach as Bix to playing 'around the melody'.

By 1924 Beiderbecke was recording with a local group of white musicians, The Wolverines, named after a Morton blues. Even at this stage, at just 21, Bix's musical conception was pretty well fully formed, as their records attest. The Wolverines were a step on from their mentors, the ODJB, in that they genuinely improvised, and their rhythms were considerably smoother and more supple, but they would not be remembered today if it were not for their cornet player. Bix's uniquely beautiful tone is evident even through the distortion of the acoustic recording process (and he played without a mute, in

direct contrast to the King Oliver tradition), his rhythmic propulsion is effortless, and his melodic imagination borders on the lyrical. Compared to him, his colleagues are primitives and, in Bix's own description of white musicians, 'corny'. Famed drug dealer and sometime jazz musician Mezz Mezzrow (1899-1972), author of a truly wild set of memoirs on his involvement in the early jazz scene, described Beiderbecke as 'a rawboned, husky, farmboy kind of kid . . . In those days he had an air of cynicism and boredom about most things, just sitting around lazy-like with his legs crossed and his body drooping, but it wasn't an act with him . . . I never heard a tone like he got before or since. He played mostly open horn, every note full, big, rich and round, standing out like a pearl, loud but never irritating or jangling, with a powerful drive

Willie 'The Lion' Smith (above left) *and James P Johnson* (above) *were the dominant stride pianists in 1920s New York. James P Johnson was also a notable composer and theoretician.*

that few white musicians had in those days.'

Being self-taught, and supremely gifted, Bix played mostly by ear, and was a poor reader until late in his career. Unlike most self-taught players, he had the same ability as Sidney Bechet to negotiate the most intricate chord patterns and come up with a solo which was truly inspired. As Mezzrow quipped, 'Bix has the most perfect instincts of all. He was born with harmony in his soul, and chords instead of corpuscles.' Unfortunately for him, the harmony in his soul was only musical. It is now clear, from the mass of eye-witness accounts, that he was a heavy drinker by his mid-twenties, and alcoholism severely disrupted and finally ended his life. At least he did not suffer from neglect. Bix was lured away from The Wolverines by a successful dance band of the time, Jean Goldkette, and recorded prolifically with him and with pick-up bands formed from a nucleus of Goldkette musicians. He toured widely with the band and became a sensation in New York, a town whose musical development up to that stage had not included the brand of 'hot' jazz cooked up by this young man from Chicago's nightspots. Late in 1927, his reputation was such that the biggest band in the business, the Paul Whiteman Orchestra, hired him as their specialist 'hot' player.

Whiteman (1890-1967) has a curious position in the evolution of jazz. His orchestra, during its peak years of popularity between the early twenties and the beginnings of the Swing Era a decade later, had only a tangential relationship to jazz, but Whiteman himself was a big fan. (He was also a first-rate self-publicist, dubbing himself at the end of the decade 'King of Jazz'.) And when he held a concert at New York's Aeolian Hall in early 1924, featuring George Gershwin playing the premiere of his *Rhapsody In Blue*, he quickly, if erroneously, became identified in the public's mind with 'hot' music. In fact, most of his repertoire at that stage were light classical warhorses re-arranged to give them new life. As the twenties wore on, his arranger Ferde Grafé (composer of *The Grand Canyon Suite*, among other works) concocted a 'symphonic' style of playing popular and 'hot' numbers which were big in the ballrooms of America.

Beiderbecke was genuinely appreciated by Whiteman, who tolerated his increasingly unreliable and erratic offstage behaviour, as well as his poor reading ability, because he loved Bix's improvisations, unequalled at that time in white jazz circles. But to wade through the scores of Whiteman sides on which Bix is present is a depressing experience, and it is without doubt that his talent was wasted in this featureless musical terrain. Clearly, it is in the sides he made with pick-up groups formed from Whiteman band members and other close associates such as Hoagy Carmichael, Tommy and Jimmy Dorsey, Frank Trumbauer, Miff Mole, Pee Wee Russell, Eddie Lang and Joe Venuti, Adrian Rollini, Benny Goodman, Bubber Miley, Jack Teagarden, Bud Freeman and Gene Krupa that the lasting legacy was created. These names make up a virtual who's who of the white jazz fraternity in Chicago and New York (although Miley was the star black trumpeter with the Duke Ellington Orchestra) in the following decade. Bix even played on the first recorded versions of Carmichael's most popular songs, *Georgia On My Mind* and *Rockin' Chair*. He was in at the beginning, and was probably the most gifted of them all, but he was the only one who failed to make the distance. Therein lies the loss, and the legend.

In contrast, trombonist Jack Teagarden (1905-1964), who was possibly the equal of Bix as an instrumentalist, with an unparalleled ease and beauty of phrasing and tone, largely fulfilled his potential in a long and happy career. Today, only diehards and students of the music are aware of his immense contribution.

Chicago had been the place where the crucial stylistic developments had taken place for the best part of the twenties, and where the music was dominated by a 'hot' and bluesy conception, whether from the Jelly Roll school, Louis Armstrong or the white boys from the Austin High School gang (a collection of talents from this suburban Chicago high school who gathered around leading personalities such as Eddie Condon, Bud Freeman and Pee Wee Russell). From Benny Goodman (then heavily influenced by New Orleans clarinettist Jimmie Noone) and Muggsy Spanier (a fervent admirer of Armstrong and Oliver) through to Armstrong sideman Earl Hines, or ex-New Orleans men such as Johnny Dodds and Freddie Keppard, every player had that urgency, that rhythmic heat and buzz laid out on an even, swinging beat that characterized Chicago jazz at its best and most typical. Yet New York had not been a musical wasteland. By the middle of this decade called 'The Jazz Age' by contemporary journalists looking for a headline (and by everybody since), New York had some fine jazz musicians settled in its midst. Virtually none of them were native New Yorkers, but the new creative vibrancy generated by what became known as the Harlem Renaissance attracted them, and some were successful enough to put down firm roots in New York soil.

A RENAISSANCE IN NEW YORK

The Harlem Renaissance was the epicentre of a general cultural and political flowering within the US black communities following the aftermath of The Great War. This massive conflict was the first time that blacks had fought overseas for the democratic ideals of American life. That they were treated as equals only when it came to dying and were let down badly on their return to the homeland undoubtedly led to the tremendous unrest of 1919, with its summer of riots whose only parallel is that of the summer of 1968 and 'burn baby burn'.

The renaissance was first and foremost a literary movement, and had been initiated by the black poet, teacher and sometime US Consul James Weldon Johnson's book of poems, *Fifty Years and Other Poems*, published in 1917. Within a short time, other literary figures and important writers such as Paul Dunbar, Langston Hughes, Claude McKay and William S. Braithwaite had come to national attention as spokesmen for a hitherto ignored stratum of American society. Soon two periodicals catering for the black population came into existence: *Crisis* and *Opportunity*. The strained and unbalanced times can be seen through the names of those two magazines. The cultural movement centred

Henry 'Red' Allen, one of the great trumpet stylists in jazz, was the first player to come up in Armstrong's shadow yet still manage to carve out a convincing personal trumpeting indentity. He was a dynamic stage performer and a greatly entertaining singer.

around an uptown section of New York City's Manhattan Island, an old German expatriate middle-class suburb, Harlem. This area, north of the business and retail centre of the city, had been the subject of intense property speculation, and when, prior to the Great War, the house market collapsed, desperate developers began renting off the unsold properties to anyone who would take them. So began the influx of negro families, and, in turn, the departure of the whites. By the end of World War 1, Harlem was the black cultural centre of the US in every way.

The city had two main musical streams – one formal, the other informal. At downtown and mid-city hotels, in uptown cabarets such as The Cotton Club and The Plantation and the high-class clubs, all patronized almost exclusively by rich whites, the early big bands entertained their high-society guests. In a town which practised strict audience segregation, all these places had a whites-only policy on the door, although, in many cases – especially when it came to playing 'hot' music – the musicians were black. The glitzier the place, the less jazz content the band had: Paul Whiteman is a neat example of this exercise in diminishing returns. At the other end of the spectrum – and town – were the little bars, clubs and private parties which showcased the talents of the solo pianists and of small groups, most of whom had constantly shifting personnel.

The great bandleader and composer Duke Ellington (1899-1974) started his career in New York after leaving his home town of Washington DC with a small core of musicians such as Harry Carney and Sonny Greer, working whatever clubs he could get into, and often having to play as a solo act. He had clear memories of these early days: 'There wasn't near enough work for everybody that could blow horns, and what musicians didn't have steady jobs would spend their days standing out on the street gabbing, always arguing about the respective merits of everybody else ... At nights everybody used to carry their horns around with them and wherever there was a piano you'd find hornblowers sitting in and jamming ... And whoever owned the place would stand drinks all night long. It was OK by him, he got free music that way.'

In this latter climate, it was the pianists who held sway. And New York even by the early twenties, was awash with major black piano talent. The father of them all was James P. Johnson (1894-1955). An extraordinary figure, Johnson had by 1916 become sufficiently popular in New York

THE COTTON CLUB: **This was one of the great night-spots in New York City for hearing good jazz and catching a great floorshow during the twenties and thirties. It was smart and exclusive in more ways than one. Its clients (below) were rich, high-society whites, many (but not all) of them jazz lovers. Both Duke Ellington and Cab Calloway began their rise to fame in the club, and for many people their names are still associated with it. Curiously, for a venue which is world-renowned for being a mecca for all that's best in the jazz of the period, it had an unpleasant door policy: whites only. The only negroes allowed in the place were the ones onstage (right).**

that he was cutting his first piano rolls, in the then ubiquitous ragtime style, but his talents lay much wider afield. He was thoroughly trained in the European tradition, had a phenomenal technique for the period, was an influential piano stylist and teacher (his most famous pupil being Fats Waller) and was a distinguished composer, not only of songs, but of extended works for the stage and the concert hall, including a symphony. Needless to say, this side of his talents went unappreciated by his normal audience and critics during his lifetime. However, his knowledge and sheer ability meant that his pre-eminence in New York went unchallenged in the period when the famous 'stride' piano style was developing. He and his two acolytes, Willie 'The Lion' Smith and Fats Waller, dominated New York piano for over a decade.

One of the forums at which the great 'stride' pianists presided in Harlem during the twenties and thirties was the rent-party. This was a phenomenon which grew out of sheer need. When some-

one was particularly hard-up, and had no other way of drumming up the cash to pay the rent and keep a roof over his head, he would organize a rent-party. This was pretty easy to do: you would spread the word around about the date and time. Then you would hire yourself a pianist like James P. (Duke Ellington once said 'Jimmy Johnson used to get all the house-rent parties to play'), ask an entry fee to cover the pianist's fee, then charge for all food and drink. By the next dawn, with everyone 'feeling no pain' and collapsed in the corner or drifting off home, the relieved occupant would have a busted-up apartment and the money to keep the landlord happy. James P.'s acolyte and performer at many such occasions, Fats Waller, later released a single, *The Joint Is Jumpin'*, whose lyrics convey the some-what illicit excitement of such nights:

'The piano's thumpin', the dancers are bumpin'
this here spot is more than hot, in fact the joint is jumpin'!
Check your weapons at the door, be sure to pay your quarter;
burn your leather on the floor, grab anybody's daughter.
The roof is rockin', the neighbours knockin'
we're all bums when the wagon comes, I mean the joint is jumpin'!'

New York was also the city where big band music came to an early fruition, mostly through the endeavours of two leaders, Fletcher Henderson and Duke Ellington. Both had learned valuable lessons at the hands of the earlier New Orleans musicians who had passed through New York, and were to incorporate much of that music's characteristics into their own. Henderson, a diffident man from a comfortable and educated background, had formed his band in 1923 according to impeccable principles from

which he never departed: hire the best men, and play the music you like, in the way you like. This led him, in 1924, to hire Louis' Armstrong as his 'hot' soloist.

Armstrong's contribution to the Henderson band was crucial: he freed up the rhythm, got the sections playing off each other, and inspired the arrangers, Henderson and Don Redman, to bring in the riff and section work within a band which became the cornerstone of big-band jazz for the next four decades. By the close of the decade, Henderson's band had a song book which included pieces which were to become jazz standards for the whole of the swing era, had matchless soloists like Coleman Hawkins, the first great tenor saxophonist, and Henry 'Red' Allen, Armstrong's great trumpet rival at the close of the twenties, and had arrangements which would remain state-of-the-art for years. They also had the smoothest rhythmic pulse this side of Count Basie, and half a decade earlier.

Duke Ellington's position was a little different. At no time during the twenties did he dominate the musical scene – that role was Armstrong's and his alone. As Ellington's trumpeter Rex Stewart recalled: 'Then Louis Armstrong hit town! I went mad with the rest of the town. I tried to walk like him, talk like him, eat like him, sleep like him. I even bought a pair of big policeman shoes like he used to wear and stood outside his apartment waiting for him to come out so I could look at him.' Ellington had arrived in New York from Washington in 1923, had scuffled with his five-piece which included Otto Hardwicke and Sonny Greer, and had finally landed the residency at the Hollywood Club at 49th and Broadway. This place was re-named the Kentucky Club, and Ellington's band stayed there for four years. After that, manager Irving Mills

got them into the Cotton Club, and also into recording. Ellington's music, as well as his band, still had a long way to develop, as Ned Williams states bluntly: 'I can't say I was too impressed with the Ellington crew on that [first] visit [to the Cotton Club]. It definitely didn't have the form and the polish that it acquired later.' But in 1928-29, Ellington was writing memorable music such as *Black & Tan Fantasy, Rockin' In Rhythm* and *The Mooche* – songs he would continue to play for the rest of his career – and the greatest composer in the history of jazz was on his way. His style was an amalgam of everything he had heard in his native Washington, in New York and in every place in between: but it was his genius which distilled all this down to the multi-faceted and endlessly satisfying tapestry of sound and rhythm which characterizes his best work.

With the thriving live circuit criss-crossing the US by the end of the twenties, the cross-fertilization of the music was producing some fabulous breeds. Jazz was developing at a pell-mell rate, listened to by an audience which was truly world-wide and which contained converts from the most everyday sections of society up to the Prince of Wales, composers Maurice Ravel and Stravinsky, and authors Boris Vian and Jean-Paul Sartre. Surely there was no stopping it now.

Well, one thing did, at least for a while: the Depression. While many struggled through it as best they could, hundreds of careers came to a full-stop. Some major artists were never to record again, while others disappeared from public life for five, ten, twenty years – or more, in the case of many blues musicians. And when the music came back again, in the early thirties, it was playing a rather different song, with a shift in mood to match.

swing street

'If it ain't got swing, it ain't worth playin'; if it ain't got gutbucket, it ain't worth doin'

Bubber Miley, *Ellington trumpeter*

AT THE CLOSE of the twenties, America entered a period of cataclysmic change. After an era of unparalleled expansion, the economy collapsed like a house of cards, bringing down with it whole sections of the workforce. As with all economic recessions, the worst hit parts of society were the most unprotected. The black workforce was decimated, and similarly the black element of the entertainment industry was dealt crippling blows.

It was hit from two sides: the rise of the film industry in the 1920s was beginning to radically alter popular forms of entertainment nationwide, as well as popular entertainment habits. The severe economic squeeze affected the public's ability to pay for live shows. With the coming of talkies, the key forms of in-person variety, such as verbal comedy and other vocal effects, could be imitated by the film screen actors and actresses. Indeed, films rapidly established themselves as America's favourite form of entertainment. This melancholy fact was reflected in the shrinkage of live venues over the first 40 years

The natural audience for dance music and swing in the 1930s were the blacks in urban centres who were ready to enjoy themselves dancing or listening to music whether it was live or from a juke box. Right: *a typical dance session from a Harlem highspot of the thirties;* (inset) *a southern states juke joint on Saturday night.*

of the century. In 1900, there were close to 5,000 theatres actively patronized throughout the US, all of which probably gave employment in one form or another to blacks. By 1940, five years after the worst effects of the Depression had receded, and ten years after talkies had commenced, only around 200 theatres were still in existence. With this rapid shrinkage came a crisis in the

stant work once they were affiliated. The most famous of these agencies was an association which specialized in touring all-black areas in cities, towns and communities throughout the midwest and the south. This was a collection of theatres formed into a booking organization called Theatre Owners Booking Association. The range of artists appearing in these travelling

schedules and the lack of major big-city venues kept them on the treadmill long after they should have graduated to better things. For this reason, the TOBA initials came to stand for 'Tough On Black Asses' among performers.

However, when the Depression and the talkies delivered two body blows to TOBA, the wounds were mortal. Between its demise in the deepest part of the

albeit under the demeaning 'race' records series titles – threw overboard all but the most popular black acts: the list of musicians who ceased recording in 1930-1931 and simply never cut a disc again, or only after 10, 20 or even 30 years, is astonishing in its completeness, especially in the blues, where even Bessie Smith, once a colossal star, did not record (apart from one session arranged by John Hammond at his expense in 1933) from 1931 until her death in 1937. On the jazz side, King Oliver, Jelly Roll Morton, Johnny Dodds, Sidney Bechet, James P. Johnson, Jabbo Smith and Noble Sissle all either never recorded again, or suffered lengthy hiatuses in their recording activities. Even as popular an entertainer as Fats Waller went three years without a record date at the height of the Depression.

an inherent balance of musical structure which makes its best records far from being simply a stringing-together of riff and solo sections, and its advanced concept of rhythmic drive.

This was one of the very first bands which really swung, four-to-the-bar. In fact it swung so much that there were often problems in the studio, as Cuba Austin recalls: 'The boys were wild with excitement about recording ... and we trooped into the studio shoutin' and rarin' to go ... We had a lot of trouble with the engineers. In those days everybody took off their shoes and had a pillow under his feet so the thud from beating the rhythm didn't ruin things. Well, on *Milenberg Joys* the band was beating a fast rhythm and then, bit by bit, the pillows kept sliding away. We ruined several takes.'

The Cotton Pickers may have been ahead of their time and had the makings of a band to challenge the best; however, the collapse of steady employment meant that they were soon on a never-ending trail of one-nighters over the midwest and southwest. As Cuba Austin put it: 'There isn't anything that can ruin a band quicker than a booker who keeps jumping it all over the country for one-nighters. You play nine to three, then hop in a bus and ride. You pull into the next stop maybe around sunset the next day. No time to get a rest in a bed or even to clean up and get the grime off you ... You've seen the boys on the stand making out they were laughing and talking with each other during the numbers – that's all in the game. You never know when you see them up there that any of those men might be in pain.'

After a while the strain began to show, with the band breaking up into factions, then key people such as Redman leaving and taking his friends with him. The

Jean Goldkette's Orchestra on a tour of New England in September 1926. Bix Beiderbecke can be seen, fourth from the left. Goldkette is in the white suit, three places up from Beiderbecke.

booking organizations which arranged the tours and ran the venues that kept these black musicians and entertainers employed.

In the decades up to 1930, specialist booking agencies had set up theatre circuits which guaranteed the performers con-

shows embraced every form of entertainment, from jugglers, magicians, dancers, comics and banjoists to the greatest of the early blues shouters. Bessie Smith, 'The Empress of The Blues', came to national attention through her many tours with TOBA. Yet despite its pivotal role in providing work for artists and entertainment for thousands of provincial blacks, few of the performers used by the organization thought well of it, feeling that the low wages, the murderous touring

Depression and the eventual upturn of live work with the Swing craze towards the middle of the thirties, there was nothing to replace it. People who had made decent livings, or got by with TOBA, simply vanished off the scene. Others worked as farm hands, cab drivers or just did not work at all until the Depression lifted.

Similarly, the recording industry which, by the end of the twenties, had become quite enterprising in its recording of black music –

EFFECTS OF THE DEPRESSION

The fate of a number of large bands, all of them active at the onset of the Depression, illustrates how chance, luck and economic realities contributed to the development of jazz as a music. McKinney's Cotton Pickers was a band which came out of Detroit, organized as it was by Jean Goldkette's management company, and often playing with Goldkette's band at the Greystone Ballroom in Detroit. Well under way by 1925, and with a number of key musicians such as trumpeter/arranger John Nesbitt (plus in 1927 Don Redman, who had recently quit the Fletcher Henderson orchestra), Prince Robinson and drummer Cuba Austin, the band made a series of records between 1928 and 1930 which demonstrates its imaginative development of contrasting instrumental textures,

Southern blacks had few diversions, especially during the great Depression. Here, some are hanging out in a juke joint, playing cards, drinking low-grade whiskey, and enjoying life as best they can. Note the impressive array of hats.

record sessions by then had stopped, and though the band limped on until 1935, its presence had become marginal.

Fletcher Henderson's fate was quite different. Although his approach as band leader was laissez-faire in the extreme, his exciting music and top-flight arrangements meant that the musicians in the band stayed loyal as the going got tough. The band continued to record right through the worst years of the Depression, and in fact made one of their most remarkable recordings, Coleman Hawkins' *Queer Notions*, which is based throughout on various applications of a diminished scale, in 1933. They had abandoned the tuba in the late twenties, and by the end of 1930 the banjo, that other vestige of New Orleans, had also gone, replaced by the rhythm guitar. As a result, their music was shaping up into something close to swing a number of years before that style's general emergence. Nevertheless, work was drying

up, as Duke Ellington remembered: 'Smack's [Henderson's] band was beginning to find the going a little tough . . . Work was scarce, but the band was so fine, and the guys so attached to it, that nobody had the heart to quit . . . Almost every individual musician had money coming to him, and yet nothing ever happened. Finally, when they couldn't hang out any longer, the whole band got together, and everybody turned in their notice at the same time. That was the break-up of the Fletcher Henderson band.'

Henderson organized other ensembles, and even continued to record sporadically right into the swing era, but his time as the hottest leader in the music had gone. However, he was to play a crucial role in the next stage of the music, because it was his band's book of arrangements which Benny Goodman was to buy and exploit with Goodman such incredible success in the space of a few short years.

Another crucial influence on the new music of the thirties, Bennie

Bennie Moten was a key figure in big band jazz. Based in Kansas City, he formed around him a nucleus of brilliant musicians and in the early 1930s he recruited Count Basie and Hot Lips Page.

Moten, also failed to make the distance, but for a different reason. Moten had a well-organized and locally popular band in Kansas City by 1923, and in the fall of that year made his first records for the Okeh label. Late in 1926, he signed a deal with Victor, and continued to record for the label until December 1932, when the contract was terminated; the band was never to record again under Moten's name. Moten himself was a musi-

cian happy to play in the current style of the period, but was also astute enough to know that he had to continue to stay abreast of with each new development to survive. By 1929, Walter Page's Blue Devils, also from Kansas City, was his main competitor. This band, which included in its ranks Hot Lips Page, Buster Smith (later to be a crucial influence on Charlie Parker), Dan Minor, Jimmy Rushing and Count Basie, had a smoother, more elastic approach to rhythm, and was generating a deal more excitement than Moten's: Moten's reaction was to absorb them into his own band and radically change his musical style. Recognizing that Count Basie was a better pianist than himself, he also more or less ceased playing piano with his own band.

Kansas City at this time provided the perfect climate for musicians of all persuasions. The town had been administered by Democratic Party boss Tom Pendergast since 1928, when he manipulated the party vote to have himself installed as Mayor. Pendergast ran the town as if

Prohibition had never been introduced, and it was an open secret that he collaborated with local hoodlums to run the town's thriving red light and vice district, exacting a cut from the takings of the best illegal dens in return for giving them his official 'protection'. With the economics of jazz so closely tied to entertainment of this kind in the twenties and thirties, this thriving illicit scene meant plenty of work for the musicians of the area.

Kansas City itself, sitting on the state line between Kansas and Missouri, was in a pivotal position in America's midwest, being a trade centre and crossroads for a huge surrounding area. The town was a natural resting point in a headlong tour across the country. Although the working conditions were atrocious and the pay not much better (about £15 a week for the average musician in 1931), everybody loved to play there. Drummer Jo Jones had very fond memories of that time: 'Some places in Kansas City never closed. You could be sleeping one morning at 6 am, and a travelling band would come into

town for a few hours, and they would wake you up to make a couple of hours' session with them until eight in the morning. You never knew what time in the morning someone would knock on the door and say they were jamming down the street.'

By 1930, a year after he had absorbed most of the Blue Devils into his organization, and three years into his Victor recording contract, Moten was beginning to nudge ahead of his rivals in the midwest, and come to level terms with nationally established orchestras such as Henderson's and Ellington's. Two years further on, Moten bought 40 arrangements from Horace Henderson and Benny Carter, direct from the Fletcher Henderson library, in an attempt to keep in the forefront of the big band business after a series of disastrous 'live' encounters with better and more modern bands. But perhaps even he, astute businessman though he was, did not realize that, by late 1932, with his Victor recording contract still intact, he was presiding over a band which was making strides into previously untouched musical terrain.

His was the first band, for example, to evolve a balance between arrangements and soloists which gave the soloists the advantage, while still giving them musical support. But, most crucially, the rhythm section of Count Basie, Walter Page, LeRoy Berry and Willie Washington was creating a smooth swinging style which was years ahead of its time, and different to anything the contemporary records by Henderson or Ellington could come up with. With soloists of the calibre of Ben Webster, Hot Lips Page, Hershel Evans and Lester Young to play over this subtly supercharged rhythm, this was the sound of the future. Unhappily, it was not to be Moten's sound: at the dawning of the swing era in 1935, with the Depression more or less successfully negotiated, Moten died in the operating theatre of a Chicago hospital after complications during a routine tonsilectomy. The man who took the band over was Count Basie.

Somebody whose career failed to survive the Depression was the former trumpet king of New Orleans, Joe Oliver. After Armstrong had left him in 1924, he continued to prosper in Chicago until a long residency at The Plantation was terminated in 1927, when the place was gutted by fire – a result of the increasing violence in the Chicago gang wars. In a bid for better prospects, Oliver took his band east to New York where he made a number of decisions which were to seal his fate; one was to over-estimate his powers as a drawing-card, and refuse the offer of a long-term engagement, for rather poor money, in The Cotton Club. The offer was subsequently made to Duke Ellington, and the rest is history.

Oliver was still recording regularly, mostly with pick-up groups, right through the first year of the Depression, but his fading powers as a trumpeter due to a chronic gum condition were beginning to show. Most significantly, the classic New Orleans style was dropping out of favour, not just in New York but also in his second home, Chicago, and by late 1931, with his last recording session behind him, Oliver was reduced to 'guesting' with other bands, or accepting poorly-paid work on disastrously organized tours of the midwest and southern states. Sometimes nights were as of old, but on other occasions, gigs failed to materialize, or were booked for a redneck dance with the band barely escaping with their instruments and bodies intact.

Oliver undoubtedly had wretched luck, with a nightmare succession of wrecked tour buses and cars, seized engines and cancelled gigs. As he once said himself, 'breaks come to cats only once in a while and I must have been asleep when mine came. I've made lots of dough in this game but I didn't know how to take care of it . . . I have written a lot of numbers that someone else got the credit and the money for. I couldn't help it because I didn't know what to do.' By late 1937, he was stranded in Savannah, Georgia, his health broken and all musical activity halted. Writing to his sister, he gives a clear indication of his situation in the winter of 1937-38: 'I open the pool rooms at 9 a.m. and close at 12 midnite. If the money was only a quarter as much as the hours I'd be all set. But at that I can thank God for what I'm getting. Which I do night after night . . . Should anything happen to me will you want my body? Let me know because I won't last forever and the longer I go the worst I'll get . . .' Two months later, on the morning of April 10th, 1938, he was found dead in his rented room, the victim of a cerebral haemorrhage. His family arranged for the body to be brought to New York, where he was buried: times

were hard, and there was no money for a gravestone. There still isn't one today.

PRECURSORS OF SWING

Swing did not officially get under way until Benny Goodman's debut at the Palomar Ballroom in August 1935 where, to his amazement, the place was packed with young fans of his 'Let's Dance' radio show who went crazy every time he played a 'hot' number. However, it is clear that swing as a style of music had arrived some two to three years before then: it just took that long for public taste, media fashions, and the music business to catch on. Three bands, in particular, had been playing swing style with great success in those years: Jimmie Lunceford, Chick Webb and Duke Ellington.

Lunceford (1902-1947) suc-

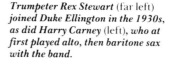

Trumpeter Rex Stewart (far left) *joined Duke Ellington in the 1930s, as did Harry Carney* (left), *who at first played alto, then baritone sax with the band.*

ceeded the gifted dancer, singer, comedian and bandleader Cab Calloway (b. 1907) at the Cotton Club in 1934 after four years of obscure one-nighter tours followed by a big success at the Lafayette Theatre in New York. Within months he had a recording contract, and made a number, *White Heat*, which became his theme tune for the next decade. Other hits followed, including *It Ain't What You Do (But The Way That You Do It)*, and the band acquired an unparalleled reputation for fast, accurate section work, insistent swing and superb lead work from players such as altoist Willie Smith, trombonist Trummy Young, and trumpeter/arranger Sy Oliver. This dynamic outfit was untouchable as a powerhouse dance band, and their records bear this out. However, Lunceford's main preoccupation remained making great music for dancers, rather than evolving within a given style. Musically, he was gradually super-

*Above: **Jimmy Lunceford and his band**, swing specialists of the 1930s. Right: **A young Ella Fitzgerald** in reflective mood with Chick Webb, the band leader who had the inspiration to recognize her talents.*

seded so that, by his death in 1947, his great years were a long way behind him.

Chick Webb (1909-39) was everybody's favourite drummer in New York in the early thirties. Born a hunchback into a poor Baltimore family, the deformity never bothered him in his professional life, nor did it bother the people he worked with. Helped initially by Duke Ellington, he ran a quintet at first, then in 1928 an eight-piece at New York's Paddock Club. In 1931 he got the job that was to set him up for the rest of his brief life: leading the resident band at Harlem's Savoy Ballroom. Although there were interruptions through band breakups, then later national tours and

other prestige one-nighters, it was at the Savoy that Webb and his band felt truly at home. The Savoy was nicknamed 'the track' because it was so vast inside, with two stages, one for each band, that it looked like a race-track. Webb, was a superlative drummer with perfect time who drove his band through his impeccable beat. With this set-up, there was nothing he liked better than to 'take on' one of the other top bands guesting at the Savoy in a 'battle' to win the dancers' approval. His mentor, Duke Ellington, said about him: 'Webb was always battle mad, and those eight guys used to take on every band that came up to play there ... Webb ate up any kind of fight, and everybody in the band played like mad at all times. They figured out a bunch of original numbers, and it was generally too bad for the guy on the opposite stand.'

As Webb's reputation grew, so did the quality of his sidemen. His big coup was to have both Taft Jordan, a charismatic trumpeter with a 'Satchmo' routine that crowds adored, and Edgar Sampson, an arranger and composer of some genius, in the band at the same time. Sampson gave Chick his first hit-songs which were later to be million-sellers for Goodman and other white bands: *Don't Be That Way and Stompin' At The Savoy* are just two of them. But the biggest break of all, and the one which keeps Webb's name alive to even casual fans of jazz, was the one he gave to an unknown girl singer who won an amateur night at Harlem's Apollo in 1934. As Mary Lou Williams tells it, dropping one night into the Savoy around that time: 'After dancing a couple of rounds, I heard a voice that sent chills up and down my spine ... I almost ran to the stand to find out who belonged to the voice, and saw a pleasant-looking, brown-skinned

girl standing modestly and sing-ing the greatest. I was told her name was Ella Fitzgerald.'

With Ella in the band, big-time success finally arrived and, in 1939, Webb had his first million-seller with a swing version of the nursery rhyme *A-Tisket, A-Tasket*. By late the same year, however, it was clear that Webb was no longer a healthy man, and he had to bring in another drum-mer to play sections of each engagement for him. Afflicted with tuberculosis of the spine, he was determined to battle on even though by early 1939 he was fainting after playing shows. At this time virtually every band-leader was desperately trying to pry Fitzgerald away from the ail-ing drummer, but she stayed loyal to the man who had given her a break: so loyal, in fact, that when Webb died in 1939, she kept the band going for a further two years before going out as a solo.

DUKE ELLINGTON: GENESIS OF A GENIUS

Although active in the twenties, Duke Ellington came to life in a completely new way during the course of the thirties. By the end of the decade he was such a force in the music that people realized they were dealing with a man who was an exception to every rule and standard in jazz. By the beginning of the Depression, Ellington had formed his first great band, and was deep into his 'jungle' period, during which his style was characterized by growl-ing trumpets, muted, wah-wah trombones, and saxophone har-monies radically different to the blandness found in the 'sweet' bands of the day. In early 1932, Duke recorded a novelty song of his called *It Don't Mean a Thing (If It Ain't Got That Swing)*, thereby presaging the swing era by over three years. At about this time he

had come to the end of his long residency at the Cotton Club and handed it over the Cab Calloway, who in turn went on to national and international prominence. In his closing period there, Ellington had been producing such music that, as Ned Williams recounts, 'Paul Whiteman and his arranger, Ferde Grofé, visited the Cotton Club nightly for more than a week, [and] finally admitted that they couldn't steal even two bars of the amazing music', while society pianist Eddie Duchin, after listen-ing one night in the Club, 'actually and literally rolled on the floor under his table in ecstasy.'

Duke had a vital and unique combination of talents: he was, for a start, a brilliant leader and inspirer of men, who understood the special qualities of every musician in his band. He gener-ated tremendous loyalty among his players, with some of them, such as Harry Carney, Sonny Greer, Johnny Hodges and Billy Strayhorn, staying in the Orches-tra 30 or 40 years. On top of this, Duke was a songwriter and orchestral arranger of real genius, and someone who, while a natu-ral, also spent long exhausting periods perfecting his craft and learning from a variety of sources. He used to delight in telling how he learned the basics of composi-tion from Will Marion Cook, the composer and orchestra leader who had taken Sidney Bechet to Europe in 1919: 'Will never wore a hat, and when people asked him why, he'd say because he didn't have the money to buy one. They'd give him five dollars and then he and I would get in a taxi and ride around Central Park and he'd give me lectures in music ... Some of the things he used to tell me I never got a chance to use until years later, when I wrote the tone poem *Black, Brown & Beige*. Beyond this, he would pick up theory and ideas from any musi-cal situation he came across. But

A 1929 photograph (right) *shows several essential musicians in the early Ellington sound: Joe 'Tricky Sam' Nanton and Cootie Williams (second and third from left), Arthur Whetsol (fifth from left), the reed section of Harry Carney, Johnny Hodges and Barney Bigard, and the bass player Wellman Braud (standing, far right). In 1943, Ellington posed with players from his then-current band* (below), *which included 1929 members Joe Nanton (trombone), Harry Carney (clarinet), Johnny Hodges (sax) and Sonny Greer (drums).*

ELLINGTON AND HIS MUSICIANS: Duke Ellington had a remarkably
stable personnel over many years and this was one of the great
strengths of his music, because it meant that he could write his
music with specific men in mind, and was consequently able to
rely on particular sounds to emerge in the blend of instruments.
Sleek and sophisticated, he was one of the first ambassadors of
jazz to Europe and became one of the most acclaimed muscians of
the 20th century.

it was his nightly experimentation with his band that gave him the greatest possible understanding of the musical process as he wished to use it.

Ellington was also unusual in his vast appetite for learning across other artistic and entertainment disciplines, and his sincere interest in other cultures. But one of his most distinctive creative patterns was the inspiration he drew from observing everyday things around him, as in *Daybreak Express*, which had liberal imitations of steam trains thundering down railroads in the US countryside, and *Rent Party Blues*, *East St Louis Toodle-Oo*, *Saturday Night Function*, or *Caravan*, all brilliantly evocative of their subjects.

In 1933, Ellington and his Orchestra toured Europe for the first time, becoming one of the first black orchestras to do so (Louis Armstrong had come to Europe the year before). The tour was both a triumph and an eye-opener to Duke and his band: Rex Stewart, trumpeter with Duke in the thirties, commented a few years later: 'You have to be a negro to understand why. Europe is a different world. You can go anywhere, do anything, talk to anybody ... You are like a guy who has eaten hot dogs all his life and is suddenly offered caviar.' Ellington received ovations everywhere he played, and his band performed at a party arranged for the Prince of Wales who, like his brother, was a big fan. Duke was surprised and delighted to find that his music was treated with great seriousness by intellectuals and musicians all over Europe, and this gave him added confidence to follow his own path, rather than succumb to shallow commercial efforts.

With the death of his mother in 1935, the year other bands were jumping on the swing band-wagon, Ellington composed his first extended work, *Reminiscing In Tempo*. Covering four sides of two ten-inch 78rpm singles, this was the first recording by a jazz musician to last longer than the three or so minutes of the average popular tune. It was a milestone that clearly marked the beginning of a new and important stage in Ellington's development, and led directly to his early forties masterpieces.

BENNY GOODMAN: SWING'S THE THING

In the same year, Benny Goodman had exploded on to the scene. Benny had been around for a long time before he finally broke through. Born in Chicago in 1909, he took up clarinet at the age of 10, and by the time he was 13 was appearing professionally around his home town. Still in his teens in 1925, he joined the Ben Pollack Orchestra and became one of its star 'hot' attractions. Even at this stage Goodman, who had a reputation as someone who declined to suffer fools gladly, was never entirely satisfied with Pollack or his music. He regularly took jobs outside the Pollack band and sometimes left for months at a time but was always welcomed back, not only because he was so good, but also because Pollack had a genuinely high regard for musicians who were better than himself. However, in September 1929, Benny left for the last time to work in New York with, among others, the jazz-tinged popular trumpeter Red Nichols. With the collapse of the economy the following month, Goodman stayed on top of things by working wherever jobs presented themselves, playing in Broadway pit bands, and doing studio session work and radio session work. As a brilliant technician and an effortless reader, Benny found no trouble getting work of this kind, and his desire to live in relative comfort meant that he had a pragmatist's approach to the jobs he played. An additional incentive was that he came from a large, impoverished family, and

Benny Goodman (left) *in his heyday, 1939, when everything he did went gold. Benny was a greatly gifted clarinettist who thoroughly deserved the success and adulation which came to him.*

Goodman (above *in the late thirties with inspirational vibist Lionel Hampton) was the first white band leader to feature a mixed-race outfit onstage. Although he did not hire blacks as regular sidemen, he featured both Lionel Hampton and Teddy Wilson in his small groups for many years. Goodman was a notoriously hard taskmaster when it came to musicianship. In the photo* (left) *, there are some pretty unhappy faces at this 1940 recording session! Note Fletcher Henderson at the piano, and a fine sax section made up of Toots Mondello, Buff Estes, Bus Bassey and Jerry Jerome.*

BENNY GOODMAN, A TRAIL-BLAZING SUCCESS: **By 1938, despite a succession of setbacks, Benny Goodman was a household name in the US and was soon to be similarly popular worldwide. He gave a generation of young, white audiences a new and exciting music to dance to. Yet what was remarkable about his music was that it was uncompromisingly jazz as he saw it and as he and his band wanted to play it. What was also notable at the time was that Goodman was willing to include black musicians such as Teddy Wilson and Lionel Hampton among his players. Goodman was the epitome of the swing era and an all-time jazz bestseller.**

when his father was killed in an automobile accident around this time, the burden of family support fell mostly to young Benny.

Goodman's methods, and his strong leadership style on a whole string of pick-up dates and recordings, meant that musicians naturally coalesced around him, even if they did not appreciate his tongue-lashings and sarcasm. The jazz producer, talent-spotter and musicians' patron, John Hammond, became involved in recording sessions with Goodman in 1933, when jazz was pretty much not being recorded at all. Hammond had agreed to do a series of recordings for English Columbia at a time that the US Columbia company had gone bankrupt. Goodman, a great hustler, persuaded Hammond to listen to his own band rather than use the top-flight jazz musicians the A&R man had originally intended.

Hammond listened and hated them, calling them the 'dreariest bunch of musicians I had ever listened to.' He persuaded Goodman to compromise on the musicians, while he agreed to allow the songs to be arranged, rather than simply 'jammed' for the recording. In this way, both Goodman and Hammond got what they wanted, and together

made some halfway decent records.

Goodman's strong will became evident once again when, having formed a big band in 1934 with the idea of playing the 'hot' music he really liked, the clarinettist found himself and his band less successful than he expected. He had rehearsed his handpicked players in readiness for the first spot at a new ballroom opened in 1934 by Billy Rose, a man whom Goodman had met through the pianist/songwriter Oscar Levant; after passing the audition the band was hired to play for both the floorshow and for the public dancers. Goodman's outfit lasted just one night as the show band, and about four months as the dance orchestra. Goodman's comment years later sums up the reasons for this fiasco: 'I thought they [the dancers in the floorshow] were supposed to follow us.' However, two months after the lay-off and the breakup of his band through lack of work, Goodman's band was reconvened to audition for a new radio show, networked right across the US. The show was 'Let's Dance', and had a format in which different types of dance bands, from smooth strict-tempo outfits through to Goodman's 'hot' band,

Three great men behind the great man: pianist Teddy Wilson (above left), who was also the leader and arranger on the famous 1930s Billie Holiday sides, Gene Krupa (right), legendary drummer and the real heart of Goodman's late thirties big band and small groups, and John Hammond (above right), self-appointed jazz benefactor and the discoverer of, among others, Count Basie, Billie Holiday, Lester Young and Charlie Christian. He was a close friend of Goodman's and helped him immeasurably in the early years of his career.

played half-hour segments on the three-hour programme from 10.30pm to 1.30am once a week.

This show, a bold venture at the time, was not only Goodman's financial lifeline in the six months of its existence (from December 1934 to late May 1935), but it also made him a national name without him even realizing it. In addition, it gave him time to build up a superbly professional band and a formidable book of jazz arrangements, not the least important being a whole sheaf of scores bought from Fletcher Henderson. With John Hammond recruiting such key figures as drummer Gene Krupa and pianist Jess Stacy, Goodman managed to create the first white big band with real jazz credentials. This, in 1934, was no mean achievement for a

25-year-old clarinettist, especially against the background of the Depression.

In this Goodman was quite clearly going against the grain of the entertainment establishment. To the average white in search of musical entertainment, Paul Whiteman epitomized jazz. What Goodman played was loud, brash, crudely rhythmic and altogether 'too lowbrow'; decent, sane people could not dance to it. John Hammond, in his autobiography, graphically paints the scene at New York's Roosevelt Grill, home of Guy Lombardo's ultra-smooth music prior to Goodman's arrival: 'I was in the Roosevelt Grill on opening night. Customers were sitting at their tables in shock. Waiters were moving through the room with

their fingers in their ears, even though Benny's brass section was muted . . . [the] engagement ended after two weeks, a disaster which forced [booker] Willard Alexander to put together a tour for him. There was no other place in New York where the band could play.'

The subsequent tour started inauspiciously, and reached an all-time low in Denver, where Goodman had to resort to quasi-vaudeville to get through the engagement in one piece. But, on reaching California, a transformation took place. At the Palomar Ballroom in Los Angeles, August 21 1935, Goodman found his real audience: or rather, they found him. By this point, Benny and the band were fed up with compromises, and cut loose with their hottest numbers: to their amazement, the crowd went wild. What Goodman didn't know was that, due to the time differences between eastern and western seaboards in the US, his 'Let's Dance' broadcasts had picked up a significantly younger audience in California, who listened specifically to him because his was the only exciting music on the air. Typical middle-class teenagers!

From that point on, Benny Goodman and his band rapidly captured the attention of the nation's youth and the media. With wild new dances gathered under the generic title of jitter-bugging being introduced to white audiences – most with their roots in what blacks had been dancing to for years – the 'swing era' was officially under way. By January 1938, Goodman had captured the nation's attention so completely that he was able to mount the first-ever jazz concert at New York City's bastion of conservative culture, Carnegie Hall. Spurred by similar events organized for Duke Ellington and Louis Armstrong in Europe, Goodman's supporters felt that the stature of Goodman's music was sufficient that he could pull it off. Not only was it an enormous success, but the album of the concert, when finally released some 12 years after the event, became an all-time jazz bestseller.

What was so impressive about Goodman's achievement was that he did it playing music he and his band liked. As Krupa saw it, 'Benny built himself a band playing musicians' music, but didn't shoot over the heads of the public . . . It allowed us to play the way we honestly wanted to play.' On that cold January night in 1938, the Goodman band, Trio, Quartet and a selection of invited guests – including Count Basie, Johnny Hodges, Lester Young, Cootie Williams, Harry Carney and Buck Clayton – made wonderful music, and jazz history, in presenting a whole evening of jazz to a sit-down audience intent on appreciating its finer points. And when they played *Sing Sing Sing* popular music was never quite the same again.

Another way in which Benny Goodman was important to jazz in the thirties was in his willingnes to hire – and record with – black musicians. His was not the first integrated band (in fact, the black stars in his organization such as pianist Teddy Wilson and vibes player Lionel Hampton only played in his showcase small groups and not with the larger aggregation), but his immense prestige and undoubted prominence in the entertainment industry helped open doors to black musicians which had previously been not just closed but hermetically sealed. The fact that Goodman's musical conception remained more or less static for the next 40 years does not detract from his achievement as a player or a leader, but it does mean that, with one single parenthesis in the early forties, he can be safely left on the night of his Carnegie Hall triumph.

Goodman's trailblazing success in giving America's youth an exciting new beat to dance to opened the way to literally hundreds of would-be challengers to the throne. In the years up to America's declaration of war on Japan and Germany in late 1941, bands such as Tommy Dorsey, Jimmy Dorsey, Artie Shaw, Charlie Barnet, Bunny Berigan, Harry James, Gene Krupa (the last two being ex-Goodman sidemen) and Glenn Miller all gathered unpre-

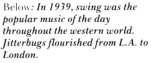

49

cedented public attention as the music got slicker and the jazz content got slimmer. By the time Frank Sinatra was debuting as the new vocalist with Tommy Dorsey's band, the big bands were so far removed from their own jazz roots that, with one or two honourable exceptions, they can be safely considered as another branch of the entertainment business, like Bing Crosby and Al Bowlly.

COUNT BASIE AND THE KANSAS CITY SCENE

Meanwhile, there had been some notable developments in Kansas City. After Bennie Moten's death in 1935, William 'Count' Basie had continued to gather around himself a nucleus of like-minded musicians who played the gin-joints and bars of Kaycee, as it was called. There was a large pool of talent in the area, all known to each other, and all the locals would play and sit in, setting up cutting sessions that ran all night and into the morning. Even some out-of-town hot-shots occasionally got caught. Coleman Hawkins, passing through one night in 1934 had got into a jam with Ben Webster, Lester Young and Hershel Evans at a little club called the Cherry Blossom. At around four in the morning, they had run through all the available pianists, so Webster went and got Mary Lou Williams out of bed: 'Hawkins has got his shirt off and is still blowing. You got to come down.' 'Sure enough,' as Williams relates, 'when we got there, Hawkins was in his singlet, taking turns with the Kaycee men ... Lester [Young's] style was light, and ... it took him maybe five choruses to warm up. But then he would really blow; then you couldn't handle him on a cutting

session. That was how Hawkins got hung up ... he kept trying to beat Ben and Hershel and Lester. When at last he gave up, he jumped straight in his car and drove to St Louis.'

Basie and his 9-piece band, playing a residency at the Reno Club, had come a long way within months of Moten's death and the band's regrouping under Basie's name. Key musicians such as drummer Jo Jones had joined the band; it had a unique, uncluttered swing which was as much the result of the spare, minimalist Basie piano style as the smoothness of the bass and drums. And, over the top of this, Basie had simply some of the best soloists in jazz history. This band, its members earning about $17 a week playing at and broadcasting from the Reno Club in Kaycee, had seemingly no other future on offer. But fate intervened. One freezing winter evening early in 1936, John Hammond, who was in Chicago with Benny Goodman's band, turned the radio on and tuned to a broadcast coming from a club in Kansas City. It was the Reno Club, and it was Basie's band. As he said in his autobiography, 'I couldn't believe my ears ... what I picked up from Kansas City was amazing ... After that I went to my car every night to listen to Basie. Once I dragged Benny out to listen with me in that cold, cold car.'

Hammond went to Kansas City soon after, and found the Basie band playing in 'a dingy building with a second floor which must have been a whorehouse, because there were girls lounging on the stairway. On the street level was the Reno Club.' Hammond, undeterred by the band's surroundings, was completely knocked out, and went back to New York enthusing about his discovery. In no time he had a deal set up at Brunswick records, and went back to Basie with a

Count Basie (above) *came to New York in 1936.* (Below): *The Basie band at the Apollo Theatre, New York City, 1939. Buck Clayton (standing) is the trumpet soloist. Lester Young is the saxophonist on the far right.*

COUNT BASIE AND THE KANSAS CITY SOUND: Count Basie first came to prominence in 1936 when, after hearing him in a radio broadcast from Kansas City, jazz entrepreneur John Hammond brought Basie's band to New York. Basie's unique style of swing was agreeably different from that of the New York bands. It was easy, uncluttered – almost spare – and rhythmically flexible. Basie also had some of the best soloists in jazz history, including Lester Young and Herschel Evans, and, all too briefly, the great singer Billie Holiday. Hammond's enterprise paid off and the band was a huge success in New York in the thirties.

Left: Lester Young, the great tenor saxophonist who blended musical thought to a pure feeling for the blues. Centre: 'Little' Jimmy Rushing, the singer also known as Mr Five-by-five for his size. He gave a sharp, raw edge to the Basie band. Right Dickie Wells, another mainstay with Count Basie, who provided a trombone style envied by almost every bandleader.

contract, only to find that an opportunist by the name of Jack Kapp of America Decca had beaten him to it, signing the band to a three-year contract which paid them a total of $750 per year and no royalties. This miserable deal meant that Basie would only earn any real money by touring.

However, a determined Hammond arranged for a small group from the band to attend a recording session in Chicago before Decca made their move. In October 1936, under the anodyne name of Jones-Smith Inc (from drummer Jo Jones and trumpeter Carl Smith), this Basie quintet made four sides of surpassing

power and originality, and recorded for the first time the tenor saxophone playing of Lester Young. Jo Jones relates: 'We made these records in one hour. All the time I was looking out of the window watching a man playing with his dog over by the lake. We were all through by 10.05 am.'

Both Basie and Young were completely mature as musicians by the time these sides were made, and what they played here was utterly new. For a start, their music dealt with the blues in a way quite different to the New York bands, and their easy, uncluttered rhythmic flow was iconoclastic for the period. When they needed a singer, they used a real blues shouter like Jimmy Rushing, not an imitation crooner. As soloists, both players made a virtue of simplicity, space and extreme rhythmic flexibility – a playfulness with their phrasing only previously matched by Louis Armstrong and Jack Teagarden. Young in particular also had a unique sound: his was a clean,

sinuous tone which ran contrary to what every tenor sax player thought the instrument should sound like at the time. Put simply, he sounded nothing like Coleman Hawkins, the first tenor sax player to develop a credible solo style in jazz, and who had a clipped rhythmic approach and heavy, tremendously robust sound.

Basie encouraged the friendly rivalry between Lester and his section-mate, Hawkins-inspired Texas tenor Hershel Evans. Billie Holiday, who was briefly the singer with the band in their initial flush of success, remembered this: 'Once Hershel asked Lester, "Why don't you play alto, man? You got an alto tone." Lester tapped his head, "There's things going on up there, man," he told Hershel. "Some of you guys are all belly." ' Both Young and Evans were with the band when their light, driving swing style, with its Kansas City riff-and-response section work, met with a big response from the crowds at New York's Savoy Ballroom and

Apollo, and the record-buying public. The great Basie band stayed more or less intact even after Hershel Evans' untimely death from heart disease in 1939 right up to America's involvement in World War 2. Then, one by one, the players were drafted or just trickled away. Young himself left in December 1940 for reasons which are still unclear, and determined to start his own small group. By that time, however, the Basie outfit had made enough 78rpm masterpieces such as *Taxi War Dance*, *Blue and Sentimental* and *Miss Thing* (the latter an extended workout on the chord base of *Honeysuckle Rose*), to guarantee their inclusion in any sane person's jazz top ten.

Members of the Basie band also participated in another series of unforgettable recordings in the years 1936-1940: those by the studio bands of Billie Holiday and Teddy Wilson. Billie (1915-1959) is a singer universally known for her turbulent life and her uniquely

moving vocal style. Fresh-voiced and still a teenager, she first recorded in 1933 within weeks of Bessie Smith's last recording session, an unknown playing with a group of top-line New York musicians. Three years later, still working as a solo in clubs around New York City, she began a studio collaboration inspired by producer John Hammond whereby, under either her own or Teddy Wilson's nominal leadership, she sang and jammed with the best and most sympathetic musicians in town. From the first time they appeared in a recording studio together in 1937, Holiday and Lester Young made special magic together: indeed, Billie later said, 'I don't think I'm singing; I feel like I'm playing like a horn. I try to improvise like Lester Young, like Louis Armstrong . . . What comes out is what I feel.' What these two felt together on a whole string of record dates is among the most moving and poetic music of this century, where two voices, one human, the other instrumental,

make perfect foils for each other. Sadly, after 1940 they were never to record together again, their poignant reunion on TV in 1957, when both were visibly in decline, was an altogether different affair.

SMALL-GROUP SWING

Pianist Teddy Wilson (1912-1986) also played a pivotal role in another famous group of the 1930s, the Benny Goodman Trio (and later, Quartet). This band was an offshoot of the successful big band which re wroto the history of American – and later, European – popular music in the mid to late 1930s. And, in its own way, it was just as groundbreaking. For a start, Goodman used the basic principle of New Orleans music where every frontline instrument was an equal voice, and extended that to every member of his group. It was called 'chamber jazz' at the time for this reason. By whatever name, the music was sparkling. And when Lionel Hampton joined the original trio to make it a quartet, something special happened: the band ignited to become one of the most exhilarating sounds of the thirties. It was like breathing in pure oxygen, the effect was so fast and strong.

Another player to make history with small-group combinations in the thirties was the godfather of all tenor saxophonists, Coleman Hawkins. A gruff, self-reliant man with a clear sense of his own

Earl Hines had been a major player in jazz circles since the late 1920s, when he made a series of sides with Louis Armstrong. He led his own big band from the piano stool for most of the thirties and forties. His solo style was modelled on the melodic and rhythmic ideas of trumpeters and saxophonists.

worth, he had left Fletcher Henderson, and America, in 1934, moving to Europe in the search for a more congenial society in which to function. The fact that he stayed for five years, moving happily between England, France, Holland, Denmark, Sweden and Switzerland, tends to suggest that he found it. However, the coming stormclouds of World War 2 finally convinced Hawkins that it was time to head home, and in mid-summer 1939 he returned. By the fall, he was fronting a band at Kelly's Stables in New York, and it was with this group that he made his famous recording of *Body and Soul*, a masterpiece of sustained improvisation over two choruses which remained the benchmark for all other tenor players to aspire to for the next 20 years. The record was also a minor hit, and re-established Hawkins with his American audience.

The area of small-group swing is of itself an extraordinarily rich one throughout this period, given the popular dominance of the big bands. Inevitably, some of the best small groups only existed in the recording studios rather than the live circuit, and many players who had been comfortable with the small group format found themselves fronting large organizations. Earl Hines (1903-1983), for example, after his innovative duets recorded in 1928 with Louis Armstrong (where the trumpet master found his own improvising discoveries coming back at him thick and fast from a pianist who would not cede second place), settled down into a 12-year residency at the Grand Terrace in Chicago with his own big band.

On the other hand Art Tatum (1909-1956), the most awesome pianist of his generation, worked either as a soloist or with a trio whether he was playing live or just cutting a record. His tech-

nique by the time he was in his late teens was such that he easily cut every pianist he met at a jam session, including Fats Waller, James P. Johnson, Willie 'The Lion' Smith and Teddy Wilson. Self-taught, his harmonic sophistication was ten years ahead of its time, and his knowledge of popular songs was immense. By the time he had established himself in the bars and clubs of Harlem and midtown, the most extraordinary figures would turn up to hear him play. On more than one occasion, conductor Arturo Toscanini and pianist Vladimir Horowitz, the greatest classical stars of their generation, would finish up a concert at Carnegie Hall, and spend the rest of the night watching Tatum, utterly mesmerized. Fats Waller, Tatum's senior by some years, revered him. One night Fats was playing The Yacht Club, a venue he was a big favourite at and did radio broadcasts from, and Art Tatum came down to listen to the band. Fats, spotting him enter, announced him to the crowd, saying, 'Ladies and gentlemen; I just play the piano, but God is in the house tonight.' Fats himself, a brilliant stride pianist, led a phenomenally successful small group right through the swing era from 1934 until his death in 1943. Called 'Fats Waller and His Rhythm', they recorded hundreds of sides for RCA Victor, a combination of Waller's own songs such as *Honeysuckle Rose* or *Ain't Misbehavin* and various tin pan alley songs which his record company foisted upon him. Fats had a devilish sense of humour and a genuinely charis-

The powerful trumpet and trombone section of the 1938 edition of the Earl Hines Orchestra. Among the trumpeters are Freddy Webster, later to be a model for many younger players; and Ray Nance, who would join Duke Ellington within two years as the replacement for Cootie Williams, who defected to Goodman.

matic vocal delivery: he could turn the worst lyric in the world into a merry-go-round of fun and games. Here is an example: a trivial lyric called *S' posin'*. Fat's interjections are in brackets.

S'posin' I should fall in love with you;
do you think that you could love me too?
(you could love me? . . . well alright that's great! – listen:)
s'posin' I could hold you and caress you –
would it impress you? (would it, huh?)
or would it distress you? (huh: would it? well answer me! . . .)
s'posin' I should say for you I yearn
(yeah I yearn; sure I do; yeah . . .)
would you think I'm speaking out of turn?

(no I'm not lyin': it's a sin to tell a lie, yeah!)
s'posin I declared it, would you take my love & share it? (hmm!)
I'm not s'posin; I'm in love with you!
(come on! s'pose with me baby! – yeah!)

Had Fats lived into the post-war period, there is little doubt he would have been as big a star as Louis Armstrong, Cab Calloway or Nat King Cole, moving beyond the jazz audience into the larger world of popular entertainment. Armstrong, incidentally, spent most of the 1930s consolidating his amazing popularity fronting a big band and, although he was no longer pushing back the boundaries of his musical form, he was still the supreme soloist and the essence of jazz vocals.

A trumpeter of the next generation who picked up the challenge thrown down by Armstrong's 1920s recordings was Roy Eldridge (b. 1911). A product of big bands such as McKinney's Cotton Pickers and Teddy Hill, he became a close friend of the gifted tenorist Leon 'Chu' Berry (1910-1941) and, with Berry, joined Fletcher Henderson's band in 1935. Within 12 months he was fronting his own outfit as a leader, and cutting the first sides under his own name, with a septet which included Buster Bailey on clarinet, Chu Berry on sax, John Kirby on bass and Big Sid Catlett on drums.

By the end of the decade Eldridge had established himself as the man to take the classic trumpet style and, by sheer force of personality, aggressive playing and phenomenal technique, push

it into the swing era with an unparalleled force. To many his sound epitomized the heart and soul of jazz: passionate, swinging, fiery, exuberant and prepared to take every risk to communicate what was on his mind. It was a sound so intensely human that no-one could walk away from it unmoved, one way or the other. By the early forties he was so much in demand that he played as a featured player with Gene Krupa's big band, where he had big hits with *Rockin' Chair* and *Let Me Off Uptown*, among others. Soon after, he was moved on to star as the hot soloist with Artie Shaw. But first racial bigotry, then the coming be-bop revolution threatened to eclipse him. With Krupa he had suffered so much harrassment from the public, hotel managements, local police and other officials that he had a near nervous breakdown. Later, with Shaw, it all came to a climax. 'I went to a place where we were supposed to play a dance and they wouldn't even let me in the place. "This is a white dance", they said, and there was my name

Coleman Hawkins (above) *was the first great tenor saxophonist. His friend and sometime partner, Roy Eldridge* (right) *was the greatest trumpeter to follow Armstrong.*

INIMITABLE FATS WALLER: **One of the great entertainers of the first half of this century, Fats Waller (above) had a singing voice which, although based on that of Louis Armstrong's, was in many ways inimitable. He certainly had one of the most infectious senses of humour to be found in music. Waller was also a brilliant stride pianist. Referring to himself as that 'harmful little armful', he would play 'some of that fine Arabian stuff' for audiences night after night, in countless record sessions between 1924 and 1943, the year of his premature death.**

Art Tatum (above) *was held in awe by every single pianist of his generation – and that included the great classical pianists as well.*

outside: Roy "Little Jazz" Eldridge, and I told them who I was. When I finally did get in, I played the first set, trying to keep from crying.' Mixed-raced groups may have been okay in the studio by then, but on the road it was still a very dangerous business.

DUKE AT HIS VERY BEST

Duke Ellington solved the problem by retaining a black line-up and, with a remarkably stable personnel, finished the decade a bigger creative force than he started it and on the verge of an astonishing period of creativity. By the end of 1939, with tenor saxophonist Ben Webster and young bassist Jimmy Blanton in the band, Ellington was inspired to write music that even today can quite simply amaze and overwhelm the unprepared listener. One additional bonus for Ellington in 1939 was the recruitment to his staff of a young composer and arranger, Billy Strayhorn, the composer of, among many others, *Lush Life* and *Take The A Train*.

It has been asserted repeatedly that Duke Ellington plays the piano, but his real instrument was his orchestra, considering the immensely personal sounds he got out of every ensemble he ever directed. This can be partly explained by some simple advice Ellington gave to Billy Strayhorn when he first joined the band. 'His first, last and only formal instruction for me was embodied in one word: Observe.' And this is precisely what Duke did himself, nurturing the characteristic talents of each individual band member. The development of his band, however, would have counted for nothing had he not been an equally inspired and resourceful composer, able to harness his outfit's disparate pieces and galvanize them into unity in his works.

This inspiration is perhaps most movingly summarized in a memorable evocation by the Duke while talking of the Harlem he had tried to capture in his piece, *Harlem Air Shaft*: 'So much goes on in a Harlem air shaft. You get the full essence of Harlem in an air shaft. You hear fights, you smell dinner, you hear people making love. You hear intimate gossip floating down. You hear the radio. An air shaft is one great big loudspeaker. You see your neighbour's laundry. You hear the janitor's dogs. The man upstairs' aerial falls down and breaks your window. You smell coffee. A wonderful thing, is that smell … You hear people praying, fighting, snoring. Jitterbugs are jumping up and down always over you, never below you. That's a funny thing about jitterbugs … I tried to put that all in *Harlem Air Shaft*.'

In the years 1940 to 1946 Ellington created a string of masterpieces, starting with his showcase piece for bassist Jimmy Blanton, *Jack The Bear* (itself titled after an old Harlem bassist), *Ko-Ko* (allegedly describing the early slave dances in New Orleans' Congo Square), *Concerto For Cootie* and *Sepia Panorama*, and culminating in his misunderstood first suite-cum-tone parallel, *Black, Brown and Beige*, the beautiful *I Let A Song*

Counting among his fans Toscanini and Horowitz, Tatum (below) *liked nothing better than to play after-hours sessions for the entertainment of friends and fellow musicians.*

Go Out Of My Heart, and a showcase for Johnny Hodges, *Esquire Swank*. There are so many miracles of creativity and musical construction within just these few pieces, let alone the scores of unmentioned ones, that it is tempting to analyse each one in turn. However, all one needs to do to appreciate Ellington's special genius is listen closely to the gathering excitement in *Conga Brava* as each new contrasting section builds inexorably to a thrilling unison brass riff before the melody's single-trombone recapitulation. With this purple period, Ellington reached a peak of development most of his contemporaries could only listen to in awe. It is a fitting place at which to leave swing street and move on to other musical highways.

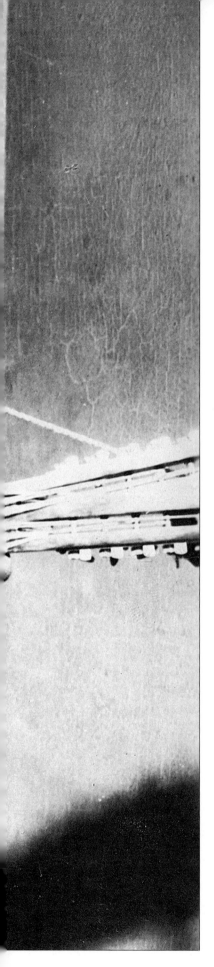

good morning, blues

"The blues? I didn't start playing the blues ever. That was in me before I was born and I've been playing and living the blues ever since." T-Bone Walker

JAZZ AND BLUES are two distinct streams from the same musical source: both ultimately derive from the unique mix of West African and European music fermented in the slave states of the US from the 17th century to present times. It is fairly certain that the blues predate jazz by a considerable period of time, and it is also a remarkable fact that, while it is perfectly possible – in fact desirable in most cases – to have

A man and his guitar: in this case the blues and folk musician Huddie Leadbetter – known to the world as Leadbelly – portraying the eternal image of the blues player. With his 12-string guitar in his hands and powerful message to deliver, he was a commanding figure and a repository of a people's history.

blues without jazz, it is difficult to conceive of jazz without at least one of the major elements of blues being present.

So what do these two musical forms share? Without becoming too technical, the vast majority of blues performers have used a certain chordal sequence which eventually became formalized as 'the 12-bar blues progression', which has been shared by jazz artists, with ever-increasing sophistication, right up to the present day. Many of the early blues artists, especially the solo singers accompanying themselves on guitar, never actually used 12-bar cycles, but would use irregular bar-lengths, or perhaps omit part of the normal chordal progression, and in some cases simply play a one chord drone for the whole of a perform-

ance. In these cases, other musical elements connect them to the mainstream. For example, there are the so-called 'blue notes', or 'blue' intervals, based around the minor third and minor seventh notes in the scale. These notes are the meeting-point of two musical cultures, the pentatonic West African and the 8-note diatonic Western scales. The non-tempered African 5-note scale and the tempered diatonic scale mesh, to all intents and purposes, at all but two places – the two 'blue notes' which the Western scale can only approximate. These notes give blues and jazz artists that peculiar 'cry' which makes the music uniquely expressive. It also accounts for the intensely vocal quality to be found in instrumental blues and jazz, where the musicians seem almost to be singing and talking between themselves and to the listener.

So, 'the blues' is at once a

specific musical form, and a general social condition: it can be a state of mind; it can also be a particular harmonic progression. It can just as easily be an inflection within the performance of a song which is not necessarily a blues song. The reason for this proliferation of meanings is that the negro verbal heritage, as African dialects slowly fused with American English between the 17th and 19th centuries, was a wholly aural one. The roots of the word's usage to describe a certain melancholic stoicism, and a particular perception of the world probably reach as far back as the arrival of the first generations of West African slaves in America. Although these people had little contact with their masters' culture, at some point they picked up the older English expression 'blue devils' – a graphic description of the demons who afflicted a person suffering from melancholia. The religious overtones of this early usage are obvious.

Most of the aural music used by the slaves of America was functional: in a sense it had to be, for the negro slave had no 'leisure time' as such, and so the music they shared related to their community, which was strictly a work community. Blues seems only to have emerged as a distinct form after the American Civil War, and the subsequent Emancipation. As the new shape of US society slowly emerged from the ruins, negroes in rural southern areas at last had time to themselves, time to be alone. Admittedly, this time was a small fraction of what the average white enjoyed, but it was a material improvement on the pre-war situation. In this leisure time, a new hybrid form was born out of the joining of the old field hollers and the ballad tradition which had its roots in white folk music. This new music spread more rapidly than any predecessor due to the relative freedom of movement accorded to migrant black workers looking for a new beginning.

Its distinguishing characteristics were the central importance of the 'blue' notes, and the unique and simple harmonic structure – the famous 12-bar structure every 3-chord guitarist in the world

knows – allied to the three-line verse where the first lyric line is usually repeated. As the music developed, the instrumental accompaniment (usually a guitar, banjo or harmonica) provided by the singer himself took over the role traditionally reserved for the call-and-response lines of the old negro forms.

Although there is some evidence for the emergence of the classic blues progression amongst guitarists in the Mississippi Delta in the 1890s, it is no longer possible to pinpoint the exact time when the blues became a distinct and mature musical style, because by the very nature of the music, it went unrecorded. It also spread far and fast, because it had no particular fulcrum, like jazz had in New Orleans.

The first people singing the blues for a living were probably musicians working with the travelling shows which mixed hokum, comedy, music and magic, along with the occasional sales pitch on some highly suspect medicine with supernatural healing or restorative powers. Others continued to sing blues purely for their own or their local community's benefit, and so the regional styles could vary im-

mensely, as well as the levels of sophistication.

Some of the blues' earliest practitioners were admired and remembered by the first jazzmen.

Jelly Roll Morton recalled: 'I do not claim any of the creation of the blues, although I have written many of them even before Mr Handy had any blues published. I had heard them when I was knee-high to a duck. For instance . . . I used to hear the following blues prayers, who could play nothing else – Buddie Canter, Josky Adams, Game Kid, Frank Richards, Sam Henry and many more too numerous to mention – what we call "rag-men" . . . Tony Jackson used to play the blues in 1905, entitled *Michigan Water Tastes Like Sherry Wine.* One can detect a slight condescension here, and Jelly indeed felt that blues musicians were of a lower class than himself, as most jazz musicians did. But that did not stop people from exploiting the appeal of this powerful and simple music. Although few blues players from the first ten years of this century are documented, the people who took the songs and published them under their own name became world-famous. Clarence Williams and W. C. Handy are two of the best-known

BLIND WILLIE JOHNSON

This new and exclusive Columbia artist, Blind Willie Johnson, sings sacred selections in a way that you have never heard before. Be sure to hear his first record and listen close to that guitar accompaniment. Nothing like it anywhere else.

Record No. 14276-D, 10-inch, 75¢

I Know His Blood Can Make Me Whole
Jesus Make Up My Dying Bed

Ask Your Dealer for Latest Race Record Catalog

Columbia Phonograph Company, 1819 Broadway, New York City

Columbia
NEW PROCESS RECORDS
Made the New Way - Electrically

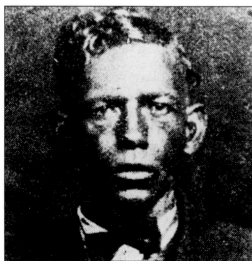

Charley Patton (far left) *and Furry Lewis* (left), *two seminal figures in country blues. Patton was the 'founder' of Delta blues, while Lewis, a brilliant guitarist, was a leading figure in Memphis.*

Above: *Although Blind Willie Johnson used all the blues techniques in his singing and guitar playing, his songs were religious – as can be seen by the titles in the records advertisement.*

composers to have done this.

All this is by the way of an introduction to the main event, because with the lack of any but a tiny fraction of blues compositions in published form, and the entire absence of all blues performers from phonograph disc until 1920, the fragmented and disparate local styles of the music can only be guessed at until heard on a phonograph record. Even after the advent of the prolific recording of so-called 'race' records (as blues and jazz was called then), in many cases the sum total of knowledge about a performer is the stark story told on a handful of 78rpm discs. No biographical details are found, and nobody else remembers him or her.

It is astonishing just how little one can be sure of in the music: something as seemingly simple as establishing an original set of lyrics for a particular blues song becomes an endless pursuit. So many of the pieces were common property, or common subjects, with verses, parts of verses or just lines or phrases passed on verbally from area to area, singer to singer, that the originals are all utterly consigned to oblivion. One has to take someone's word for it that they 'wrote' a particular song, or 'learned it from' some other singer.

DELTA BLUES STYLE
One of the first rural blues artists to escape the general anonymity of early country blues was Charley Patton (1891-1934). Known as 'the father of the Delta blues style', Patton learned guitar while

Left: *Mamie Smith (with her Jazz Hounds, including a young Willie 'The Lion' Smith on piano) made the first so-called 'race' records in 1920. She had a massive hit with Crazy Blues.*

living on one of the huge old plantations in the Mississippi Delta, and by 1910 had written many of his most famous pieces, which he would perform at the functions held around 'Dockery'. This plantation had about 1000 negroes living and working there as tenant farmers, so Patton had a large ready-made audience.

Charley accompanied his stark vocal lines with a driving and original guitar style of astonishing intricacy. His themes were the close concerns of his life and of the lives around him: the Mississippi flood of 1927 in *High Water Everywhere*, drugs and high living in *Spoonful*, the harshness of his life in *Screamin' & Hollerin' The Blues* and *Going To Move to Alabama*, drunkenness and scrapes with the law in *High Sheriff Blues*, and the pursuit of women in any number of his songs. His delivery of these themes was accomplished with a searing vocal style pitched for the most part in the higher baritone range. The darkness and menace of this voice has to be heard to be believed.

In person, Patton was a dynamic and vastly entertaining performer with a whole repertoire of novelty tricks he could pull to keep his audience spellbound. He mostly played material suitable for rough-and-tumble dances that had a solid one-two beat as its basis, and this explains the tremendous driving rhythm in his work. He had to wait until 1929 to make his first 78rpm record for Paramount discs, after being 'discovered' by H.C. Spears, a Paramount talent scout with a furniture business in Jackson, Mississippi. But the effect of his records was immediate; for one thing, he was thrown off the plantation and so started moving around the Delta, playing at dances and other functions to make a living. The dangers of this sort of life were made all too real

to Patton in 1933, when he had his throat slit at an over-rowdy dance. Although he survived this attack, his health and his voice were impaired. He died the following year of a long-term heart ailment.

Patton's Delta contemporaries, such as Skip James, Son House, Bukka White, Mississippi John Hurt and Blind Willie Johnson, all had similar personal histories, coming from country areas, plantations and the like, and alternating between music and manual labour for a living. Each had brilliant and individual approaches to guitar playing, reflecting their differing temperaments and the uses to which they wanted their guitar put in their music. People like Son House and the intensely religious Blind Willie were consummate players in the bottle-neck style (using a broken neck of a bottle, or some other smooth object, to run up and down the frets and produce a wild singing effect) and also possessed huge, gravelly voices which even today can dissect the listener's nervous system through the gruff power of their delivery. Son House generated thrilling levels of intensity in his vocal and instrumental delivery – a rough power unmatched perhaps until Howlin' Wolf's emergence some 20 years later. James and Hurt, on the other hand, were communicating on a much more intimate level, James with a purity of voice and intense melancholy which can be deeply disturbing, while Hurt's gentle good humour is evident in his lyrics and easy, soft voice.

Robert Johnson, the greatest of the Delta blues players, was born in 1912 in Robinsonville, Mississippi, (although even this information is no more than a probability) and died just 25 years later in December 1937. Johnson approached life from the dark side of the road: his inspiration was undoubtedly touched by the fires of hell. Just a glance through his brief discography (a mere 29 songs, recorded over four sessions between November 1936 and June 1937) reveals titles such as *Hellhound On My Trail, Me And The Devil Blues* and *If I Had Possession Over Judgement Day*. Johnson sings and plays like a man demoniacally possessed on all his recordings. His brilliant guitar playing, inventive at any speed from slow drag to break-neck, offsets the searingly intense imagery of his work, often delivered in a voice not far from a frenzied screech. His lyrics, even when they are reworkings of familiar or traditional material, have a hard, clear poetry in them unrivalled in country blues. For example, *Stones in My Passway* brilliantly contrasts natural imagery and personal agonies:

I got stones in my passway and my road seems dark as night (twice)
I have pains in my heart, they have taken my appetite.

I have a bird to whistle and I have a bird to sing (twice)
I've got a woman that I'm lovin' – boy she don't mean a thing.

Now you'se tryin' to take my life, and all my lovin' too,
You laid a passway for me, now what are you tryin' to do?
I'm cryin' please, please let us be friends,
And when you hear me howlin' in my passway rider,
please open the door and let me in.

Johnson's influence has never waned since his early death. His songs have continued to be recorded by others right up to the present day. *Dust My Broom, Crossroad Blues, Love In Vain* and *Ramblin' On My Mind* are all familiar from hundreds, if not thousands, of performances by young white r&b bands during the sixties blues renaissance, as well as in recordings by The Rolling Stones and Cream. Robert Johnson's life and death echo the harshness of his lyrics: just six months after his last recording session (held in Texas) he was poisoned by the roadhouse owner at The Three Forks, in Greenwood Miss., (the last job Johnson ever played) who had already warned the sexually insatiable Johnson to stay away from his wife. His songs are littered with references to evil urges and temptations he could not renounce, and this rush to self-destruction proved unerringly effective.

TEXAS TWISTERS

Another southern state, Texas, had its own definite country blues flavour. One of the earliest blues troubadors, Blind Lemon Jefferson, came from there, and he possessed more than a touch of the 'driven' quality of Robert Johnson, only he displayed it within a different style. Jefferson was a friend and travelling buddy of Huddie Leadbetter (universally known as Leadbelly and born in 1889), and they played a lot of the same places and got into the same scrapes throughout the southern states in the first 20 years of this century. They also shared a common repertoire, which was not merely the blues.

The two men, travelling and performing the same songs as long ago as 1912, according to Leadbelly himself in his reminiscences of Lemon, began to tread increasingly divergent paths as the century progressed. Leadbelly, in fact, came to be known primarily as a folk singer, rather than as a blues artist.

One important point of divergence was that Blind Lemon was a songwriter himself, while Leadbelly was a superb interpreter of others' music. Blessed with an incredible memory, he could recall, late in life, performing *St Louis Blues* when it was still a traditional song.

It is tempting to speculate that Leadbelly's celebrated prison sentence for killing a man in a brawl also arrested his music style for the 17 years he was in Angola State Prison Farm, Lousiana. It could be said that he created a musical time-capsule of songs, shouts and dance rounds which, in the world outside, had been discarded and forgotten by the majority of performers as their audiences demanded something new.

Blind Lemon, meanwhile, progressed out in the real world. One man who knew him, Sam Price, described him as an independent, jaunty type: 'He had a really uncanny sense of direction. He'd walk around those Dallas streets singin' the blues – a chunky little fellow wearing a big black hat. Everybody knew him.' Still a

Gertrude 'Ma' Rainey (left and, above, with her Georgia Jazz Band in 1925) was the first great female blues singer whose voice found its way onto a phonograph record. Her direct communication on disc made her innumerable fans.

young man in the twenties (he was reputedly born around 1890, but no-one knows for sure), Lemon shed most of his buck-dance material (which Leadbelly studiously retained and played for the rest of his life) and with it, the crude one-two rhythm, chordally-based guitar style so suited to enlivening dances and stomps. Instead, he developed a complex guitar style which amounted to a dialogue with the vocal line.

Jefferson made a great many records in a relatively short time – over 100 sides between January 1926 and September 1929, and so his music was quickly dissemi-nated over a wide area of the US, influencing countless other blues-men who never met him or saw him live. Although he travelled extensively around the south and midwest, playing on the streets, at dances and to bar-room crowds wherever possible, his records got the message across on a much wider scale.

The blind Texan was another casualty of the Depression. After his last session for Paramount, he virtually disappeared: to this day nobody knows when or where he died. Leadbelly, on the other

hand, survived to become a worldwide celebrity. The other key geographical centre for early country blues was Memphis, Ten-nessee.

MEMPHIS MASTER

Typical of the players steeped in the Memphis idiom is Robert Wil-kins (1896-1987), who came from a Mississippi town just south of Memphis. Wilkins was another exceptional blues man whose recording career got under way just prior to the Depression, and who never really recovered from its blows. He recorded just 12 pieces between 1928 and early 1930, another five in 1935, and then took up the life of a preacher. This gentle, sensitive artist wrote pieces of great subtlety, often with long instrumental gaps between lines and verses where he demonstrated his versatility and expressiveness on the guitar.

His instrumental backgrounds are unusually varied, with choppy chords in 'travel' songs suggest-ing movement, long single re-petitive riff lines in more personal

EMPRESS OF THE BLUES: Bessie Smith was known – rightly – as The Empress of the Blues. A strikingly handsome and vital woman (left), she could sing like no other, and her interpretations remain definitive.

No matter who accompanied her, she created triumphant music which to this day communi-cates uniquely. Her backing musicians included Louis Armstrong and Fletcher Henderson: no-one willingly missed a Bessie Smith session. As a young woman of 25 (right), she already had her own show and was beginning to attract wider attention in touring venues. By the late twenties and early thirties (far right) she was at the height of her achievements.

songs, and dance-type rhythms which display a technique clearly derived from the banjo. On a bitter love ballad like *I Do Blues*, the guitar provides a fascinating musical dissection of the main melody and harmony, mixed with the rhythm of the song. In some songs a constant re-arrangement of the vocal line in the guitar accompaniment reveals a careful compositional hand even though the lyrics give the impression of great simplicity and starkness. And the lyrics themselves are timeless:

Ah woman I do, woman god knows I do (twice)

I ain't doin' tho' for you what any poor man would do.

I done did everything woman but die for you (twice) Woman can you tell me what more woman do you want me to do?. .

Now if you don't want me give me your right hand (twice),

I'll go to my woman and you can go to your man.

Better come here woman, sit down on my knee (twice)

Oh we can talk all night, and you can tell me what you please . . .

'Cause I'd rather be dead, buried on my face (twice) Than to love you, and be treated this-a way.

But I don't want nobody say they don't want me (twice)

I'd rather be somewhere praying bended on my knees

I'm done gone up the country, won't come here no mo' (twice)

I love you woman but you always treat me so.

Other vital Memphis artists from this period include Frank Stokes, probably the first great bluesman of the era and a man who had a parallel career as a blacksmith, the incredible guitarist and lyrical blues singer Furry Lewis who, like Wilkins and Stokes, straddled the different streams of black folk music, and the highly successful Memphis Jug Band.

A jug band was an amazing concoction of joyful celebration and fun conjured up from various liquor bottles, jugs and pitchers, each with its own timbre and pulse, with a highly colourful vocal skating across the bizarre sounds thus produced. These bands, often with washboards used as rhythm accompaniment, produced an enormous number of sides of wildly varying quality, but the Memphis Jug Band was, along with Cannon's Jug Stompers, undoubtedly one of the best. Jug music, deemed to be of no musical value what-soever at the time of its greatest popularity, was the first folk style to be dropped by the ailing record companies in 1930. The solo country blues artists soon followed in its wake.

CLASSIC FEMALE BLUES

Country blues, however, was not the only style of blues being played, even in the deep south. Another whole area of the blues – what is known today as the 'classic' blues style – had been thriving, both in person and on record, in the decade prior to the stock market crash, slowly evolving from travelling vaudeville shows and reviews of the turn-of-the-century period. This style predated country blues on record by close to five years, and its major artists – all women, as it happens – were internationally known (though few if any of them left America to tour) by the mid-twenties. The style was clearly identifiable from its country cousin by the instrumental accompaniment – usually piano or small groups of jazz players – and the more urban subject matter of the lyrics.

In February 1920, a singer called Mamie Smith cut two sides for the Okeh label. Neither were strictly blues, but their sales were exclusively to the black community. And to the record company's surprise, *That Thing Called Love* and *You Can't Keep A Good Man Down*, aimed only to the 'race' market, sold in phenomenal numbers. In August of the same year, Mamie recorded *Crazy Blues* which, though again not exactly a blues, started the avalanche of blues recordings which continued unabated throughout the rest of the twenties.

Mamie Smith was closer to popular and vaudeville music than blues or jazz, but the people signed up in the rush to emulate her success remain to this day some of the greatest blues artists of all time.

Although not the first to be signed, Gertrude 'Ma' Rainey (1886-1939) had an influence which can hardly be over-estimated in the development of the early urban blues style. She ran her own minstrel show with husband 'Pa' Rainey, called the Rabbit Foot Minstrels, from the early years of this century. This troupe had the deep south for its core audience, and its repertoire covered every aspect of negro entertainment at this period, with cakewalks and coon dancing, comedy numbers, minstrel routines and popular songs of the day.

In this, the show was a dramatic link between what people in the country districts had grown up with and the emerging blues forms which would soon entrance the urban negro populations. Rainey also eschewed the guitar-and-vocal approach of country blues, being more comfortable with either piano or with a small instrumental group. Indeed, this was how she cut her first records in 1923 with Lovie Austin and her Serenaders, (a group consisting of Lovie Austin on piano, New Orleans trumpeter and partner to Sidney Bechet Tommy Ladnier, and clarinettist Jimmy O'Bryant).

'Ma' Rainey's recordings for Paramount at that time were a judicious mixture of old and newer styles, and the blend proved very successful. She also continued to record with Tommy Ladnier as often as possible, and he is often the featured player in her regular backing group, Ma Rainey's Georgia Band. Rainey's style of singing is quite unadorned, but her ability to play with a set of lyrics, extracting a whole range of new meanings from them, is immensely impressive in its implied sophistication. After all,

Ma had been a professional for just on 20 years by the time she first entered the recording studio. Her sophistication is also evident in the choice of musical partners, where she always plumps for first-rate jazzmen (Louis Armstrong appears on a couple of sides).

'Ma' Rainey's presence both off stage and on was overwhelming, and gave later artists a clear direction to follow. A large, rather ugly woman, bedecked in jewels, and much given to flamboyant clothing decorated with feathers, furs and other animal skins, she used wonderfully expressive facial and bodily gestures to enhance the magic of her vocal

delivery; by the mid-twenties she could mount one-nighters which regularly pulled in 1500 eager people to see the show. In an age when women were not usually seen as leaders, she managed to run a successful touring company while holding together a fine recording career. She also produced a selection of songs which have stood the test of time, such as *Shave 'Em Dry*, *Screech Owl Blues* and (with Bessie Smith) *Don't Fish In My Sea*. Ma retired in 1933, the year her sister and mother both died, and five years after her last recording session. The change in public taste away from female blues and the collapse of the 'race' market in the

Depression convinced this seasoned professional that it was time to go.

Rainey's kind and generous nature is remembered by everyone who worked with her and knew her well, and it is a matter of fact that she nurtured the young Bessie Smith, her eventual successor as 'Empress of The Blues'. Bessie, however, was a very different character. May Wright Johnson, wife to pianist James P. Johnson, recalls: 'Yes she was terrific, and there's been nobody ever since that could sing the blues like Bessie Smith. She would come over to the house, but, mind you, she wasn't my friend. She was very rough.'

Born in Chattanooga, Tennessee in 1895, Bessie Smith was performing as a teenager around Atlanta, Georgia just prior to the Great War. At that point, as entrepreneur Irvin C. Miller says, 'She didn't know how to dress – she just sang in her street clothes – but she could wreck anybody's show.' A beautiful teenager, her skin a very dark hue and her face wonderfully regular, Bessie gradually developed her onstage presence and her approach to the music. By 1920, the year Mamie Smith launched the blues on record, Bessie had her own show, and was beginning to encounter real success further afield than just the far south. Appearing in places like Philadelphia and Atlantic City, she was being recognized as something rather special by the white as well as the black clientele of the theatres she was playing.

In 1923, Bessie relocated to New York and signed to Columbia, and her startingly

Although no one came even remotely close to Bessie Smith, there were many other brilliant women singing and playing the blues in the 1920s and beyond. One of the best was Victoria Spivey, an artiste who was still recording in the 1960s, 40 years after her heyday.

successful career as blues performer and recording artist was under way. Right from the start it is clear that she had the power to mesmerise both through her voice and through her stage presence. As guitarist Danny Barker recalls: 'She had a church deal mixed up in it. She dominated a stage. You didn't turn your head when she went on. You just watched Bessie. You didn't read any newspapers in a night club when she went on. She just upset you ... if you had any church background, like people who came from the south as I did, you would recognise a similarity between what she was doing and what those preachers and evangelists from there did ...' Bessie was a natural, with a stupendous voice which could

wrap itself around any lyric, any line, inject tremendous vitality into it, and unerringly flavour it with a blues feeling which no-one could possibly have thought it had before. This is all there on the 160 or so sides she made for Columbia between 1923 and 1933.

She also had a marvellous ear for the best talent when it came to accompanists: Fletcher Henderson was her normal pianist on record dates, and he would bring along people from his band such as Coleman Hawkins, Don Redman, Joe Smith, Buster Bailey and, on a couple of memorable occasions in 1925, Louis Armstrong. Bessie had the good luck to have special powers of interpretation as well. Often thought of as a one-groove singer without

ETHEL WALTERS, A GREAT SURVIVOR: By the time of Bessie Smith's death in 1937, the craze for female blues singers was almost over. One who stayed the course and indeed renewed her career in the forties was Ethel Waters. Although working mainly in cabaret from the forties on, she had a parallel career as a film actress, following her success in a dramatic role in the play Mamba's Daughter in 1939. She appeared in such films as On With the Show, Tales of Manhattan and Pinky and many others. She resumed her solo career in the fifties and, in the sixties, featured on many television shows. She continued working until her death in 1977.

the wit to change and adapt, she was in fact capable of a wide range of musical styles, all touched with the blues nonetheless. In her last years, after her contract with Columbia records had expired and the rise of the movies had eroded a large part of the travelling shows' natural audience, the classic blues style became something of an unfashionable leftover from the reckless twenties. Bessie, however, adapted her approach to the style of the day, bringing in popular songs of the thirties to her repertoire, and making every effort to stay fresh and contemporary for her audiences.

Even with all the enormous success she enjoyed, it was just appallingly bad luck that Bessie did not live long enough to see a revival of her fortunes. She had fallen during the Depression years from previous dizzying heights and her records now sold as pitifully as the rest of the blues market's. The Empress of The Blues, who could once tour the country in her own show with a cast of nearly 50 people, secure in her own luxury train from the problems of racial segregation, was reduced to support status by

Ethel Waters started her career as a blues singer, but soon moved into a wider entertainment role – one of the first black women to do so. She is seen (left) *in a still from* On With The Show, *a 1929 Warner Bros production; the pensive portrait* (right) *dates from a year later, while the dance routine* (below right) *is another still, from the 1943 movie* Cabin In The Sky.

the mid-thirties. In a cruel twist of fate, just when her indomitable spirit had brought her back to the brink of national acclaim, she was involved in a car crash while driving to her next date on a southern tour and died in September 1937 as a result of her injuries. Thus, within three months of the same year, black music was deprived of two of its greatest interpreters, Bessie Smith and Robert Johnson. Both had died violent deaths, consistent with the hazardous lifestyle blacks had to adopt to pursue a career in music at the time. With Johnson, there is no trace except the music. At least with Bessie, there is the marvellous film short *St Louis Blues*, made in 1929, which preserves her unique presence, both singing and acting.

Although Ma Rainey and Bessie Smith dominated the classic blues style of the twenties, other women made worthwhile and significant contributions. Namesake Clara Smith, who actually made some blues duets with Bessie until a fistfight between them one night at a show put an end to the friendship, was a rough, take-no-prisoners type who appealed to the lowest stratum of the coloured blues clientele. She made a lot of money and met with popular success in the twenties, before she made her last record in 1932, succumbing like the rest to a poverty stricken and fickle public.

Ida Cox (1889-1967), who was a big success on the vaudeville circuit before moving into the studios for Paramount, also met the same fate. Born with a powerful contralto, she commanded attention with her tales of hard times, low-down lovers and the money she never had; her mix with the jazz musicians she regularly used as accompanists such as Lovie Austin and Fletcher Henderson proved to be a telling combination of sophistication and forcefulness.

Cox, and women like Bertha 'Chippie' Hill, Victoria Spivey and Alberta Hunter all made important and hugely enjoyable contributions to the development of the classic blues styles: many of them were to return to the scene years later when the earlier blues styles captured the interest of of young white audiences. Others faded away completely. The international star Ethel Waters, on the other hand, made a great many records between 1921 and 1929, often featuring top jazzmen of the period, and her revue-style delivery, often coquettish and beguiling, is more blues-based than blues singing. In the 1940s Waters went on to make the music which would secure her reputation as a brilliant and moving singer.

Meade 'Lux' Lewis (far left) *was the most popular boogie pianist of the 1930s, and best known for his million-selling single,* Honky Tonk Train. *Big Bill Broonzy (left) enjoyed a local reputation in the 1930s before post-war success.*

When the Depression receded, and the 'live' circuit had finally adjusted to the killing impact of the movies (which were often transported around the country areas and shown in the same tents as the great vaudeville stars used to perform in), a very different type of blues performer began to emerge. For reasons tied up with public taste and the economics of live work, most of them were men, performing alone or with a regular partner.

PIANO BLUES AND BOOGIE WOOGIE

As the great age of classic female blues was fading, new blues strains, such as piano blues, were gaining national (and international) attention. For one thing, piano blues styles were coming into their own for the first time.

In 1929, blues pianist Pine Top Smith recorded a song of his own called *Pine Top's Boogie Woogie.*

It was the first instance of the phrase 'boogie woogie' occurring as a musical description. This instrumental blues style itself seems to have been slowly developing throughout the twenties, as piano bass figures (those played by the pianist's left hand) evolved from plain dance-step accompaniment to completely articulated, recurring patterns – which is what happens in classic boogie-woogie. Pine Top himself, a rather unlucky man who got himself killed by a stray bullet in a bar-room brawl just before he was to record a follow-up to his big hit, does not seem to have thought of boogie-woogie as anything else but blues piano: it was only later that the two terms came to represent different schools of pianists.

This is borne out by the titles of two other outstanding early boogie-woogie performances – *Cow Cow Blues* by Cow Cow Davenport from 1928 (although a rather different version featuring vocals had been recorded four

years earlier) and *Honky Tonk Train Blues* by Meade Lux Lewis, recorded in 1927. Both of these pieces went on to become boogie classics; *Honky Tonk Train* was one of the biggest hits of the thirties when reissued and re-recorded by Lewis.

Honky Tonk Train also gives a clear suggestion as to where one of the main sources of inspiration for the left-hand style came from: the insistent, unbroken rhythms of the train and its carriages which Duke Ellington, in his rather different way, had found so evocative. Meade Lux, in the meantime, had met with so little success that, by the early thirties, he was working in a Chicago carwash, only finally to be located by John Hammond in time to appear with fellow boogie pianists Albert Ammons and Pete Johnson at Hammond's 'Spirituals To Swing' Carnegie Hall concert in mid-1938. Within a short time, boogie-woogie had become the latest musical craze of white teenage America, and all three pianists

had considerable hits. This was a pleasant contrast to the time when the main thing Lewis and Ammons had in common was that they both worked in the same taxi company! Predictably, however, it was the white cover versions which really reaped the commercial rewards while the fad lasted, with vocal novelty numbers like *Beat Me Daddy, Eight To The Bar* taking the public by storm.

Other pianists with boogie in their left hand included Louise Johnson, who only made four sides in 1930 but whose greatness is instantly apparent to anyone who hears her, Jimmy Yancey, whose more primitive style set him apart from most, and Cripple Clarence Lofton, who was wildly extrovert and always willing to take a bushel load of chances in a performance, rather than stick to the same old showbiz routine. Four pianists with a more relaxed, bluesy feel in their playing in the early thirties were Leroy Carr (mostly teamed with guitarist Scrapper Blackwell), Roosevelt 'The Honey Dripper' Sykes, Peetie Wheatstraw and Walter Davis (who had a very successful and prolific recording career on the Bluebird label). These players also had a developed singing persona, so their piano was not the showcase instrument that it was for the strictly boogie-woogie performers. In fact it is fair to say that a considerable amount of their continuing success was due to the role vocals played in their music.

Two piano blues practitioners whose careers began in the thirties but who effectively span the pre-and-post-war periods were

Memphis Slim and Big Maceo Merriweather. Both pianists began their careers as the piano foils for important vocalist/guitarists, and clearly learned a great deal about their craft from them. Slim was the partner of Big Bill Broonzy (for many years simply known as 'Big Bill'), while Maceo formed a memorable duo with Tampa Red. Red and Maceo made many records for Bluebird

such as *Chicago Breakdown* and *Texas Stomp*, both together and separately, and had an easy, loping delivery which could be quite beguiling on the right sort of number. Memphis Smith went on to become one of the most prolifically recorded bluesmen of the post-war period, but his work with Broonzy kept him for the most part in a subsidiary role. This is hardly surprising, considering Broonzy's massive presence as a performer.

A country boy from Arkansas, Big Bill Broonzy (1893-1958) became familiar with the Chicago scene by the early thirties and made the crucial adjustment in his performing and composing style by structuring his music to include piano, and occasionally brass and reed accompaniment, in his guitar-and-voice approach. This helped him survive the declining popularity of the country blues, a style which he had been part of prior to the Depression. A former preacher, Bill one day quit and went to music. 'I'm not a church man,' he later said. 'When I wanna hear some real good singin', that's where I go. As for spirituals, let them alone until the feelin' comes.'

Broonzy's other distinction was to sing blues which were friendly and reassuring in their delivery, no matter how bitter the lyrics' message. Big Bill recorded scores of sides in the decade prior to World War 2, some of them big hits for him, such as *Milk Cow Blues*, *The Sun Gonna Shine In My Back Door Someday* and *I'm Gonna Move To The Outskirts Of Town*. His increasing confidence and sophistication meant that he recorded with a variety of groups during these years, and his popularity remained undimmed, especially in Europe, where he became a major cult figure in the 1950s. His work in the late thirties and early forties with groups using amplification were pointers to the future of Chicago blues in particular. In this sense, he was a leading representative of an evolving blues tradition, while performers such as Sonny Terry and Brownie McGhee stayed within the pre-war acoustic tradition – something which gradually lost them their original following, but in time created an eager new set of fans in the young white enthusiasts of the post-war period.

Another significant figure in pre-war blues was guitarist Lonnie Johnson (1889-1970). Born in New Orleans, Johnson was comfortable with both jazz and blues, as befits someone from that city: as Big Bill once observed: 'In New Orleans they don't raise no cotton. They raise sugar cane. That's the difference between Mississippi and New Orleans blues. Only time New Orleans cats see cotton is in bales on a boat or train. The feeling of a man – that's what he sings from.' Johnson was an outstanding member of Louis Armstrong's Hot Five and Hot Seven, playing both guitar solo and accompaniment. But he also had a successful recording career in the thirties with sexually-based material such as *Don't Wear It Out*, and had a major hit in *Tomorrow Night*, where the roots of rhythm and blues are there for all to hear. Yet time was running out for people like Lonnie Johnson, Leroy Carr and others: blues styles were about to be revolutionized by the introduction of the electric guitar, amplifier bass and harmonica, and the older players would be swept away in the tide, or forced, like Johnson, back into the jazz orbit.

In the years 1941 and 1942 blues researcher (and discoverer of Leadbelly) Alan Lomax made latter-day forays deep into Mississippi on behalf of the Library of Congress. On those field trips, he recorded blues veteran Son House, a seminal influence on acoustic blues, in a fine set of performances which updated his 1930 recordings and placed him back in the forefront of the country blues tradition. On the same set of trips, he recorded a young blues guitarist and singer who had been greatly helped and influenced by Son House. The youngster's name was McKinley Morganfield, and at this stage of his life he was a fine slide guitarist and vocalist in the country tradition. Within a few years, he was to move to Chicago, change his professional name to Muddy Waters (a childhood nickname), and become a vital contributor to the evolution of the post-war electrified Chicago sound.

In his story is the wider story of post-war US blues development, while in Son House, we have an example of the neglect and obscurity which most early blues singers suffered right into the 1960s. Only then would those few surviving blues artists (House included) have their careers resuscitated, and on a scale larger than anything they'd previously experienced.

dizzy atmosphere

"What the hell is that up there? Man, is that cat crazy? That horn ain't
s'posed to sound that fast!"

– **Ben Webster**, *on first hearing Charlie Parker, Minton's, 1941*

IN THE TWO
years following the outbreak
World War 2 in Europe, a
major shift in playing attitudes and personal goals
began among the younger
generation of US jazz musicians. This watershed in
playing approaches even-
tually coalesced around a
small number of late-night
bars and clubs in New
York's Harlem; but, as far
back as the closing year of
the 1930s, the harbingers of
change had been appearing,
for the most part isolated
and in ignorance of each
other, in different parts of
the country.

Probably the first musician of a
decidedly modern bent to attain
public recognition was guitarist
Charlie Christian (1916-1942), a
young player from Dallas, Texas,
who in 1937 had taken up electric
guitar: his introduction to the
mainstream of jazz came through
Benny Goodman, after a manic
piece of arm-twisting by Goodman's friend John Hammond. In
August 1939, within a month of
Coleman Hawkins' return from
Europe, and acting on a tip from
pianist friend Mary Lou Williams,
Hammond arranged for a studio
audition of the unknown guitarist
with the Goodman band. Christian was flown in specially by
Hammond from Oaklahoma City,
but the try-out was a turkey from
the beginning, with a preoccupied
Goodman giving the player no
chance to even play.

That night, determined to make
Goodman listen, Hammond

*Right: A typical night in one of New
York's 52nd St clubs, The Three
Deuces. 52nd St, or 'Swing Street'
as it was known in the thirties,
gradually became the home of the
new jazz played by Dizzy Gillespie,
Charlie Parker and Thelonious
Monk. By the end of the forties,
however, it had been overtaken by
strip joints. Today, it is the home of
giant office blocks.*

arranged for his protégé to sit in unannounced on the Goodman small group set at the Victor Hugo Restaurant in Beverly Hills. Christian, still dressed in his Oaklahoma City clothes – large hat, purple shirt and bright yellow shoes – walked up onto the stage and plugged in. As Hammond relates, Goodman, 'looked around the room until he spotted me, and zapped me with the famous Goodman "ray" ... his face expressionless, his eyes boring like laser beams, a devastating, silent reprimand. But before the opening-night audience there was nothing he could do but go along for at least one tune. He chose *Rose Room* ... I am reasonably certain Christian had never heard [it] before ... No matter ... All he had to do was hear the melody and chord structure once and he was ready to play twenty-five choruses, each more inventive than the last. Which is what happened.'

Hammond swears that, with the crowd screaming encouragement, the one number lasted some 45 minutes, and ended with perhaps the biggest ovation Benny ever received. By early October – just nine days before Hawkins recorded his classic *Body and Soul* solo – Christian made his debut on disc with the Goodman Sextet. From then until his death in early 1942 (from complications brought on by tuberculosis), Christian was a permanent fixture with the Goodman organization, and this exposure meant that musicians world-wide were hearing the first modern sounds played on an electric guitar.

The young guitarist's importance in the development of a new jazz language lay in two areas. One was in his ability to improvise at the highest level, with incredible rhythmic ease and fluency and true blues feeling, through the electric guitar's facility to sustain single notes as a wind

instrument can, and as an acoustic guitar cannot. The other was his tirelessly enthusiastic jamming at after-hours dives in Harlem, helping to develop ideas, thrusting into new territory himself, and encouraging other young players to try their own ideas. He is the central musical figure on a series of amateur recordings made in 1941 at two clubs, Minton's Playhouse and Monroe's Uptown House, playing in a fully-developed, urbane and exciting new style. Others on the same sessions, such as a young Dizzy Gillespie, the revolutionary musical thinker Thelonious Monk and the respected tenorist Don Byas, show either a clear allegiance to the then-current swing style, or merely tentative glimpses of bolder ideas. As the leader of the house band at Minton's drummer Kenny Clarke once remaked, 'There was a lot of sitting in. Charlie Christian was there a lot. He and Monk were hand in glove. If Charlie had lived, he would have been real modern. Charlie was so sold on what we were doing he bought an extra amplifier and left it at Minton's.'

All of Charlie Christian's surviving recorded efforts are worth seeking out, but one in particular commands attention. This was a rehearsal session by the Goodman Septet featuring Christian with Count Basie, Buck Clayton and Lester Young. It yielded just four sides, none of which were commercially released, but the music created, especially by Christian and Young, is of the very highest order. The two men's styles are very close, and it is evident that the guitarist learned much from Young. On one blues title, Young plays a stop-time introductory phrase to his solo which is so rhythmically advanced for the period that he temporarily loses the entire rhythm section on re-entry. Christian in similarly inspired.

BIRD PARKER, THE NAME AND ITS LEGEND: Charlie Parker acquired the nickname 'Yardbird' – shortened to Bird – in 1936. According to the legends, it derived from his fondness for fried chicken but may also have been related to his experiments with drugs and alcohol. One of the greatest artists in the history of jazz, Parker's talent was astonishing, as was his dedication to the music. They were matched by his self-destructiveness; Parker died in 1955, aged 35.

Another player who learned a great deal from Lester Young was Charlie Parker.

CHARLIE PARKER: EARLY BIRD

Born in 1920 in Kansas City, he spent the first 17 years of his life in and around Kaycee. From an early age, he was hanging around

the seedier end of what was still the wide-open town which the corrupt mayor Tom Pendergast ran for his own profit and that of his gangland friends. The music Parker heard, from the likes of the Basie band, Buster Smith, Ben Webster and the players who drifted through with touring bands, inspired him to try his hand at music; when he dropped out of high school at the age of 14, he was already spending most

of his spare time learning to master the alto saxophone. Although from 1936-38 Parker played in local bands run by well-schooled musicians such as Tommy Douglas and Buster Smith, he was virtually self-taught. What is extraordinary is the comprehensiveness of his musical education: most self-taught musicians, especially in those days, learned just enough to get by on. They attained tech-

Left: *Two of the all-time jazz greats, Max Roach (centre) and Charlie Parker (right), greet each other at the 1949 Paris Jazz Festival. Sven Bolheim looks on.*

Right: *Charlie Parker, the alto saxophonist who shaped a generation's musical thoughts. This picture, taken in L.A. in 1947, shows him at the peak of his astonishing powers.*

Below: *1949 saw the opening of a plush New York nightclub named after Charlie Parker, Birdland. Opening night, 15th December, saw (l to r) Max Kaminsky, Lester Young, Hot Lips Page and Charlie Parker onstage together: musical champagne for the launch!*

nical parity on their instrument with their peers, and also the rudiments of harmony. Few players of melody instruments such as the saxophone, trumpet or clarinet, even bothered to learn the major and minor scales to all 12 keys of the western system: only a handful of keys were ever used in most jazz of the time.

Parker, however, stuck at it and learned them all: his ambition drove him to it. Ambition also drove him to imitate his hero Lester Young in tone, rhythm and phrasing, and then add things only he heard in the music. By 1940, when he joined the Jay McShann Big Band, the last great Kansas City band of the Pendergast era, he was sufficiently adept to hold down lead alto chair and be one of the key soloists in the outfit. At the end of 1940, the band made a series of radio broadcasts in Wichita which somehow survived, transcribed onto old metal discs, although they did not appear publicly until the early 1970s. The five tracks recorded by the McShann band show Parker to be at a pivotal stage of his development, with an intriguing mixture of old styles and ideas, plus a clear, silvery tone, rhythmic sophistication and harmonic daring which – when it all clicks – is in advance of anything else in jazz at the time.

Parker has often been quoted as saying that he first made his stylistic breakthrough during a jam session in New York in 1939. He was playing the old Ray Noble tune *Cherokee* and found a new way of negotiating the chords. From the McShann transcriptions and the 1942 commercial records by the band on Decca, it is clear that his harmonic adventures had yet to surpass what Coleman Hawkins and Art Tatum, for example, had already achieved. Still, no-one else had either, and Parker was just 22 when he made his 1942 debut on record. But what was really impressive about the Decca recordings was Charlie's particular combination of qualities, and above all his sound. His tone and phrasing, and his very choice of notes across a harmonically hum-drum background, captured a vital spark of expressivity which thrust out past

previous instrumental voices, and spoke to the new generation, just as Lester Young's eloquence had done in 1936. Charlie Parker was to be the voice of the next decade of jazz and a landmark in its development.

HARLEM HAPPENINGS

Meanwhile, back in Harlem, Parker's future collaborators were collectively coming to grips with musical questions similar to the ones he was beginning to answer on his own. As Dizzy Gillespie explained: 'No one man or group of men started modern jazz, but one of the ways it happened was this. Some of us

Left: Kenny Clarke after his army discharge in 1946: it was he who carved out a new role for jazz drummers during the nights of experimentation at Minton's in the first years of the 1940s.

began to jam at Minton's in Harlem in the early forties. But there were always some cats showing up there who couldn't play at all but would take six or seven choruses to prove it. So ... Thelonious Monk and I began to work out some complex variations on chords and the like ... to scare away the no-talent guys.' Milt Hinton, a swing bassist with a definite liking for the modern music, remembers another such hangout, Puss Johnson's where jam sessions started at about 3.00 a.m. and lasted past breakfast. 'Charlie Parker was never there. Dizzy was everywhere at the time. He was a mischievous guy, and he was also trying hard to accomplish what he eventually did. Diz at that time was practically ignored by the veteran musicians.'

Trumpeter Gillespie (b. 1917), originally from South Carolina, was mostly self-taught, but also had occasional formal musical training as a youth. By 1935 he

Ben Webster in the 1940s went from international fame as featured soloist with Duke Ellington to obscurity as bebop became the jazz language for the youth of the day, and New Orleans jazz hardened into an orthodoxy.

had moved to Philadelphia, hardly a thriving centre of anything, but he made a living playing professionally within the swing tradition, then relocated to New York where, in 1937, he joined Teddy Hill's band, with whom he made his first records. This proved to be a fortuitous meeting for Gillespie because, when he was finally fired from Cab Calloway's band after two years in the trumpet section (1939-41), he was able to use Teddy Hill's influence as manager of Minton's to sit in there on the jams. It was here that he gradually formed, with Kenny Clarke and Monk, the nucleus of like-minded souls who would nurture the new jazz. Not that he had wasted his time with Calloway: bassist Milt Hinton, who played with Calloway for over a decade in a variety of roles, worked with Diz on evolving many of his harmonic progressions. Guitarist Danny Barker sometimes joined their sessions together: 'Dizzy and Milt, between those two-and-a-half hour shows at the Cotton Club, would retire to the roof. Dizzy would blow his new ideas in progressions, and he and Hinton would experiment . . . they would suggest that I come up and join them. But after that two-and-a-half hour show, sometimes I'd go up and sometimes I wouldn't . . . I couldn't see going up there and wasting energies on something not commercial.'

Thelonious Monk (1917-1982) was also wasting a great deal of time on uncommercial activities. Born in North Carolina but from the age of five a resident of Harlem, Monk took piano lessons as a child, and as a teenager played a variety of gigs, including rent parties and bars, in and around New York. After a bewildering amount of freelance work during the mid to late thirties, Monk finally landed the pianist's chair in Kenny Clarke's house band at Minton's from 1940 to 1942. Once there, he concentrated exclusively on developing his musical theories and style, often in tandem with Dizzy Gillespie, who would drop by after finishing Cab Calloway's Cotton Club show for the night. A remarkably taciturn man, he only bothered communicating with a small circle of colleagues, and made no attempt to sell the new music to a wider public than the musicians who frequented Minton's. Teddy Hill, the manager there, had a theory as to why: 'He was living at home with his own people. Maybe if the guy had to stand on his own two feet it might have been different. But knowing that he had a place to eat and sleep, that might have had a lot to do with it. Dizzy had to be on time

to keep the landlady from saying, "You don't live here any more." Monk never had that worry.'

At this distance it is impossible to say who came up with the ideas first, and the point is probably an academic one. But everyone agrees that Monk, Dizzy and Kenny Clarke were the organizers of the new music, the creative sparks who drove on everyone else. Mary Lou Williams believes that 'Monk, Charlie Christian, Kenny Clarke, Art Blakey, and Idrees Sulieman were the first to play bop. Next were Parker, Gillespie, and Clyde Hart, now dead, who was sensational on piano.'

Monk's innovations were harmonic and structural: he thought deeply about the music, and had a very fixed idea about how it should be played. He also became less and less the full-blown piano player, in the conventional sense, as time went on. For him, evolution meant playing less, not more. Most people expected the opposite, especially in an age when Parker and Gillespie were setting new standards in virtuosity almost every night. But Monk was resolved to stick to what he wanted. This intransigence, plus his often remote personality, made him a natural for a long stay in oblivion while others moved on. And so it was. As Teddy Hill commented, 'He just doesn't seem to be present unless he's actually talking to you and then sometimes suddenly in the middle of a conversation his mind is somewhere else . . . When I had him here, the band used to come to work at ten. He'd come in at nine, but at ten you couldn't find him. Maybe an hour later you'd find him sitting off by himself in the kitchen somewhere writing and the band playing didn't make any difference to him. He'd say, "I didn't hear it."'

As a result, Monk played briefly in a few good bands, such as Coleman Hawkins' fine sextet

Charlie Christian was not the first electric guitarist, but he was the first to fashion an individual voice for it. After joining Benny Goodman in 1939, Christian was in the forefront of jazz, until his death from TB in 1942.

from 1943-5, but gained little other exposure and did not record in any significant way until 1947. By then he had completed writing the body of compositions his reputation rests on today, although, apart from *Round Midnight*, *Epistrophy* (co-written with

Kenny Clarke) and *52nd St Theme* few had been heard publicly. The discovery of his unique talents by the larger world would not take place for another decade.

Everybody talks about Kenny Clarke (1914-1985) as the essential rhythmic ingredient in the evolution of what came to be called 'bop', but few give his contributions their due weight. This may have something to do with his being a drummer, and the critical prejudice against a drum-

mer ever doing anything musically significant. However, rhythm has always been of central importance to jazz, and the shift in rhythmic emphasis in each period of jazz's development has involved drummers of superior musical talent and insight. It is the rhythmic inflexion of a music which is its special signature, or identifying trait, and it is generally agreed that Clarke was the first to apply the new rhythmic patterns which would free the soloist to develop new solo cadences. It

Below: *The Dizzy Gillespie Band at a New York jazz concert in May 1945. Hal West is on drums, Curly Russell on bass and Dizzy on trumpet.*

DIZZY GILLESPIE: With Parker, Dizzy Gillespie was the most brilliantly influential musician of the late forties. His gift for music was nearly matched by his talent for survival in a notably short-lived profession. Additionally, he was a superb self-publicist. He was called Dizzie because of his antics on the stands, which did little to endear him to other players. This was especially so at the outset of his career when he was unproved. Another gimmick, his specially bent trumpet (left), was produced in 1955, allegedly so that Dizzie could hear himself better. But it caused tremendous controversy among jazz enthusiasts.

may have helped that Clarke knew his way around the piano and vibes, but after about ten years playing orthodox swing patterns in various groups, Clarke became bored, and started experimenting, reckoning, as all good experimenters do, that 'there must be more'.

What resulted was a means of keeping up the beat through the use of recurring patterns, rather than a constant 'heartbeat' time-keeping. Clarke then went further by developing the use of the snare drum as a means of cutting across the metric beat with independent patterns and 'punctuation marks', thus opening the door for the drummer to actually respond to little ideas and passages from the soloist. This simultaneous lightening and intensifying of the beat, by carrying the time on the ride cymbals and pushing the soloist through constant snare and bass drum interjections, was quickly adopted by other young drummers such as Max Roach and Art Blakey, and the style became the new music's signature. Clarke was also capable of writing music, and two of his co-compositions, *Salt Peanuts* (with Gillespie) and *Epistrophy* (with Monk) are still bop staples today. Unhappily, Clarke lost his central role in the music when he was drafted into the Army in 1943. By the time he was back in New York in 1946, events had overtaken him. Carmen McRae recalled: 'They drafted Klook [Clarke] at a time when he was really on his way to presenting this new jazz to the people. He was kind of a bitter guy for a while when he came back and found how different things were.'

WARTIME REFUGES

By 1943-44, the slow decline and demise of the big swing outfits (in the mid-forties), the rise of the popular vocalists such as Mel Torme, Billy Eckstine, Ella Fitzgerald and a skinny kid called Frank Sinatra, and the devastating economic effect of the war against Japan and Germany, were making jazz a tricky business for musicians to survive in, especially black musicians. This was compounded by a recording ban imposed by the musicians' union between late 1942 and, in some cases, late 1944, which hurt everyone and helped no-one. Glenn Miller, by this time a band leader with only an oblique connection to the jazz mainsteam, solved the economic and logistical problem by signing up and organizing a band to play for the US Services. Major Glenn Miller continued to function successfully in this role until his death in 1944. Artie Shaw also tried this route, meeting with less success and finally pulling out of the whole venture. Other white band leaders simply hired young vocalists and sweetened things up in an attempt to stay in touch with changing public taste.

All of these domestic factors, plus the constant drain of men being drafted into the services which further depleted the natural audience for the music, meant that the live circuit was drying up as venues closed due to wartime conditions. There was less work around, and additionally there was no money to be made in the studios for two years. As often happens in extreme situations, things polarized, and the people left in the middle were the ones most hurt. A large number of musicians born and bred in the swing era veered off down the road to rhythm and blues, the music newly popular with America's urban blacks, while the more sophisticated caught the wave of new music as propagated by Monk, Parker, Gillespie and others. A little later on, as Parker

and Gillespie began to make public headway, a severe backlash in certain musical circles led to the revival of New Orleans-style music, and a resurrection of the careers of many retired or semi-retired players, who found that they had an enthusiastic new audience, mainly made up of earnest young whites. Later still again, there was an explosion of what came to be known as 'Dixieland'-style white bands, especially in northern Europe and Britain, and which experienced its final incarnation in the late-50s 'Trad' craze.

Those left scratching their heads in the middle, playing high-class music in yesterday's style, quickly found work drying up and careers, at least in the short term, blighted. Roy Eldridge was such a player, as was Ben Webster after he left Ellington in 1943. The only sanctuary for these players were the big bands, struggling on as best they could in wartime America. For the younger players who did not end up serving in the forces, these conditions meant that they had to work even harder for the breaks which would launch their subsequent solo careers.

There were two bands which were refuges for these players. Earl Hines, who left the Grand Terrace in Chicago in 1940 to go out on the road with Billy Eckstine as singer and front man, listened to his vocalist's ideas and hired Dizzy Gillespie and Charlie Parker, as well as a further selection of promising young players with modern ideas. None of this band's music was recorded due to the recording ban of that time. Later, when Eckstine went out on his own, he took Dizzy and Bird with him, and hired people such as Budd Johnson, Dexter Gordon, Sonny Stitt, Gene Ammons (Albert's son), Art Blakey and Fats Navarro. Hines stuck to the modern sounds even after this defection, and gave work at important times to men of the calibre of Wardell Gray.

Charlie Parker had joined up with Hines after leaving Jay McShann's band in 1942 as it was about to return to Kansas City for a residency there. Bird was determined to stay on in New York, and so went freelance. During his last period in New York with McShann he had begun to build close associations with the players at the uptown jam sessions, astounding them with the total fluency of his new style. It had been his new friends from Minton's who had made the necessary contacts to get him work with Hines, after Parker had come close to starving through lack of paid work.

Neither Gillespie nor Parker stayed with Eckstine for long. Both men were capable of, and ready to, lead their own groups,

and the exposure Eckstine in particular had generously given them had helped establish them sufficiently for this idea not to be entirely impractical. Gillespie, ever the organizer, formed a succession of groups in early 1945, one of which was a quintet featuring Parker and swing drum star Big Sid Catlett, a player with great sympathy for the emerging style and a beautifully unforced way of driving a band along. This group was to be the first to make uncompromised recordings of the new music, in 1945, for the Guild label. Within a short time, the two men were fronting their own bands in the tiny clubs on New York's famous 52nd St – then known as Swing Street, and after the triumph of bop, simply as 'the Street'.

52nd Street, in New York's midtown area on Manhattan Island – virtually at the epicentre of the

city – had a deserved reputation not unlike the hot spots of New Orleans 30 years earlier, or Kansas City under Pendergast. It was a single block of New York brownstone houses, long vacated by their more affluent owners, which had degenerated into a warren of down-at-heel studios, detective agencies, insurance offices, mail-order companies, and various other low-rent, bolt-hole operations. 52nd Street had started to develop into a major area for live music in the mid-thirties, and by the time Gillespie and Parker began to headline there, it was entering its last few

Artie Shaw (below) *and Glenn Miller* (right) *both led bands to entertain the armed services during World War 2, Miller in Europe, and Shaw in the Far East. Shaw, pictured in 1943, pulled out after a traumatic period, while Glenn Miller, seen here in England in 1944, died in a plane crash.*

years of musical activity. It was well away from corresponding Harlem clubs such as Minton's or Monroe's which were much further uptown, and not surprisingly the clientele was very different. This was especially true during the war years, when the usual white audience was greatly supplemented by uniformed servicemen on leave and looking for a good time.

The block which housed the majority of clubs was the one closest to 5th Avenue (there were a few lesser places, such as Kelly's Stable, between 6th and 7th Avenue). Dingy and tired by day, at night it had its own shabby magic, with neon signs announcing the clubs and bars carrying live music, and the sun-bleached marquees looking smart and jaunty under the cover of the neon night. For clubs which enjoyed worldwide reputations, places such as The Famous Door, Jimmy Ryan's, The Thee Deuces, the Spotlite Club and the Downbeat were all spectacularly unimpressive. Situated either on the ground floor or in the basements of the old brownstone residences, they were mostly very small (bandleader Woody Herman described one as 'a ratty, overcrowded basement'), with primitive facilities, no fire precautions, chairs that made you feel you were lucky not to find one to sit on, and a customer turnover policy guaranteed to offend anyone who came to actually listen to the music. After the end of each set at most of these clubs, all the customers were ejected, and they either had to fork out another entry charge, then buy a fresh round of drinks, or go on to the next club and do the same. If not, they could always go home.

For a short but important period of time, the Street reflected the changing musical times by booking some of the more important new individuals and groups into the different clubs, thereby giving these controversial musicians much-needed work and income. Still, in bad times, work had to be found all over New York and beyond. By late 1945, the Street was being hit by exactly the same problems Storyville had experienced: a crackdown by the authorities worried about morale among stir-crazy servicemen waiting for demobilization. This, added to the gradual dwindling of patrons, as marines and sailors packed up and went home, meant that the clubs were either closing due to economic crises, or were being forcibly closed by the authorities for all-too-evident infractions of the law. Within two years, almost the entire street had been transformed, with the vacated premises turned into strip joints and stag bars. Times were hard.

Gillespie's response was to look for work outside New York. His booking agent, Billy Shaw, secured a residency for his small group, which at the time included Charlie Parker, at the famous Billy Berg's in Los Angeles, a large, opulent club frequented by Hollywood's finest. It was to run for December 1945 and January 1946. Bop, as the music was being labelled by people outside the business (it was never called 'bop' by the young musicians themselves until the media made the name unavoidable), was an unknown quantity in California at this time, and the group had a rough ride there. Gillespie cut his losses and flew back to New York, and in early 1946 organized a big band which, notwithstanding personnel changes and close shaves, survived until 1950. During that time it toured both the States and a number of European countries, and did a great deal to popularize the new music internationally.

Parker's West Coast sojourn turned into a nightmare. A con-

firmed heroin user, he had found himself unable to score the drug after his regular L.A. supplier was jailed in San Quentin. After using his air fare back to New York to buy drugs he became marooned in L.A., and slipped into a vicious circle of scuffling for drugs and trying to find sources of money. Suffering from withdrawal symptoms, malnutrition and alcoholism, he went through a nervous breakdown during which he set fire to his apartment. Friends managed to have all resultant criminal charges dropped, and instead he was sent to Camarillo State Hospital for rehabilitation.

Parker had, with Gillespie, originally been booked for an eight-week engagement at Billy Berg's. It was not until April 1947 – over 15 months later – that he saw New York again. By that time, he had regained his health, was off drugs, and played better than ever. Typically, he was soon once again back on the sad slide into 'the scene'.

TADD'S DELIGHT

Throughout the forties, the newer forms of jazz, and the bands that played them, were slowly moving away from purely dance-based music towards music that could be fully appreciated only when sat and listened to. People in search of live jazz to dance to could still go to the Savoy and dance to the swing-based bands such as Lunceford and Lionel Hampton. Alternatively, people could dance to the shows or records made by the white bands of Goodman, Shaw, Dorsey and Miller, and snuggle up close during the vocal numbers.

The music these white bands and their successors were playing became progressively more remote from its original jazz base, and as World War 2 came to its close, there was a slow realization that the key to economic survival was to follow public taste back towards romanticism and sentimentality. The vocalists were taking over, and would hold sway with the populace until the rise of rock & roll, when another generation would get excited by black-based rhythms.

Compelled to turn their backs on all of this, the younger jazz musicians pursued their aims in whatever groups or bands were progressive enough to allow experimentation. Arranger/composer Tadd Dameron (1917-1965) was one of the key figures at the beginning of the forties whose compositions and arrangements showed big bands the way to exploit the new ideas.

Dameron, a gentle, diffident man, once described himself as 'the most misplaced musician in the business, because I'm a composer. I'm not an arranger or a pianist. They forced me to be an arranger, because nobody would play my tunes unless I would write them out. I don't like to arrange music.' Whether he liked to or not, he was very successful at it. His misfortune was to be a creative spirit, just as Ellington was, but not the type of character who could form and maintain a band so that his compositions were played to their best advantage.

Neither was he a virtuoso instrumentalist, able to dominate bands by the sheer force of his playing. As a consequence, he found himself writing music privately, for his own satisfaction, and earning a living by arranging for a succession of bands. He wrote two be-bop anthems, *Good Bait* and *Hot House*, for orchestras which never recorded them (Count Basie for the former, and Vido Musso for the latter). Both were made famous by Gil-lespie and Parker, with Gillespie keeping *Good Bait* in his band's book for many years.

Dameron actually worked as arranger/composer for Gillespie's late-forties big band, and in 1947 co-led a small group with young trumpeter Fats Navarro, but his influence was never exactly a personal one: his ideas were passed from musician to musician, often in unattributable ways, and so his contribution, though vast, is rarely drawn attention to. People such as Horace Silver and Benny Golson learned much from his work and incorporated it on later styles of bop. But Dameron was a romantic, in his music and in life, and what he did musically was subtle rather than shocking. Late in the 1950s, he was arrested and sentenced for heroin use. During his time inside, he did community service by working for a local family who encouraged his composing, and kept in touch with him after his release. To Dameron, tired of the pressure of his old existence, this kindly family 'influenced me a lot: I began to realise that people can be nice.'

BIRD'S CHILDREN

Most changes come in waves, and the shakedown initiated by Monk, Parker, Gillespie and others produced a new generation of performers intent on building upon their breakthroughs. Most of them fell under Parker's spell, for his virtuosity and his enigmatic emotionalism, as well as his ultra-hip lifestyle and personality, had a hypnotic effect on those on the way up and looking for a role model. In this way, Bird had the same overwhelming influence throughout the music that Louis Armstrong had once enjoyed: each instrument was playing patterns and phrases

Above The street of jazz in New York for nearly two decades: 52nd St in all its glory. It is possible from this photograph to judge just how small and cramped the average 52nd Street club was.

Left: Outside the 3 Deuces in 1947: Erroll Garner and his trio. The great bassist and cellist, Oscar Pettiford, is seen here on the far right.

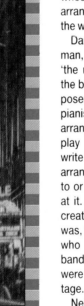

52ND STREET CLUBS: The Three Deuces was one of the most famous of the 52nd Street clubs in the late thirties. Dingy, small and housed in near derelict brownstone buildings, clubs like this, the Famous Door and Jimmy Ryan's came alive at night when garish neon lights gave them a certain artificial glamour.

which had originated with Parker, or adapted its usage to fit in with those patterns. Crucially, drummers altered their approach and began using some of the unusual rhythmic patterns and emphases which Parker relied upon to shape his whole style. The second generation of drummers, such as Max Roach (b.1924) and Art Blakey (1919-1990), both came of age professionally under the influence of Bird in the early years of the new music. Rather than functioning merely as timekeepers, they developed the language of Kenny Clarke into an explosive and challenging rhythmic environment for the soloist to inhabit.

Another area which Roach, in particular, made his own, was the breakneck tempo so beloved of Parker and Gillespie. If there was one single aspect of bop which frightened and discouraged people accustomed to the older jazz styles, it was the delight in virtuosity so evident in Bird and Diz

Above: The great gypsy guitarist Django Reinhardt with his French partner, Stephane Grappeli.

Right: Django pictured with Duke Ellington during the guitarist's 1947 U.S. visit.

and their disciples. So great a figure as Louis Armstrong found it hard to stomach the new subdivision of time which meant that, even at average tempos, these soloists sounded as if they were on a racetrack. 'Some of them cats who play it play real good, like Dizzy, especially. But bebop is the easy way out. Instead of holding notes the way they should be held, they just play a lot of little notes. They sorta fake out of it . . . It's all just flash. It doesn't come from the heart the way real music should.'

A listen to any solo from the 1940s by pianist Bud Powell (1924-1966) would put the lie to Louis' complaint. The emotions are all there: it was just a case of training the ear in a new way to locate where and how they were

being expressed in the music.

Powell was not the first be-bop pianist, nor even the first pre-eminent one: Dodo Marmarosa would probably be most people's candidate for that honour. But when he emerged in 1944, Bud's overwhelming talent, coupled with the intense, driven quality of his music, quickly elevated him to the top of the tree. But there was a reason for the intensity, and a price to pay for it. Powell had a history of mental problems and,

from the age of 21, periodically underwent psychiatric treatment. Between 1945 and 1955, he was institutionalised five times, and on many of these sojourns received electric shock treatment. From the first he was a competitive and difficult young man; a member of trumpeter Cootie Williams' group in 1943-44, he once refused point blank to play a number the leader had called for, folding his arms in front of him and saying 'I won't play it.' On another occasion,

years later, he sat and listened to Art Tatum, whom he idolized, in a New York club. When Tatum had finished playing, Powell walked up to the pianist and said, 'You made five mistakes in that last piece.'

Powell undoubtedly formed his musical style from Parker and Tatum, with a liberal dash of Monk's harmonic theories. The florid approach to ballads (often his own compositions), the formidable harmonic sophistication

Above: Earl 'Bud' Powell, the most influential pianist after Art Tatum and a surpassingly brilliant player whose stature is undimmed today. Mental problems shortened his career and his life, in 1966.

and the perfect articulation all reflect a deep study of Tatum's playing. But Powell had taken Parker's sub-division of the basic metric time unit, from four to eight notes in a common-time bar, and brought pianistic improvisation to new virtuosoic heights at impossible tempos.

The fascinating thing about Bud, moreover, was that he never merely copied Parker's 'licks', or pet phrases: he created his own melodic and rhythmic patterns. As a general rule, when jazz musicians play at very fast tempos, they either play preconceived little patterns, or they simply follow their fingers, with little or no thought as to what the eventual outcome will be. What made Parker and Gillespie so exceptional was that, at the

fastest tempos, they were thinking, and shaping phrases. Powell not only shared that ability, but he was creating utterly individualistic music, often at white heat. There is more than a hint of the demoniac in what Powell played when he was at his peak from 1945-1951.

It is not surprising that Parker and Powell rarely played harmoniously together: both were supreme egotists, and Powell never lost an opportunity to try to ruffle Parker's feathers. There are transcriptions of radio broadcasts in existence where Bird deliberately cuts Powell's solos short, or muscles in to play the recapitulation of the theme before Powell has even had a chance to solo. And on one climactic evening early in 1955, just months before Parker died, the two of them played in the same band at New York's Birdland, a club named after the saxophonist. Powell was drunk and erratic even before the music began, but once it had, he

Above: Sidney Bechet, along with many other New Orleans players, enjoyed a marked return to favour in the 1940s. Here he is caught in action with ace swing trumpeter Oran 'Hot Lips' Page.

simply played a different song from the rest of the band. After a violent verbal altercation with Parker, who himself was in a bad way, Powell stalked off the stage. A visibly distraught Parker walked to the microphone and intoned 'Bud Powell, Bud Powell', over and over, in a lifeless voice. The rest of the band stood rooted to the stage, and gradually the club cleared as onlookers became unnerved. The bassist, Charles Mingus, came up to the microphone after Parker had abandoned it, and said, 'Ladies and gentlemen, please don't associate me with any of this. This is not jazz. These are sick people.' Parker never played at the club again.

The other spectre which hung over so much of the new music-

making of the forties was narcotics. If the twenties and thirties had been the age of alcohol and marihuana for musicians either intent on a good time or just getting through the punishingly long hours of night-club playing, the 1940s saw widespread abuse of much harder drugs. In this, Charlie Parker was something of a reluctant leader: himself an addict on and off since the age of 15, he had such an overwhelming impact on his followers that many of them copied his lifestyle as well as his music. This caused him great distress, and he publicly declared: 'Any musician who says he is playing better either on tea, the needle, or when he is juiced, is a plain, straight liar . . . It isn't true, I know, believe me.'

Many gifted players succumbed to the lure of heroin during these years. Some of them survived it; others did not. Many players wasted their most fertile years strung out and off the scene, either in gaol or too

wasted to land a paying gig. The two most talented black tenor saxophonists of the forties, Dexter Gordon and Wardell Gray, both supported heavy habits, as did Sonny Stitt. Gray finally died in 1955 at the age of 34, as a result of mixing with the wrong people in the wrong town, trying to make a connection. Gordon lost his 'cabaret card', a document authorizing entertainers to work legally in New York State, for many years, and was therefore deprived of the main outlet for his talents. The most naturally gifted trumpeter of the movement after Gillespie, Fats Navarro, was blessed with an unending font of ideas, a bright, jubilant tone and unlimited technique; he was an inspiration to every group he played in. He picked up a habit, developed TB in his enfeebled state, and died young. Singer Carmen McRae recalled sadly: 'I met Fat Girl when . . . he was a fat, lovable character, playing the most beautiful horn, forever prac-

Flip Phillips (left) *and Roy Eldridge* (right), *here caught during one of their blistering sets at a Jazz At The Philharmonic concert.*

tising and forever striving . . . He was still in his twenties when he died. I hear he was down to one hundred and ten pounds, and he used to weigh one hundred and seventy five at least, and he wasn't tall, just fat, you know.'

THE NEW ORLEANS REVIVAL

Meanwhile, the conditions which had eventually enabled bop to

flourish against stern opposition, also encouraged a quite remarkable rebirth of interest in the first generation of jazz musicians. Those who had survived were now mostly in their fifties or sixties, and many had left the music business altogether, discouraged and disillusioned by their experiences in the Depression and its aftermath. By the mid-forties, however, there was a fresh generation of enthusiasts, predominantly white and middle class, who were discovering the old recordings of people such as Kid Ory, Sidney Bechet, Jack Teagarden, and even people like Bunk Johnson, who had been in the Eagle Band in 1910. They also digested the recordings of the

greats who had died earlier on, like Beiderbecke and Jelly Roll Morton, and were hungry to hear this music recreated by the surviving players who were still capable of music 'within the tradition'.

This led to the somewhat bizarre spectacle of players being encouraged out of retirement to lead bands specifically to play to this new audience, and record new versions of old material for enthusiasts. Some of the music thus created has stood the test of time. Some of it is best left in the oblivion it soon went back to. But the best of it has an important place in the history of jazz. Sidney Bechet, for example, anticipated the trend in a series of recording

sessions in the late 1930s with various line-ups and for various labels. One series of recordings in 1938 organized by French critic Hughes Panassie created a stir, especially in Europe, but it was the minor hit he had in 1939 with his sensational recording of *Summertime*, the Gershwin song from *Porgy and Bess*, which really pushed things along. The song at that point was still only two years old, and had been extracted from an opera which had failed at its premiere. Having been turned down by one company, RCA Victor, with the idea, Bechet was given the opportunity by Alfred Lion of the small independent Blue Note records.

In those same two years there

were two important events which helped set the revivalist bandwagon rolling. Firstly, John Hammond organized his enormously successful 'Spirituals To Swing' concert at New York's Carnegie Hall, which brought a new public to many older musicians (including blues men) as well as to the swing musicians, such as Benny Goodman and Count Basie, who were the stars of the concert. Those participating included: Ida Cox, Big Bill Broonzy, Pete Johnson, Albert Ammons, Meade Lux Lewis, Sidney Bechet, Tommy Ladnier, and Sonny Terry. Many of these artists had not been in the public eye for many years.

The second event was the publication in 1939 of the book *Jazzmen*, by two classic jazz enthusiasts, Frederick Ramsey Jnr and Charles Edward Smith. This pioneering work, written with enormous verve and enthusiasm, talked about long-forgotten places and musicians in a way which brought the full romance of the old stories to the readers. As Nat Hentoff, later a respected critic, put it, 'I was fourteen when *Jazzmen* came out, and it hit me so hard that I kept reading it, for the rest of the year and for years thereafter. This was the first book I knew that not only was about the music, but had the music in it.'

It does not matter that subsequent research has proved many of the stories and anecdotes in the book to be wrong: what was important was the rekindling of interest. Enthusiasts went in search of the men talked of in the book, and started demanding recordings by them. For the first time in jazz's short history, old records began to be reissued, on small enthusiasts' labels, while people like Bunk Johnson, after 30 years of playing – and seven years out of the business entirely – were given their first-ever record dates.

The whole enterprise was laudable, and a lot of fine music came out of it. However, a couple of the side-effects were pernicious, to say the least. Firstly, there was the business of music being created (more accurately, re-created) for a specific clientele. While it is good to have your own audience assured, things go hay-wire when the audience starts telling you what to play, and how. An instance of this is pointed out in John Chilton's book on Sidney Bechet. The great saxophonist was signed to an RCA Victor recording deal in which it was originally intended that he play with fine musicians from across the stylistic range of jazz, such as Lionel Hampton, Fats Waller, Tommy Dorsey, Charlie Barnet and Duke Ellington. Ellington was even to be commissioned to write two songs for their date. But critical and public opinion had hardened: they only wanted Bechet teamed up with the classic New Orleans instrumental formations. This was a sadly limiting approach, heralding what was to become a bitter war between jazz generations.

The second side-effect was critical line-drawing. Up to the advent of bop, there had been little controversy in jazz between styles and schools: you were either good at what you did, or you were not. People and styles may have come in and out of fashion, but there was a general consensus that, whether you played New Orleans or Kansas City, trumpet or drums, you were playing jazz, and you were serious about the music. By the time bop came to be recorded, this consensus was seriously breaking down. Certain musicians, and certain musical styles,

A seminal big band in bop: The Billy Eckstine Band in 1945. L to r: Art Blakey, Tommy Potter, Budd Johnson, Junior Williams, Fats Navarro, Billy Eckstine, Chippy Outcalt, Gene Ammons.

came to be championed by critics and opinion-makers at the expense of others. Some radio stations in the US banned what they regarded as 'bop' records, although this term was often misunderstood and misappropriated. In March 1946, *Time* magazine pontificated: 'What bebop amounts to is hot jazz overheated, with overdone lyrics full of bawdiness, reference to narcotics, and doubletalk.' In fact, it would have been very difficult to find a so-called bop record with any lyrics at all in March 1946. They simply didn't exist.

Worse than this, critics who were promoting the revival of what they saw as 'real' jazz (i.e. in the New Orleans tradition) referred to the music of Parker, Gillespie and their followers as 'antijazz' – an absurdity, but one which did much damage at the time. The younger players and their champions reacted by dismissing the old-time musicians as

irrelevant, and their champions as 'mouldy figs'. The controversy lasted for most of the forties, and reached a peculiar intensity in France, where critic Hughes Panassie, who denounced the younger players, and his challenge Charles Delauny who derided the classic jazz men, ended up not even on speaking terms.

There were positive developments from the New Orleans revival, and one was the discovery by young musicians in many countries around the world that they wanted to, and could, play the classic jazz styles and make a living at it. Up to this point, jazz in

other countries had been lacklustre, with only a genius and free spirit such as gypsy guitarist Django Reinhardt cutting through the mire and making a tangible contribution to the development of the music. Django (1910-1953), through his commitment to the Hot Club de France and its Quintet, wherein he played with Stephan Grappelli, brought many of his gypsy music techniques and ideas to jazz. His phenomenal technique, his unabashed lyricism and his wonderful élan won him admiration worldwide, and during the mid-forties he actually toured in the US with Duke Ellington. But he was alone

in his greatness, and it was decades before another European made such an impact on the world stage. Still, the seeds had been sown, and bands like Humphrey Littleton's in England, and Graeme Bell's in Australia, became worthwhile proving grounds for many fine musicians of the next generation.

THE BIG BAND PROGRESSIVES

Another proving ground, especially for young white American musicians, were the so-called

'progressive' big bands of leaders such as Woody Herman and Stan Kenton. Kenton's contribution to the music is still the subject of much argument, more than ten years after his death in 1979 at the age of 67. Woody Herman's position, however, is much clearer. He was a generous and much-loved boss, beginning his career as a bandleader in the mid-thirties when he was elected by his colleagues to take over the Isham Jones band on Jones's retirement in 1936. For the first eight years of his stewardship, the music they played was down-to-earth, bluesy swing, led by Herman's gutsy clarinet and alto

Stan Kenton, below and right (at the Palladium), was another progressive big band leader of the 1940s who stayed the course until his death in 1979. He was a controversial figure, often accused of being too grandiose and neglecting to swing. But much of his music has stood the test of time and is still listened to today.

Woody Herman, an exciting clarinettist and an important bandleader for over 40 years, had his most musically significant Herds – the First Herd and the Second Herd – during the 1940s.

saxophone playing. Herman had a smash hit in *Woodchoppers' Ball*, which sold over a million copies worldwide, and he continued to plough that particular field for many years. However, by 1944, he had built up a particularly strong personnel line-up, and had also taken on board some unusually talented composers and arrangers. Herman himself came up with such scorchers as *Apple Honey*, *Blowin' Up A Storm* and *Goosey Gander*, while Neal Hefti, Ralph Burns, Shorty Rogers and Bill Harris all contributed memorable compositions. The soloists were also strong, led by trombonist Bill Harris, tenor saxophonist Flip Phillips and trumpeter Pete Candoli. But it is probably the contributions of pianist Ralph Burns which have endured more than any other.

By 1945, the Herman band had been christened The Herd (later to be known as the First Herd, as other line-ups followed), and was creating music which was actually new to jazz. It had a rhythm section which probably swung as much as any big band's outside of Basie's, with guitarist Billy Bauer, bassist Chubby Jackson, and drummer Dave Tough generating incredible drive. But what was so remarkable about his band was that, like Ellington, it could combine truly advanced musical ideas about form, harmonic progressions and voicings with an exhilarating ability to swing out which carried its audiences all the way through the trickiest musical equation. As Herman himself said, many years later, 'Let me clear something up right now. We were making money, please believe me – money you don't make today.

That was one of the highest salaried bands of all time.'

Ralph Burns, given the freedom to develop his ideas by Herman, came up with music such as *Bijou*, a feature for trombonist Bill Harris, and *Lady McGowan's Dream*, a mysterious-sounding feature for the whole band, but his greatest achievement was *Summer Sequence*. This unique suite of four parts has a wonderful poetic feeling throughout, evoking strongly the differing moods of summer. It shows hints of Ellington, but more revealing perhaps is that Igor Stravinsky's *Ebony Concerto*, commissioned by Herman and debuted by him at his 1946 Carnegie Hall concert, shows a large debt to the tonal palette utilized by Burns at this time.

Herman's Second Herd was perhaps even more famous than his first, debuting the *Four Brothers* as a song and as a saxophone section (Zoot Sims, Stan Getz, Herbie Steward and Serge Chaloff). Getz at this time was still a teenager, but his solos on this title and on *Summer Sequence Part 4*, later retitled *Early Autumn*, made him an international star overnight, with his cool, pristine tone and rich lyricism.

Stan Kenton (1912-1979), on the other hand, has always been controversial. His idea of good jazz is many people's idea of a nightmarish headache, and it is not entirely inaccurate to describe his concepts and aspirations as Wagnerian, despite a singular lack of vocals in his more portentous music. It serves little purpose to go into the arguments surrounding Kenton, apart from to say that his detractors felt his bands never swung or made anybody feel remotely like dancing, while his fans felt that what they had experienced, in concert or on records, was akin to a nerve-shattering revelation of some vital

musical truth.

Kenton had his fair share of hits in the mid-forties, such as *Artistry In Rhythm*, *The Peanut Vendor*, *Eager Beaver* and *Intermission Riff*. He also became increasingly elaborate and extreme in his musical pursuits, presenting scored works such as *City Of Glass*, which perhaps were more at home in the concert hall. The impresario, Norman Granz, felt, 'It's a shame; this could have been a real swinging band, but it failed because Stan read a book or something. He had some wonderful raw material, eager young musicians, and music; but as Stan is verbose, his band is the same way.'

In the final reckoning, it may be that Kenton's launching of the careers of so many fine young players (all of them white, incidentally), such as Shelly Manne, Art Pepper, Lee Konitz, Maynard Ferguson and Frank Rosolino, will be his most enduring achievement.

By the close of the forties, jazz had developed into a number of vigorous stylistic streams, all running parallel to each other, with very little interaction between them. As the fifties opened, the current styles, including bop, had begun to exhibit signs of tiredness and strain. It was time for another new synthesis, to help people out of the prevailing straitjacket. This synthesis, arriving quietly in 1949 and then making headway slowly both in California and New York, was to come from a mix of the most unlikely musicians. And in Miles Davis it would, for a time at least, find a charismatic new figurehead.

cool and beyond

'I think that the United States, to make up for what happened to Charlie Parker, and to make sure that there are no more geniuses going to waste like Charlie Parker, should subsidize jazz. Jazz is the only true art form that this country has come up with . . . except maybe the atomic bomb.' Jackie McLean

IN RETROSPECT, the emergence in the early fifties of so-called 'cool' jazz, and the attitudes which went with it, was inevitable. In a real sense, it was an orderly progression from the revelations of bop. Dizzy Gillespie's big bands notwithstanding, the essence of bop was spontaneity, individual improvisatory brilliance and as little written or arranged material as possible so as to free up the soloists. The other key ingredient, of course, was personal expression at white heat. Given this recipe, there was little likelihood of the music remaining fresh in its original form for very long. After a few years of constantly having to respond to the demands of the moment within a few tried and tested chord structures, only the most gifted of players were not reduced to recycling personal clichés and formulas, in a simulation of the fire and inspiration which had been the original reasons for playing such music.

So what was 'cool'? The cool style was not a reaction away from bop, but a parallel development to it, using some of its innovations, but also picking up other equally important influences along the way. Its roots go

Left: *Chet Baker, the epitome of 'cool', lounges in between takes at a mid-fifties recording session.*

deep into the big band era, as one of the major attributes of cool was the importance of imaginative and unusual arrangements of the basic material. With this insistence on the advantage of form and balanced structures, the role of the soloist was forcibly changed. Rather than being the prime (and in many cases only) reason for the performance, the soloist had to recognize himself as an element in the overall

composition at the Cincinatti Conservatory in the early thirties. His band of 1941-42 gave him a major hit record in *Snowfall* which in some ways anticipated the later style. Thornhill's music lay outside the mainstream of swing big bands, with an extreme sophistication of sound, and a relative disinterest in dance music. What he and his arrangers were mostly looking for were expressions of atmosphere and

the band's charts, while Thornhill himself often contributed distinctive arrangements of his own. By 1946, he had re-organized his orchestra, and encouraged Evans in particular to contribute arrangements which utilized many of the rhythmic and harmonic devices of the new music of the moment, bop. Evans even arranged three Charlie Parker songs for the band, using such unusual instruments for jazz as

theorist/pianist/composer George Russell, and pianist John Lewis, later to be the guiding spirit behind the Modern Jazz Quartet. Blossom Dearie, the exotic pianist/singer, was also a regular. Gerry Mulligan remembers that they used Gil Evans's place as a meeting-point. It was 'a room in a basement on 55th Street. Actually it was behind a Chinese laundry and had all the pipes for the building as well as a sink, a bed, a piano, a hot-plate, and no heat.'

In late 1947, Evans met trumpeter Miles Davis (b. 1926), and the two quickly realized that they had a great many common interests in music. Davis was drawn into the Evans circle, and quickly became the driving organizational force behind a rehearsal band specifically formed to experiment with new musical forms suggested by bop and other contemporary progressive music. After a period of settling down, what emerged was a nonet made up of a trumpet, trombone, French horn, tuba, alto and baritone saxes, piano, base and drums. This nonet rehearsed music produced specifically for it by Evans, Mulligan, Davis, John Lewis and John Carisi, and almost a year after its inception, played a two-week engagement at the Royal Roost. That, apart from another equally short session about a year later, was about all the live work the band ever did. However, due to Miles' perseverance and one of those unfathomable policy decisions at a major record company, the band got a contract to record 12 78rpm sides. Although it took over a year (from January 1949 to March 1950) to record all 12 compositions, when the singles finally began to be issued they had a profound impact on the nonet's contemporaries.

Another group of players had formed in New York around the blind pianist, theoretician and

teacher, Lennie Tristano (1919-1978). Tristano had received a thorough musical schooling as an adolescent and young man in Chicago, graduating from the Conservatory there in 1943 with a B.Mus. From 1945 onwards he began to attract gifted pupils to him, and his move to New York in 1946 consolidated his position in this respect. By 1948 his regular pupils included alto saxophonist Lee Konitz, guitarist Billy Bauer and tenor saxophonist Warne Marsh, all players of the highest calibre and the intellectual inquisitiveness to accept Tristano's discipline and reap his rewards. What Tristano offered them was a thorough grounding in modern music theory, including altonality and the 12-tone approach, as a basis for playing music which preserved a remarkable outward calm, but was in fact extremely daring and imaginative. He particularly stressed the importance of grasping immediately by ear the underlying harmonic basis for every note played by the group a musician participates in. It was an ability he saw as essential to the successful experimentation of collective improvisation against exotic or non-existent harmonic backgrounds. This extremely straightforward demand conceals a lifetime's dedication to accumulating sufficient musical knowledge to recognize and then act upon each musical context as it arises. Needless to say, few players had the determination and self-discipline, as well as the humility, to undergo such a training.

Not surprisingly, Tristano's school remained somewhat hermetically sealed from other players, although Tristano was widely respected and was a welcome guest musician with people of Gillespie and Parker's calibre. However, his approach and ideas had a widespread impact when the cool style was at its peak: his

Claude Thornhill's Orchestra (above) *was an important early harbinger of things to come. Here the band is pictured in 1947 at the Hotel Pennsylvania, NYC. Claude Thornhill is at the piano,* far left; *Lee Konitz is fifth from the right.*

tapestry. This meant a certain amount of subsuming oneself to the greater good. Many players actually welcomed this approach, because it fitted their personal aims and styles better than the harder edge of bop.

The movement's widely-acknowledged ancestor was the Claude Thornhill Orchestra, a forward-looking group with a leader who had studied piano and

mood. Consequently, outside of the obvious commercial numbers recorded to keep the record label happy, that is what he concentrated on. At the time, this was a highly irregular attitude, and one that probably stemmed from his exposure to classical music during his formal training, as well as his sideman work with the Ray Noble and Benny Goodman outfits.

By 1942, Thornhill had in his band a number of people who would be important creative personalities in the cool sound of the decade's close. Pianist/arranger Gil Evans (1912-1988) and arranger Bill Borden supplied most of

the French horn and tuba to gain a unique sound. In the same line-up Thornhill also had the young altoist Lee Konitz, and baritonist Gerry Mulligan: both players would develop into central figures of the cool approach as the fifties dawned.

By this stage of the band's history, Gil Evans had taken up the position of informal focal point and in-house guru for the younger band members who were experiment-minded. Evans had also taken into his circle some musicians from outside the band who were following similar paths, such as composer/arranger John Carisi, the brilliant

Gerry Mulligan (above), baritonist, composer and arranger, was a seminal West Coast figure as the fifties progressed. The Gene Norman 'Just Jazz' concerts provided vital exposure in the late forties for many modernists. Left: At a 1947 gig are, l to r, Wardell Gray, Shorty Rogers and Art Pepper. Above right: Lennie Tristano, pianist, teacher and theorist, in New York in 1946.

period of greatest recording activity coincided with the rise of the 'cool' school, and his acolytes such as Konitz and Marsh became international stars in the fifties.

WEST COAST WHITE: CALIFORNIA COOL

California in 1949-50 was a long way short of being the contemporary jazz capital of the world. Virtually every above-average young musician with any aspirations left such cities as L.A. and San Francisco and headed east as soon as they could. But in 1950 a bunch of white players from Stan Kenton's band came off a concert tour and decided that they wanted to stay in L.A. They had had enough of the road, had no desire to re-enter the New York steeplechase, and wanted to establish a lifestyle which was a cut above the usual East Coast struggle for existence.

Some of these young players felt that this security would help them to establish more adventurous jazz forms. In reflecting on the different attitudes of night club owners from East and West Coast, French horn player John Graas commented: 'Out here some of the jobs are about as close to permanent as a night club gig can get. Some guys have had jobs that have lasted for years. ... Maybe it's because the rent of most of the clubs here is lower ... anyway, eventually a listening audience begins to develop and it becomes a steady one.'

Up to this time, California had been a musical backwater, apart from a time in the mid-forties, when impresario Norman Granz had begun his jazz career in L.A., building up his annual series of concerts at L.A.'s Philharmonic Auditorium through a judicious mix of mainstream and contemporary musicians. By 1946, he could take a touring troupe from coast to coast and release recorded highlights from such line-ups as Charlier Parker, Coleman Hawkins, Lester Young, Dizzy Gillespie and Buck Clayton, all on the same stage at one time. However, Granz moved on as the size of his operations grew, and California in particular got caught up in the Dixieland end of the New Orleans revival.

By 1950-51, when men such as Shorty Rogers, Art Pepper, Bud Shank, Shelly Manne, Jimmy Guiffre and Bob Cooper first settled in L.A., the local staple diet was solid Dixieland. One man, however, was to prove instrumental in changing that to the new arrivals' advantage: trumpeter Shorty Rogers. Rogers (b. 1924) had broadened his scope and abilities during his years with Woody Herman (1945-50) and Stan Kenton (1950-51) so that, when in 1950 he came to settle in Los Angeles, he was an experienced composer and arranger with plenty to offer his fellow musicians. He was also, like his trumpet model Miles Davis, a great motivator and organizer of musicians. John Graas adds: 'Shorty was a large influence in making modern jazz catch on. He began getting gigs and record dates and he'd give us – all the ones who had been together at the beginning – first crack at them, like when he did his album for Victor, the people there had never heard of us, but Shorty insisted that we be used.'

Rogers, a man who had studied extensively while still pursuing his professional career, also became a respected teacher. He was especially skilled in counterpoint and theory, and wanted people to be able to apply such lessons to their jazz work. Graas commented on this aspect: 'Is there anyone on the Coast who didn't study with Shorty? He made us listen to Basie, Dizzy, Bird, Lester Young etcetera. He said Parker knew every note Lester Young played. We listened in record store booths to everything.'

The influence of Lester Young was especially important. After suffering something of an eclipse in the mid-forties, when his saxophone innovations had been superseded by Parker's, Young's professional career had reached a vaguely satisfactory state of equilibrium even if his personal life was deeply unhappy, but his unknowing influence on the young cool players was vast. It was felt especially in the area of tone. Lester had always possessed one of the purest, most beautiful sounds in jazz, and the

new modern players, looking for a sound which could best present their ideas, took it up and modified it for their own ends. It was probably this pure, vibratoless sound, shared by reed and brass players alike which, more than any other single ingredient, lent authenticity to the 'cool' term. Even baritone saxophonist Gerry Mulligan, who moved to the West Coast in 1950 and shortly afterwards started a pianoless quartet which was to enjoy tremendous public acclaim worldwide, had clear roots in Young's style and tone.

There was one other small West Coast group of young musicians coming of age in the late forties and early fifties who were to have a tremendous popular impact on the jazz world. Dave Brubeck and Paul Desmond, Cal Tjader and Vince Guaraldi all hailed from San Francisco, and each of them was in the process of carving out an original style unparalleled among leaders of jazz small groups. In this loose grouping, Brubeck (b. 1920) was the theoretician. He studied music at college, and took frequent lessons early in his career from French expatriate composer, Darius Milhaud. An intense, committed individual, his piano playing and composing has always had an 'angst' about it which found its perfect counterpart when, in 1951, alto saxophonist Paul Desmond (1924-1977) joined his trio to make it a quartet. Desmond was a quiet, unassuming man with a fully-developed though rather wry sense of humour (which often showed in his improvising), tall and thin and ever deferential to the claims of his more thunderous colleague. Critic Nat Hentoff once described the pairing of Brubeck's ebullience with Desmond's limpid musical beauty after seeing them play together in 1952: 'Brubeck, utterly without guile or humour, a man of invincible in-

BRUBECK THE INNOVATOR: Brubeck's great hit *Take Five* was one of the earliest pieces in which jazz musicians improvised in a tempo other than 4/4. In 5/4 time, it was conceived almost by accident. 'I just pounded out the time to keep us together,' said Brubeck.

Dave Brubeck (right) *and his Quartet were from their inception in 1951 one of the most popular groups in jazz until their break-up in the late sixties. Saxophonist Paul Desmond's* (below) *liquid tone and Brubeck's drive proved an irresistible formula. The Quartet was at its peak in the early sixties when Paul Desmond's composition,* Take Five, *topped the charts. The classic band* (above): *Dave Brubeck, Paul Desmond, Joe Morello and Gene Wright.*

nocence, played the piano as if he were clearing a life-long trail through a forest of sequoias. Paul Desmond leaned against the piano, hands folded ... and seemed to be in a reverie amid the hearty clangor. An amiable solitary at the revival meeting.'

There was a frisson between these two dissimilar players which their audiences instinctively responded to. Brubeck's particular brand of bombast, where he could quote chunks of well-known classical music in the middle of a solo on *Love For Sale*, or where he could build a massive edifice of locked-hands chords and insistent rhythms over some five or six minutes of memorable insanity, was a particular hit with young white students. Brubeck helped them feel intellectual. Desmond, on the other hand, was pure romance. His tone was one of the purest and most ethereal in the history of jazz, and he had a way of caressing a melody which could send shivers through even the most casual of listeners. Such a happy contrast of characteristics gave the Dave Brubeck Quartet a considerably wider potential appeal than most jazz small combos. Brubeck was aware of this early on, and it was partly his enterprising approach to the group's public relations that gave it such a good start.

Brubeck, for example, was one of the first jazz musicians, black or white, to realize the enormous untapped potential of the college campus circuit. He gave his music to these people in all sincerity, and they loved him for it. An open-hearted man, he took them on his personal odysseys, and showed them what he had discovered. This simple act was to have as profound an effect on the future of the music as anything else which occurred in the fifties, because it was to open up an entirely new audience in Amer-

ica to modern, as opposed to New Orleans, jazz. This was the audience which in Europe, and especially France, had been attracted to all forms of jazz for over a decade, but which had never been seriously addressed by jazz musicians or promoters in the US, Norman Granz being the honourable exception.

It is interesting to speculate whether another of the main reasons for Brubeck's and Mulligan's success was the relative lack of freneticism in the music. One of the cornerstones of bop had been the sheer rush of adrenalin generated by listening to a player career through a series of chord changes at some impossibly fast tempo. Add to this a rhythm section which could at times be positively volcanic in its response to the music coming from the front line, and you had music which, to unsuspecting ears, could sound confused, harsh and 'difficult'. If you slowed the tempos to medium, restrained the rhythm section to a time-keeping role not dissimilar to what they used to do in the swing era, and softened the actual attack of the instruments, then the same harmonic and rhythmic advances which bop engineered could be presented to an audience which found itself actually eager to hear more.

Clearly there were other issues at stake, one central one being that of race. Of the first wave of be-boppers in the mid-forties and beyond, only one white man, pianist Dodo Marmarosa, was making a significant contribution. The West Coast successes were, in the main, conspicuously white. Additionally, as the fifties dawned, America was settling into a period of political conservatism and social complacency which was not seriously disturbed until the early sixties. Still, music must have a contemporary attractiveness for people to be seduced

by it, and at least one new audience strand was developed for jazz by the efforts of Brubeck and his colleagues. As Brubeck himself commented: 'I've come to believe that any music that expresses emotion is the only music that's going to live.'

In 1952, baritone saxophonist Gerry Mulligan (b. 1927) formed a quartet featuring trumpeter Chet Baker (1929-1988) which combined several strands of his thinking at that time. Mulligan had already been a professional for close on a decade when he made this important move, and was regarded as an original and accomplished arranger as well as a fine instrumentalist. His musical approach had always been to

Right: *Session at the Lighthouse on Hermosa Beach in California: saxophonist Bob Cooper and bassist Howard Rumsey get grooving.*
Below: *The graceful yet muscular saxophone of Zoot Sims.*

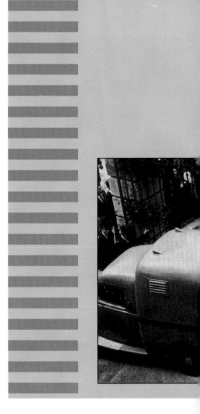

look for ways of combining challenging musical material with a severely circumscribed tonal range. John Graas felt that 'Mulligan's main contribution was to bring jazz dynamics down to the dynamic range of a string bass – and then to use counterpoint in a natural, unschooled way . . . and I think we were all secretly happy at the success of Chet Baker, a guy who used about one octave in a dynamic range of *ppp* to *mf*.'

The way Mulligan made this chamber-like approach work was to dispense with the piano. He and Baker, both barely into their mid-twenties, had sufficient musical knowledge, and quick enough reflexes, to make the weaving of two lines in support of each other an effective and indeed very attractive way of making music. The quartet's success was almost instant, and was also repeated in Europe; both Mulligan and Baker rapidly became immensely popu-

lar figures, partly for reasons that had nothing to do with their excellent music: Baker, and to a lesser extent Mulligan, were handsome, young, charismatic stage presences whose music was pretty enough to be ignored if you did not want to be distracted by such things. This is not to dismiss their efforts on the unrelated basis of their good looks, but just to comment on the odd places where creative music-making and showbiz can coincide.

The Mulligan quartet with Baker did not last long: they had a 'hit' with their intimate version of *My Funny Valentine*, and then Baker was tempted away by a major contract as a solo artist with Columbia. There he lost much of the impetus he had sustained with Mulligan, branching out into albums with strings, and even collections of songs with his vocals adorning the melodies. By the end of the

decade he was supporting a major heroin habit, and had largely dropped from view. Mulligan, a more stable and resourceful personality, kept his mind on the music, and during the rest of the fifties ran a series of musically intriguing groups, including a tentet which had as its model the nonet rehearsed by Miles Davis at the opening of the decade (with which Mulligan had enjoyed a direct involvement). His mid-fifties sextet, featuring West Coast friends such as tenorist Zoot Sims (1925-1985), trumpeter John Eardley and Baker's original replacement in the quartet, valve trombonist Bob Brookmeyer, managed to inhabit a convincing middle-ground between quartet and tentet, using harmonic colour and contrapuntal techniques to create that unique Mulligan sound.

The baritonist was also a professional sitter-in with other

<small>DRUGS SCENE: **Dependence on narcotics was an occupational hazard of jazz musicians. The habit was fostered by the often deprived upbringing of many players combined with an insecure and irregular lifestyle. Among his contemporaries, Chet Baker was merely one victim; others were Art Pepper and Dexter Gordon.**</small>

Trumpeter Chet Baker (right) *has more than his fair share of self-inflicted catastrophes, many of them associated with his drug habit. In 1960, he was arrested in Italy* (left) *for narcotics offences. Later that decade, he had all his teeth knocked out by hoodlums persuading him to see life their way in a dispute involving drugs.*

groups and many records resulted from his casual initial involvement (and, in fact, a jam with Dave Brubeck led many years later to his joining the pianist's successor outfit to the quartet with Desmond). Two outstanding quartet dates with Paul Desmond, a hugely enjoyable session with Thelonious Monk from 1957, and a string of co-led albums with saxophonists such as Getz, Hodges and Webster are among the most memorable of the ad-hoc associations.

Other West Coast players got around a lot in the studio, while the generally more relaxed atmosphere on the coast led to bands with long-lasting residencies. Some of these, although under the nominal leadership of one person (Howard Rumsey's Lighthouse All-Stars, for example), allowed virtually anyone accepted by the leading players to line up and be recorded. Notable leaders at this time were Shorty Rogers (running a sequ-

Wardell Gray (above) *and Stan Getz* (right) *were two superlative tenor players who first appeared in the latter part of the 1940s. Both showed clear allegiance to Lester Young in their style and sound. Gray was a brilliant stylist whose career was cut short in Las Vegas in 1955: Stan Getz is now accepted as one of the music's greats.*

ence of groups as varied as Mulligan's), Shelly Manne (who brought such talents as Russ Freeman, Charlie Mariano, Leroy Vinnegar and Richie Kamuka to public attention, and ran a poll-winning trio with André Previn and Leroy Vinnegar which had a major hit album with their jazz treatment of *My Fair Lady*) and later in the decade, Jimmy Giuffre the clarinettist. Giuffre (b. 1921) was in fact a featured artist in Rogers' small and larger groups, live and in the studio, from 1951 onwards, and also played and recorded a great deal with Howard Rumsey's Lighthouse All-Stars. By 1957, this quiet, deep-thinking clarinettist and saxo-

phonist had moved away from his initial stylistic base (he had composed the famous *Four Brothers* for Woody Herman in 1948) and successfully experimented in unusual chamber-like music with such sensitive sidemen as guitarist Jim Hall and trombonist Bob Brookmeyer. He appeared, famously, in the opening minutes of the film of the 1958 Newport Jazz Festival, *Jazz On a Summer's Day*, playing *The Train and The River*, and was later to become that extreme rarity, a popular avant-garde artist.

West Coast jazz of the fifties is often seen as emotionally limited music played by whites for an audience that was unprepared to

take in the wider jazz scene. Indeed, there was a lot of over-organized noodling at an emotional tempo somewhere below freezing which has simply not stayed the course; (Nat Hentoff once remarked 'much of the "West Coast" jazz that followed in Mulligan's wake has since submerged deeper than Atlantis').

WEST COAST BLACK: CALIFORNIA HOT

There was, however, another vein of music running through the

decade which was committed to expressing a much broader range of human emotions. In most cases, this music was made by black musicians.

Towards the end of the forties, L.A. was still a segregated town when it came to music-making, with white and black musicians having two separate Musicians Unions. As a result of the organizational efforts and personal courage of people such as Charles Mingus and Buddy Collette, Jerry Fielding and Milt Holland, the two Unions were finally amalgamated in 1951 after fierce resistance from conservatives. This led to blacks and whites pitching for the same jobs and working together

Two institutions of the post-war US jazz scene: drummer Shelly Manne (left) and the Newport Jazz Festival (above). Manne, a brilliant and unusually receptive drummer, also co-owned the Los Angeles nightclub, Shelly's Manne-Hole. Newport, Rhode island, was the scene for the first major annual jazz festival in the US from 1954 onwards.

in the same bands on gigs, and it also sanctioned the later entry of black musicians into the lucrative work to be found in the Hollywood studios.

During the forties, however, many first-rate black players, such as tenorists Dexter Gordon and Wardell Gray, had abandoned L.A. in search of steady work for their type of music. Gordon was to remain in New York for years to come, but Gray returned to California in 1951 after touring with Benny Goodman and Count Basie. The rest of his short career was spent in and around L.A. and Las Vegas, playing in the style which had brought him initial acceptance. Gray himself intro-

duced a number of young black West Coast musicians to the wider world on his first recording session since his return to L.A., held in January 1952. Two who would go on to build international reputations were trumpeter Art Farmer (b. 1928) and pianist Hampton Hawes (1928-1977). Farmer was doing most of his playing in big bands, but he had already written one of his best-known compositions, *Farmer's Market*, which was recorded at this time.

Hawes stayed closer to the bebop tradition, actually working with both Charlie Parker and with Parker's former colleague and sideman, trumpeter Howard

McGhee. He also stayed loyal to the idea of small group playing, rather than joining a big band, and continued to make gigs with a select pool of talented, bop-based players like tenor saxophonist Teddy Edwards, bassist Curtis Counce and alto saxophonist Sonny Criss.

All of these players had a difficult time of it on the West Coast in the first half of the fifties, as their styles were simply unfashionable to most audiences. Even the great Dexter Gordon, out of gaol in 1955 after convictions on narcotics charges, found the going very tough and his hard-driving style completely out of key with the prevailing mood. Very few

records were made by these men in the early 1950s. But as the decade wore on and the high tide of cool began to fall back, they gradually found the opportunities to record and play meaningful residencies. Hampton Hawes began making a number of records for the L.A.-based Contemporary label which were critically acclaimed before he, too, fell foul of narcotics agents and started the first of a series of long stretches inside.

One of the few white players with a similar bop-based drive and fire in his playing, Art Pepper (1925-1982), also suffered major disruptions of his life and career through drug-related sentences: at one stage in the mid-sixties he had spent more of the previous 15 years in gaol than out of it. However, Pepper enjoyed a period of relative stability in the late fifties, and at that stage made the records on which his reputation is based. The emotional

strength and the attractive flow of ideas made these sessions popular and influential in their own time, and helped steer the middle-class white public, who had earlier embraced Mulligan, Brubeck, Lennie Niehaus and others so willingly, back towards more weighty music.

Chico Hamilton (b. 1921) and Harold Land (b. 1928), both black players with strong bop foundations, initially made their names playing with famous groups before going out on their own in the mid-fifties. But they went in very different directions. By 1955 Hamilton was a veteran at the age of 34, and had been drummer behind Lena Horne for just on seven years with only one break, in 1952, when he was the drummer in Gerry Mulligan's quartet with Chet Baker. When he formed his own quintet in 1955, he opted for a combination unique at that time: reeds, cello, guitar, bass and drums. However, the presence of the cello, plus the absence of any real attacking edge from the reeds or guitar, meant that the music in general had all of the problems of chamber jazz, and not too many of the advantages. Hamilton's group proved to be enormously popular in jazz terms as the fifties drew to a close, but today sounds curiously stilted. Even the arrival in the band of Eric Dolphy (1928-1964), a musician dedicated to fiery self-expression as well as a superbly complete multi-instrumentalist, only managed to light a fire under the group when he was soloing.

Harold Land, in contrast, had no trouble in moving amongst uninhibited players. As his first major job in the business, in 1954 he landed the tenor sax chair in the exciting new quintet led by Clifford Brown (1930-1956) and Max Roach, replacing tenorist Teddy Edwards. Land was a highly original saxophonist and a close friend of Eric Dolphy in the early fifties: 'Eric Dolphy and I were very close, even before I moved to Los Angeles. He'd come down to San Diego and we'd play together, and when I moved up here, we'd go over to his house and have sessions that would last from morning until night . . . everybody loved to play so much.' After Land decided to come off the road with the Roach/Brown group and settle again in L.A., he joined another group with definite intentions of playing hard, powerfully rhythmic and advanced music. This was the Curtis Counce Quintet.

It is symptomatic of the period that this fine L.A.-based outfit, was largely ignored by the jazz press at the time partly because of geography: New York had plenty of hard-bitten post-bop bands of its own. So, given the same music and players living and recording in New York at this time, they would undoubtedly have enjoyed an entirely different history. A similar fate would await the next outstanding homegrown L.A. quintet playing attractive, updated variations on bebop: The Jazz Crusaders. This group, which included pianist Joe Sample, saxist Wilton Felder and trombonist Wayne Henderson, persevered with their music far into the sixties, finally succumbing to critical and popular indifference in 1971 when they changed their name to The Crusaders, and their style to sophisticated instrumental funk. Listening to their exciting originals and imaginative

solos on such albums as *Lookin' Ahead* and *At Newport*, it becomes clear that the loss was clearly the jazz public's.

LIFE AT THE TOP: MILES DAVIS AND STAN GETZ

There were two other jazzmen, one black, one white, closely associated with the cool period and style. Both of them, however, were too large and too complex as musical personalities to fit so neatly into such a pigeonhole. They were Miles Davis and Stan Getz.

When Getz left Woody Herman's Second Herd in 1949, he was able to form a popular small group on the back of his success with the dazzlingly beautiful solo he had taken on Herman's *Early Autumn*. Getz's sound and melo-

dic conception were both clearly descended from Lester Young, but from the first Getz had an individuality which has always set him apart. His approach combined a wonderful sensuality with a pristine clarity, and his relative rhythmic orthodoxy, compared with Young's radicalism, meant that he quickly developed an instantly recognizable musical persona. Getz may have had the reputation of being an imperturbable stylist, coolly spinning out elegant long phrases which had the emotional impact of a raised eyebrow, but he never accepted that verdict. In 1950, after making a more 'assertive' album, Getz remarked, 'It's fun swinging and getting hot for a change instead of trying to be cool. I don't want to become stagnant: I can be a real stomping tenor man.' Thinking on this, one recalls that Getz's nickname, bestowed by other musicians, was 'Stanley The Steamer';

hardly the label you would stick on someone with ice in his veins.

Getz's fondness for jamming with other musicians, and for really stretching out to play, also sets him aside from many of his West Coast contemporaries. His record label, Verve, (owned by impresario Norman Granz) recorded its star tenor in many settings during the fifties, from his own quartets (the preferred line-up was tenor, piano, bass and drums – no other horn being present) through to full-scale jam sessions featuring upwards of five saxophonists. Notable impromptu records were made with musicians as diverse as Lionel Hampton, Dizzy Gillespie, Oscar Peterson, Coleman Hawkins, Sonny Stitt and Wardell Gray, while Getz also appeared as featured soloist later in the decade on a neglected but beautiful album accompanied by strings, *Cool Velvet*. One other

asset Getz has always had as a player, which stood him in particularly good stead when playing with virtuosos like Dizzy Gillespie, is his complete mastery of his instrument, so that even when the tempo is mercilessly fast (and with Dizzy it often was), Getz not only glides along with the tempo, but continues to create dazzling melodic patterns.

Getz remained at the top of his profession for virtually the entire decade, which is strong evidence of his strength and vitality as a player, but a move to Europe in 1958 with his Danish wife took him from the public's eye, and his career to a temporary standstill. His return to the US in 1961, however, set in motion a series of musical events which so heightened his popularity that, like Brubeck, Miles Davis and precious few others, he crossed over to a public which rarely, if ever, came into contact with jazz in any form.

Miles Davis also started the decade as the epitome of cool. A sharp dresser and, like Getz, an unusually handsome man, he lent that indefinable quality – style – to everything he touched. He started the fifties with the last of the nonet sessions he had arranged with Gil Evans and Gerry Mulli-

gan, but for the next few years fell prey to a narcotics habit. Not until 1954 did he successfully shake it off (in a manner fully consistent with the iron determination he has shown all his life, by sweating it out – cold turkey – on his own) and settle down to reclaiming the lost initiative surrendered to lesser imitators. As yet without a permanent performing group, he managed to make a series of definitive albums with talents as large as Sonny Rollins, J.J. Johnson, Horace Silver and Thelonious Monk. On these classic dates, the full glory of the mature Davis tone is at last unveiled, and his patented method of improvisation is fully formed. He balances carefully weighted phrases with equally considered silences and pauses, and rides beautifully over the uncomplicated medium tempos on numbers such as *Walkin* and *Oleo*. On the date with Thelonious Monk – another master in the use of space in music – there is an almost unearthly quality to the playing on numbers such as *The Man I Love and Bags' Groove*. These tracks, all recorded while Parker was still alive and while the other main bebop players were still adhering closely to the busy,

John Coltrane (far left) *was a late starter in jazz terms, and only came to prominence when he joined Miles Davis in 1955, at the age of 29. Don Byas* (left) *similarly made his international reputation late, when he was into his thirties and bop was evolving in the forties. He is pictured here during a stint with pianist Erroll Garner at New York's* Small's Paradise.

at times frenetic musical styles Parker had created, demonstrate just how much Miles had become his own man.

The popular and critical success of these albums meant that Miles was added to the bill at the second annual Jazz Festival at Newport, Rhode Island. This was a crucial career break, as The Newport Jazz Festival, begun in 1954, was the first ever regular open-air jazz festival and, as such, an unprecedented musical and cultural event, attracting new and younger audiences to the music. He appeared there with a pick-up group of Gerry Mulligan, Zoot Sims, Thelonious Monk, Percy Heath and Connie Kay. The three numbers played that July day, *Hackensack*, *Round Midnight* and *Now's The Time* (two Monk tunes and one Parker) proved to be a watershed in Davis's career, and he was enthusiastically welcomed back onto the scene by both the audience and the critics. Miles responded in typical fashion by claiming not to know what all the fuss was about: 'I don't know what all those cats were talking about. I played the way I always play.' This disingenuous comment only confirmed the Davis mystique.

Fortified by this triumph, Miles set about forming an organized performing band. He chose a rhythm section which combined the two essential qualities for any Davis band – fire and space. The fire was provided by the hard-driving drummer Philly Joe Jones, while the space was crafted by pianist Red Garland, an imagina-

tive accompanist and soloist whose style was, for that time, astonishingly free of Bud Powell's influence. Davis had originally wanted Sonny Rollins as his other frontline player, but fate had decreed otherwise: Rollins of his own volition was temporarily off the scene for personal reasons, so Miles followed Philly Joe's recommendation and hired a virtually unknown tenor man whose career, it seemed, was going nowhere. His name was John Coltrane.

Initially, nobody was very impressed by anyone in the band apart from Miles himself and the 18-year-old bassist, Paul Chambers. Miles replied in his usual self-confident manner, 'People used to tell me Trane couldn't play and Philly Joe played too loud. But I know what I want, and if I didn't think they knew what they were doing, they wouldn't be there.' What Miles was after was a new and fresh combination of sounds and attack. His rhythm section combined lightness of touch and extreme aggression, and his front line mirrored that new balance. Miles himself continued to mine the rich vein of understatement and economy of musical means, while his partner, Coltrane, thrust ahead with a tumbling, turbulent approach, presented through a tenor sax tone which was searingly intense and almost wholly new. The listening public responded rapidly to this, and Miles was very quickly established as one of the top draws on the night-club circuit.

From the formation of what became known as 'the classic quintet' to its eventual demise close to four years later, Miles didn't put a foot wrong either with his public or with the critics. His public appearances were invariably sell-outs, and each album released by the group (it became a sextet in 1958 with the addition of altoist Cannonball Adderley)

became an instant classic. Miles had achieved that rarest of dualities, popular success and critical endorsement. Not the type to rest on his laurels, Miles pushed ahead with a series of parallel recording projects which were to become as equally influential as his own trumpet style and the masterpieces his quintet was making.

The first of these was a collaboration with his old nonet partner, the arranger Gil Evans. The result, the album *Miles Ahead*, featured Miles as the flugelhorn soloist over full orchestral arrangements of a series of modern classics such as Dave Brubeck's *The Duke*, Ahmad Jamal's *New Rhumba* and J.J. Johnson's *Lament*. The use of the softer-toned flugelhorn gave Miles a more restricted decibel range and less bite in general, allowing him to blend beautifully with the rich orchestral colours Gil Evans was giving him as a backdrop. The sound achieved was new to jazz; not even the 1949-50 nonet had achieved such refinement and such sophistication in its use of the raw materials chosen.

Davis and Evans repeated the dose in 1958 with an imaginative reworking of portions of Gershwin's opera, *Porgy and Bess*, but that year's major achievement lay with his sextet's album, *Milestones*. The album finds Miles and his group moving into new musical areas, where stark blues material is mixed with open-ended pieces such as the title track, *Milestones*, which hint at the modal excursions the trumpeter would soon wholeheartedly embrace. It is astonishing to recall that the session was conceived and recorded only three years after Charlie Parker's death in 1955 at the age of 34, from a combination of ailments probably most easily summed up in the phrase 'The Jazz Life'.

Even more astonishing are the two projects from 1959. In the spring of that year Davis once again took his sextet into the studio. By this time, although the two saxophonists Adderley and Coltrane, and bassist Chambers remained, pianist Red Garland had been replaced by Bill Evans, and Philly Joe Jones had ceded the drum stool to Jimmy Cobb. The album they produced, *Kind of Blue*, is still today universally regarded as a pinnacle of modern small-group jazz. On it, Miles fully fleshes out the tentative modality heard on *Milestones*, an approach which was to be massively influential in the years to come. This musical technique revolved around the creation of material which abandoned a conventional song-like structure, such as main melody, variation, bridge, then main melody again, each section containing its own set of chords for harmonic accompaniment. Miles' new direction first of all identified the scale around which a piece would revolve (usually two, sometimes

Above: At a West Coast recording session in 1954, trumpeter Clifford Brown's poise and vitality are evident. Trombonist J.J. Johnson (right) shown here with Kenny Clarke in the early sixties is, like his music, cool, relaxed and incisive.

more, alternating or in sequence) and then hung a theme on it. This was paradise for improvisers possessing the imaginative musical qualities of Davis, Coltrane and Adderley. As Coltrane later said, 'This approach allowed the soloist the choice of playing chordally (vertically) or melodically (horizontally) ... Miles' music gave me plenty of freedom. It's a beautiful approach.'

Both Davis and Gil Evans were well aware of the many connections between Spanish music (which has a unique combination of Western and Moorish influences) and the usage of scales which Miles was becoming fascinated by. After a few months of planning, he and Evans had prepared an album's worth of arrangements consisting of two pieces by the composers de Falla

and Rodrigo, and three originals by Evans, based on traditional material. This was, to say the least, an audacious step, for it took the two friends a long way outside the contemporary notion of 'jazz'. As Miles commented during the actual sessions, 'You know, the melody is so strong there's nothing you have to do with it. If you tried to play bebop on it, you'd wind up being a hip cornball.'

Sketches of Spain created a sensation on its initial release in 1960, and brought Davis a new level of public appreciation. The following year, he would hold a triumphant concert at Carnegie Hall (in the footsteps of Goodman and Ellington), confirming his ascendancy in the contemporary jazz world.

J.J. Johnson and Erroll Garner were two other artists who

started their careers in the forties, and although neither of them were at any point associated with the cool school, both achieved perhaps their biggest successes in the cool decade.

Genius Gets Popular

Johnson had been the man who, in the mid-forties and after, translated Gillespie's and Parker's advances onto the trombone – by no means an easy accomplishment, considering the actual construction of the instrument, which actively discourages the fast runs and precise articulation which bop thrives on. Like many of that time, he found that what he was playing in the early fifties was distinctively out of style. For two years he worked in a job totally unconnected with music, but then a fortuitous request in early 1954 by record company Savoy to record a two-trombone album with Danish trombonist Kai Winding led to a sudden breakthrough

with the public. 'Jay and Kai' became a hot item and for two years were one of the biggest acts in acts in jazz. On disbanding in 1956, they went their separate ways. Johnson, always a man with a broader interest in life than most, summed up: 'It suddenly occurred to me that I needed a change, and I even began to wonder was it possible that a musician or artist could be much too dedicated – so much that he lived in a very narrow world.'

In his own playing, Johnson had not been narrow-minded: recordings and concerts with the likes of Stan Getz, Thelonious Monk, Miles Davis and Sonny Rollins demonstrated that. But it was in his composing that Johnson revealed the true breadth of his musical perceptions. Miles Davis had been the principal soloist on Gunther Schuller's recording of Johnson's *Poem For Brass* in 1956. In 1959, as the result of a commission from the Monterey Festival, Johnson composed *El Camino Real* and *Sketch For Trombone And Orchestra*, and

in 1961 on a commission drawn from Dizzy Gillespie, he delivered an album's worth of a suite called *Perceptions*. By the mid-sixties, Johnson would be recording some beautifully-constructed big-band sessions of his own for RCA Victor, which still sound vital today.

Erroll Garner had trodden a very different path. Completely self-taught, naturally left-handed, a small, powerfully-built man, he arrived in New York in 1944 at the age of 23 and within a few months was recording prolifically with his own trio. Although not then fully mature as a stylist, he still sounded different to any other pianist. This is partly explained by the fact that he never learnt to read or write music, reliant as he was on his enormous natural talent. By the start of the fifties, he was already one of the most popular pianists in jazz and had begun composing his own material. In 1954, he recorded his own song *Misty*. This has since become one of the most-recorded and best-known songs of this century.

Garner had a fantastic ear, and could play anything, in any key. He learnt his repertoire from the radio, as pianist/arranger Nat Pierce recalled: 'He would listen to the radio ... a lot of it he learned wrong, because he would turn on the radio and listen to eight bars one day, and the next day that eight bars would be gone, and the next eight bars would be coming up. When he put them together, it wouldn't always be correct, but that's what his ear told him.' Garner had a phenomenal musical imagination, and it is a shame that his career was such that he was never encouraged to develop it further. Nat Pierce remembers teaching Garner some new pop songs from sheet music: 'Erroll would be walking around looking out the window, smoking a cigarette or something. Before I knew it, he's at the other piano; he would have a symphony composed from this silly little ditty I was playing.'

Inklings of this scope come through on some of his records, especially the solo piano recitals.

101

Tadd Dameron (pictured here in 1962) was a crucially important arranger and composer of the forties and fifties. His unusual melodic and harmonic imagination was undervalued for many years.

Garner hardly needed accompaniment anyway: his left hand was so strong he could have carried a big band on it. And with no-one else around, he could construct elaborate fantasies out of the most unlikely material. On the album *Afternoon of an Elf*, recorded on one afternoon in March 1955, Garner constructed magnificent improvisatory edifices from songs as disparate as *Don't Be That Way* and *St James Infirmary*.

Garner's single biggest breakthrough came with the release of a concert recorded at Carmel, California, in 1955, almost by accident. It was broadcast by a local army base radio station, and when Garner's manager heard the quality of the performance, she pressurised Garner's record company into releasing it. George Avakian, who had the unenviable task of cleaning it up for release, commented: 'I was floored by the poor sound quality. ... On the other hand, the performance was fantastic. It took two weeks of hard labour, inventing filters and boosters as we experimented our way through the murk, but we managed.' It was fortunate that they did; *Concert By The Sea* became the biggest-selling piano album of all time.

One other pianist, Ahmad Jamal (b. 1930), had a major impact on the sound of the fifties. He formed his first trio in 1951 at the age of 21 and landed a record deal in 1952. Originally from Pittsburgh, he felt great affection for his home town: 'I was fortunate enough to grow up with and around such musicians as Tommy Turrentine, Joe Harris ... and also share the rich heritage that Pittsburgh has – Roy Eldridge, Erroll Garner, Dodo Marmarosa, Ray Brown ... Pittsburgh is still a formidable territory for transient musicians, with sessions going on into the early hours.' Jamal is a true original. He is a well-schooled pianist with an immaculate technique who worked out at an early stage what approach he wanted to take to jazz.

His style has been much more influential than most people realize. For a start, he has always taken popular songs, or his own material, and worked out such detailed arrangements that the piece is virtually re-composed. As Cannonball Addorloy oom mented: 'Ahmad's not like the average jazz musician who uses the pop tune as a vehicle. He approaches each number as a composition in itself, and tries to work out something particular for each tune.' One of Jamal's favourite devices has always been to insert space and clarity into a song. He will often take one section of a piece, or just one chord, and sustain that chord across a static rhythmic background until all forward movement in the listener's mind is arrested, creating real dramatic tension. Then he will move on with a flourish and perhaps a swooping run on the piano. His bassist and drummer are worked fully into these arrangements, and are never just 'playing time'. What they play adds rhythmically, har-

Mary Lou Williams was one of the great jazz pianists and a fine composer to boot. Although she was playing professionally in the 1930s, she gained wider recognition in the following decade, when she worked with Duke Ellington and (briefly) Benny Goodman. A performer of great intelligence and wide abilities, she was one of the first to work in extended forms, and was a constant experimenter, fitting easily into the artistic ferment of the forties. She continued to grow as an artist right up to her death in 1981.

monically and structurally to the development of the piece.

Jamal is a master at creating mood. He is also very strongly rhythmic in his own playing, and this ebullience has often been overlooked by people who only catch his surface coolness and poise. His influence has been broadly felt because he had such a profound effect on Miles Davis for most of the fifties. Miles even went as far as to record cover versions of Jamal pieces with exactly the same arrangements as the originals. He also took over the idea of ostantino sections in songs, which in turn was adopted by John Coltrane – and later by almost every modern jazzman playing music after 1960. As Miles said in 1958, 'Listen to the way Jamal uses space. He lets it go so that you can feel the rhythm section and the rhythm section can feel you ... Ahmad is one of my favourites. I live until he

makes another record.' Jamal suffered in the eyes of critics from the curse of popularity: his album *But Not For Me*, recorded live in Chicago in 1958, was a worldwide hit and for a number of years he had the same support given earlier in the decade to Mulligan, Barker and Brubeck. Nonetheless, the musicians knew.

BROWNIE, BLAKEY AND SILVER

Clifford Brown (1930-1956), who started his professional recording career with rhythm and blues group Chris James and the Blue Flames, a group and leader well-known to Jamal, had no such problems gaining critical recognition. From an early age his exceptional abilities as a trumpeter were in demand from a number of big-name leaders. He played in

1953 with Tadd Dameron, and in the same year joined the Lionel Hampton big band, making it as far as Paris with them. Then in 1954, he teamed up with master drummer Max Roach to form the Max Roach-Clifford Brown Quintet.

In the two short years before Brown, along with pianist Richie Powell and his wife, was killed in a car crash, the band created a body of music virtually without parallel in modern jazz. Brown, although clearly influenced by bop trumpeters like Gillespie and Fats Navarro, was one of the most complete musicians jazz has known. His tone was rich and vibrant, his technique secure, his musical imagination limitless. As Max Roach later said, 'He practised all the time. And just as important, he listened. A lot of kids now don't listen. The great ones are also great listeners.'

Brown, while playing in the Roach-Brown band, developed a wonderfully rounded instrumental style: his perfect technique enabled him to execute any idea with the maximum of power, control and expressiveness. What he had to communicate was in itself excitingly full and warm. His astonishing maturity was evident on an album he made with a string ensemble where, playing with tremendous authority, he never over-elaborates in the course of stating a melody, thereby gaining in emotional power. Brown's playing was blessed with perfect balance and poise, even when playing at impossibly fast tempos. The group played music which was within the bop tradition, but put more emphasis on ensemble figures and full arrangements for songs in an effort to evolve a more completely personal sound. It is no wonder, then, that Brown and the band became the model for an enormous number of trumpeters and other leaders. Lee Morgan, Donald Byrd, Booker Little and

Freddie Hubbard spring most immediately to mind as players immutably stamped in the Clifford Brown mould.

Those who picked up on and developed Brown and Roach's ensemble approach were also deeply influenced by pianist/composer Horace Silver (b. 1928) and drummer Art Blakey. Silver came directly from the Bud Powell tradition of bop piano, and played in Stan Getz's group for a year in 1950-51, before moving to New York and signing to Blue Note records in 1952. He stayed with this record company for close to 30 years, and in that time created a whole style of post-bop playing. He and Art Blakey teamed up in 1953 to co-lead a group called The Jazz Messengers. This band, with trumpeter Kenny Dorham and saxophonist Hank Mobley, developed a style of bop parallel with that of the Brown-Roach group, but which gave even more emphasis to an earthy blues feeling, a settled rhythm often punctuated by a backbeat, and touches of sheer gospel preaching in the band's soloists. When The Jazz Messengers split in 1956, Silver formed his own group, while Blakey kept up the Jazz Messengers name. Both leaders stayed close to the style they had built up together, and towards the end of the fifties both had sizeable jazz hits.

Silver, a gifted composer of blues-and-soul-inflected songs, brought into jazz a body of compositions which are still perceived as jazz standards by young musicians playing today. These include *Sister Sadie*, *Song For My Father* (covered by Steely Dan), *Doodlin*, *Nica's Dream* and *Senor Blues*. His personnel in the fifties was remarkably stable, with just one reshuffle in 1958 bringing in tenorist Junior Cook and trumpeter Blue Mitchell.

Blakey was not a composer of any note, but a volcanic drummer

and a fine leader. He constantly found new musicians who were also talented writers and arrangers, then coaxed them into composing in the style he preferred. In this way, tunes written by members such as Benny Golson, Bobby Timmons, Lee Morgan and Wayne Shorter all became standards in the band, and in time, standards in the wider jazz community. In 1959 Blakey had a major hit with a track, written by the band's pianist Bobby Timmons, called *Moanin'* which to many epitomized so-called 'hard bop' at its best, at the point where it merged with 'soul'. The composition is blues and gospel drenched, the beat medium tempo and insistent, and the solos fresh and vigorous, while still retaining a fair degree of real sophistication.

Also developing a distinctive and ultimately profound influential style from instrumental soul, funk and gospel roots was organ-

ist Jimmy Smith. Smith abandoned the piano in 1954 for the Hammond organ, spent nearly a year learning its potential and developing a style, then launched himself on the public with a trio which was to revolutionize jazz, spawn thousands of imitators and by the late sixties make Smith one of the few household names in jazz. What has often been overlooked in all the fuss is just how accomplished a musician he is.

The Modern Jazz Quartet, although it had an outstanding interpreter of the blues in vibist Milt Jackson, certainly never even attempted to compete in such circles. Its musical goals were light years removed from that. The band, when it first recorded in 1951, was known as The Milt Jackson Quartet and featured Oscar Peterson stalwart Ray Brown on bass. By 1954, the group, bolstered by the reception of their first records, began to perform live and, by 1955, had

Saxophonist Sonny Rollins in typical garb and pose, pictured here in the early 1960s. Rollins was the tenor player all others looked to.

established the personnel it still has today. Right from the start theirs had been a philosophy matched by few others elsewhere. Pianist John Lewis, one of the deepest thinkers in jazz, once defined his ideal as 'the spontaneous playing of ideas which are the personal expression of each member of the band rather than the arrangers or composers.' He added, as an afterthought, 'I don't think it is possible to plan or make that kind of thing happen. It is a natural product. All we can do is reach and strive for it.'

The way Lewis, the main composer for the group, managed to achieve this goal was by providing constantly stimulating material, or arrangements, which had economy of means as their philosophy. Lewis would take infinite pains to ensure that nothing was overwritten, and that a soloist, and especially a soloist with the class of Jackson, should feel that the accompanying players fitted him like a glove, rather than tied him down. What was so remarkable about the M.J.Q. at their peak was that their compositions combined rigorous formal discipline with remarkable freedom. And the group never at any stage lost contact with the deeper emotional levels. Lewis's most famous piece, *Django*, is a memorable lament on the death of a great guitarist, and a celebration of his talents. It is a dramatic composition, understated and beautifully paced, bearing out Lewis's convictions about structure: 'I think the audience for jazz can be widened if we strengthen our work with structure. If there is more of a reason for what is going on, there'll be more overall sense and, therefore, more interest for the listener. The total effect must be within the mind's ability to appreciate through the ear. Also, the music will have to swing.'

The group's approach proved so popular that by the late fifties

Lewis was writing film scores, the group was performing non-stop around the world, and the M.J.Q. became initials understood by a vast audience stretching far beyond the normal jazz coterie. The serenity, strength and tenderness evident in their best work had a universal appeal which showed that the group spoke a common language uncommonly powerfully and well.

IN WALKED MONK

Thelonious Monk, when he spoke at all, certainly never spoke a language that the majority could understand. And his music, up until 1957, remained a mystery to all but a select few. This situation certainly prevailed in part because of Monk's own unwillingness to sell himself to the public – any public – or dilute his angular, difficult music in any way. But probably the single most salient factor was that, between 1951 and 1957, Monk was refused a Cabaret Card by the New York

authorities. This card was an essential item in a musician's life, as it enabled him to play in New York, jazz capital of the world. Without it, you were in trouble. For Monk, it was a particular nightmare, because, from the age of four, New York had been his home and base for all operations. The absence of live work in his home town, plus a contract with a record company, Prestige, which clearly did not believe in him as a long-term prospect, meant that Monk was an obscure and unhappy innovator for the first half of the fifties.

A change of record label, to Riverside, in late 1955, was the first sign of things looking up, Monk's third date for that label, *Brilliant Corners*, featuring players such as Sonny Rollins and Oscar Pettiford and recorded in late 1956, produced a wave of positive reaction which set the resurgence of Monk's career in motion. By the middle of 1957, he had a residency at New York's Five Spot Cafe, and had coaxed John Coltrane, newly inspired after kicking a heavy drug habit,

into his quartet. This quartet quickly became the touchstone by which all other modern groups were judged. Coltrane later said, 'Working for Monk brought me close to a musical architect of the highest order. I felt I learned from him in every way – through the senses, theoretically, and technically. I would talk to Monk about musical problems, and he would sit at the piano and show me the answers just by playing them.'

Watching Monk play music was a bizarre and inspiring sight. A tall and well-built man, slow in movement and taciturn in the extreme, he would come onstage and move slowly to the piano, without acknowledging the existence of the outside world. When the music started, the first revelation occurred, because Monk played in a manner unlike that of any other pianist. He was all elbows and weird angles, with the fingers in his hands stretched out straight as if he had a permanent electric shock. The physical presence of the man helped explain the angles in the music. Then, when the spirit took him, Monk would

dance to his own band. It didn't matter who was soloing – bass, drums or sax – he would get up from the keyboard, and shuffle in a rhythm contrary to the band's, round in little circles, eyes raised and shut, enveloped in a private ecstasy.

This could, to the cynic, sound like a bunch of eccentricities calculated to intrigue and take in an audience already bemused by his reputation for weird music and weirder hats. But Monk's sole preoccupation was the music: he did not care about the rest.

Monk's music at this time did not influence anybody directly, but it did have an enormous impact in terms of what became acceptable, and even hip, for a fan of modern jazz to like. Apart from the first-rank quality of his composing, and the unique, often humorous qualities of his piano-playing, his off-the-wall approach helped pave the way for the avant-garde storm-troopers of the sixties. That he would not be remotely interested in them or what they played is hardly surprising considering his immersion

John Lewis, MJK's pianist, who infused European influence.

Connie Kay, the drummer who fused MJQ's different strains.

Concentration: *Milt Jackson poised in rhythm at the vibraharps.*

Bassist: *Percy Heath's supple hands express a rich musical sense.*

in his own world. But this does not detract from the important role he played as the fifties drew to a close.

Monk may have had to wait a decade for recognition, but he was more fortunate than pianist Herbie Nichols, who had perhaps as much to give as Monk but who never managed to run his own band, and spent most of his career in Dixieland and r&b groups. His few records for Blue Note show him to be a strikingly original genius who simply did not fit what most people wanted in the fifties. His career is summed up by the fact that the only magazine interview he ever gave, to *Metronome* in 1963, the year of his death, did not appear until his passing, as the magazine closed down prior to its publication.

PURE GENIUS: SONNY ROLLINS AND CO

Sonny Rollins, the first tenor saxophonist since Lester Young to break through into new ground, made a series of significant recordings under his own name in the late fifties, after playing with important leaders and bands such as Miles Davis and The Max Roach-Clifford Brown Quintet. His qualities as an improviser were fully on display by 1956, when he recorded the famous *Saxophone Colossus* session with its *Blue Seven* solo which, according to critical analysis at the time, was one of the first-ever perfectly-constructed jazz solos. Sonny was just as amazed as everyone else at this, and for a while it upset his equilibrium. However, the natural fountain of inspiration he was blessed with, along with a commanding sound and indomitable technique, stood Rollins in good stead. By the time the fifties came to a close, he was number one tenor man in jazz, his deep creativity in all areas impossible to refute.

The same fifties pre-eminence could be claimed for bassist/composer Charles Mingus, except that he achieved so much in his career, it is impossible to neatly divide his life story into segments. After Mingus had left L.A. in 1951, he settled in New York and played with many leaders and bands, including Charlie Parker on numerous occasions. An irascible man, and one with high standards in all questions of music, Mingus set up his own label, Debut, in 1952, but underfunding and other problems soon accounted for it. Mingus by the middle of the decade had become involved in a number of music workshops, and ended up calling one of his groups the Charles Mingus Jazz Workshop, in an attempt to publicly define what he was attempting to do as a composer and player. He was a dynamic and demanding leader,

MJQ: Pianist John Lewis, drummer Connie Kay, vibraharpist Milt Jackson and bassist Percy Heath have for over thirty years constituted one of the most well-known, popular and consistently stimulating small groups in jazz: The Modern Jazz Quartet, or MJQ for short. Their music, while subtle and outwardly imperturbable, rewards the closest scrutiny.

and he had a pool of musicians to whom he invariably turned when he wanted something done properly. One of these was the young altoist Jackie McLean, who commented: 'As far back as 1957, I've had moments on the bandstand when Charlie had roused me into going into things I didn't know about. I turned to Charlie one night when he taught me a new tune and asked, "What are the changes?" He said, "There are no chord changes." I asked "Well, what key am I in?" He said "You're not in any key." This left me in a hung-up situation. But when I got out there and played, I felt something different.'

Mingus was a virtuoso as a bassist, taking the instrument into new areas and patterns as a soloist, and as accompanist. As a

Charles Mingus (left) *and Thelonious Monk* (below), *two of the greatest figures in jazz. Both were able to consistently strike that most difficult of balances: that of being a vital instrumentalist, bandleader and composer. Their recorded and compositional legacy is at the core of post-war jazz.*

composer, he was again doing things no-one else had conceived of. He was experimenting with atonality, with complex metre changes, with extended form and at one point with what could only be described as 'soul jazz'. His versatility was astounding, but what was more impressive was the sheer quality of everything he did. Nothing was superficial, and nothing cheap. His knowledge of jazz history was unusually detailed – one of his best-known pieces was called *My Jelly Roll Soul* – while his observation of the world and people around him was acute. When Lester Young died in 1959, Mingus wrote one of jazz's greatest melodies in the tender, enduring tribute, *Goodbye Pork Pie Hat*. The song has since become a classic, performed by people as diverse as Jeff Beck and Joni Mitchell. Similarly, Mingus was one of the few jazz players to take music and spoken word seriously, and his experiments along these lines have worn much better than all the rest put together, including the re-

citals by Ginsberg and Kerouac themselves. All of these traits were to deepen in the sixties, and bring forth even more rewarding musical fruits.

Similarly innovative, and largely unsung as an influence, was theorist, pianist and composer George Russell. For most of the four decades up to 1990, Russell has worked on and refined his so-called 'Lydian Concept' of harmonic theory, and has led challenging bands playing his stimulating music during much of this time. Starting in the fifties, his albums have featured people such as Bill Evans, Eric Dolphy, Don Ellis, Sheila Jordan and Jan Garbarek.

Finally, in a decade rich with musical developments from young and exciting players, two old stagers made remarkable comebacks. At the 1956 Newport Jazz Festival, Duke Ellington came out of five years of hard times and faltering creativity to be the hit of the Festival and spark off a near riot with a number, *Diminuendo and Crescendo In Blue*, he had written 20 years before. The hysteria started in the course of a rocking 27-chorus solo taken by tenor man Paul Gonslaves which linked the two halves of the piece. George Avakian, the Columbia producer who recorded the event, wrote later: 'At about the seventh chorus, the tension, which had been building both onstage and off since Duke kicked off the piece, suddenly broke. A platinum blonde girl in a black dress began dancing in one of the boxes .. and a moment later somebody else started in another part of the audience. Large sections of the crowd had already been on their feet ... there were frequent bursts of wild dancing, and literally acres of people stood on their chairs, cheering and clapping.' At the end of the piece, pandemonium broke loose. 'Duke', Avakian continued, 'sens-

ing that to stop now might actually cause a riot, chose instead to soothe the crowd down with a couple of quiet numbers.' From that night on, Ellington's live career was reborn and relaunched with a vigour it was not to lose again until the great bandleader's final illness in 1974.

Similarly, Count Basie, reduced at the turn of the decade to a mere Octet, had his fortunes revived through the release of his classic two *Count Basie Dance Session* albums in the early fifties, and by the end of the decade had assumed the tight-knit ensemble style and settled big-band personnel which would see him and his band successfully through to the eighties.

One the creative front, Ellington also recorded and released a suite commissioned soon after Newport, *Such Sweet Thunder*, perhaps the best of all his later work. This work, a result of Duke's involvement in the Stratford Ontario Shakespeare Festival, was a suite of pieces of such infinite subtlety and variety that their source of inspiration – William Shakespeare, no less – was richly appropriate.

p o s t w a r

b l u e s

"Hey everybody, let's have some fun –

you only live but once, and when you're dead you're done,

so let the good times roll; let the good times roll.

I don't care if you're young or old;

get together and let the good times roll!

– Louis Jordan, 1944 *(lyrics by Sam Theard)*

As THE BIG band era lurched to a close in America, and the young turks of the jazz scene were striking out for new musical territory, a whole new explosion of black popular music was sending shock waves through the country. Out of step with and alienated from the high-gloss sophistication of the latter-day swing bands run mostly for and by whites, the urban blacks had been turning to more fundamental, hard-hitting music for their kicks. The worst days of the Depression were in the past and many people with money were able to look optimistically to the future again. The majority wanted to hear good-time music, and the advent of the Second World War in the US was another reason for a music-loving nation to seek entertainment which enhanced or celebrated life, rather than dwelt in the dark realities of a nation at war.

Right: Hysteria, noise, hootin' saxophones, smoke, booze and music: what rhythm & blues was all about in the early fifties. Pictured here lying on the stage with a few of his fans appreciating the finer points of his embouchure technique is Big Jay McNeely.

The music which came roaring through to capture the urban black audience's minds and feet at first had no distinct name of its own, but by the end of the war it was known to its fans as rhythm and blues, or 'r&b'. It roots went back into a late-thirties phenomenon, the 'jump' bands. These little big bands, or big little bands, had grown directly from small-group swing music, emphasizing the rhythmic concepts so beloved of boogie pianists and blues men (shuffle beat or even occasionally a back-beat), and going in big for the blistering sax or trumpet solo. It was ideal music to go crazy dancing to. Some of the most popular bands had vocalists up front, or featured a vocalist for novelty value.

The man generally credited with getting the 'jump' style up and running was alto saxophonist Pete Brown (1906-1963). Brown came up through the swing bands and for a while played with trumpeter Frankie Newton (1906-1954) in bassist John Kirby's band. After that, both men gigged around, often appearing together in various units, and stuck to the small-group style they preferred. Brown, by the time of his first recordings in 1937, had a fully mature saxophone style which generated tremendous rhythmic propulsion against a swinging beat, a gritty, vocal sound, and clipped, ebullient phrasing. Although never a big star or member of a smash-hit group, Brown's influence was extensive, his style suggesting as it did an alternative (and more exciting) approach to swing sax playing. Tenor saxophonist Al Sears, who managed a successful five-year stint with Duke Ellington as well as a later career as a hard-bitten r&b stylist, was one of the more prominent examples of Brown's impact.

Louis Jordan (1908-1975) was a bandleader with a unique style, but his alto sax playing showed definite Pete Brown touches. After a couple of years with the great Chick Webb's band, he formed his own small group in 1938, The Tympany Five. Initially Jordan concentrated on being a ballad singer, but as his confidence grew, he moved into the 'jump' style, and added his unique vocals to the already heady brew. As he later said, 'I worked with Chick Webb and Ella Fitzgerald, and I played jazz. And then I switched over. I didn't think I could handle a big band. But with my little band, I did everything they did with a big band. I made the blues jump.'

Jordan did that and more. An engaging performer with flawless timing when it came to delivering lyrics, Jordan gradually built up a book of what were then called 'novelty' songs, but which were in reality the first songs dealing with urban negro street life, sung in street language, to hit the wider public. The response was overwhelming: Jordan had hit after hit with songs like *Five Guys Named Moe*, *Saturday Night Fish Fry*, *Caldonia* and *Is You Is Or Is You Ain't My Baby?* right through the forties, and his earthy, driving combination of blues and swing forged a new path for popular black music. His brilliantly-arranged and punchy outfit kept everything on a raw edge of excitement, while his vocals intrigued and entertained. His singles crossed over, too, reaching a large white market, just as his live show did.

Jordan had a sure-fire way of discovering what songs to record next, to keep the hits coming. His manager Berle Adams described that method: 'When we found

Mr R – Billy Eckstine, vocalist and heart-throb to millions in the forties, and a figure for countless imitators to look up to. He also played a keen trumpet, and had an excellent ear for good music, whatever style it was played in.

something we liked, an arrangement would be made up and we'd play it on the one-nighters. The songs that the public asked for again and again were the songs that we recorded. When we walked into a studio to do a record date, we knew that the four songs would be hits – we'd pre-tested the market.'

The proof of this assertion is in the fact that, in seven straight years of hits, 1942-1949, Jordan's Tympany Five had no less than five million-selling singles. He continued to perform and record right through the fifties and remained active up till his death in 1975. In 1954, he found his style and his act being imitated by Bill Haley, to the latter's advantage, and watched as white players took over. He later expressed some very strong views on this: 'There is nothing that the white artist has invented or come along with in the form of jazz or entertainment . . . Rock & roll was not a marriage of rhythm and blues and country and western. That's white publicity. Rock & roll was just a white imitation, a white adaptation of negro rhythm and blues.'

In Jordan's wake came a whole wagon-load of groups and solo acts using the same combination of wit, deep blues feeling and rhythmic drive in their music. Artists having juke box and chart hits in the first half of the forties with that easy-rockin' style included Lil Green, Billy Eckstine, Slim Gaillard, Etta Jones, Helen Humes, Cecil Grant and a young Nat Cole, who at this stage still thought of himself primarily as a jazz pianist (and a very fine one he was, too!).

All these artists were making use of that special American

invention, the jukebox, to spread the good news about themselves and their records. The jukebox eventually became ubiquitous throughout not only the US, but also other affluent western countries before it began to die out in the early eighties. Sitting in the corner of a bar, pool hall or other local hangout, it contained all the latest releases and hits from the so-called 'race' record catalogues, and at the drop of a coin someone's favourite tune came blaring out into the thick, smoky air. The new drive and flair of the 'jump' and embryo r&b records cut through the din and confusion of a bar a lot better than a ballad. And with acts like Louis Jordan refusing to play the black clubs (the money was too poor), and only playing to negroes at large theatres, the jukebox was often the average hipster's favourite means of hearing his kind of music.

The other kind of music which was muscling in on the charts in the early forties was a more direct descendant of big band jazz. It took two forms: the purely instrumental boogie-based backbeat-driven material, and the shuffle-based vocal blues material. Both varieties were normally backed by a roaring big band well versed in how to shout the blues. Beyond this, it was not too difficult to locate the direct influence of gospel sounds and gospel techniques in the music's presentation.

LIONEL HAMPTON: FLYING HOME

This was particularly true of the Lionel Hampton Big Band. Hampton had come up through the thirties with an impeccable swing pedigree, starting in 1930 with Louis Armstrong and moving on to Les Hite's tight and swinging outfit. His breakthrough to the big

time came when he joined the Benny Goodman Quartet (later the Quintet and Sextet) in 1936, staying on board until 1940 and thus crossing over with the formative electric guitarist Charlie Christian. To that august outfit he brought such fire and enthusiasm that he virtually transformed it into one of the hottest small groups in jazz. In 1940 he formed his first big band, and kept faith with his basic principles. The band from the first was designed to create maximum excitement.

Hamp took the boogie beat, married it to the riffing style of big band jazz made famous by Kansas City bands such as Count Basie's and Jay McShann's, then seriously overheated it by pitching the trumpet section way up at the top of their range, getting the sax section growling and riffing like a bear pit, and then sending out into the spotlight a tenor sax player ready to rip up the joint and shoot out all the lights. A drummer himself as well as a two-finger pianist, Hamp would often have two drum kits onstage so that when the spirit took him, he could join in on nailing down the backbeat along with the regular drummer. With two drummers pounding out a boogie beat, and the band riffing into a new dimension of delirium, Hamp could get a crowd into such a frenzy that his shows were sometimes like a Baptist revival meeting way down south.

Needless to say, his erstwhile admirers in the jazz world were horrified by this development, and Hampton became a name synonymous with sadly shaken heads and patronizing expressions of loss. As Lionel said: 'They used to call my band a circus just because I'd jiggle my sticks or clap my hands. Well, what I did was never a routine.' Hamp's strong point in all this was his sincerity, and this certainly came across to the crowds

who flocked to see him, as well as to his record-buying public, who faithfully bought his new sides as they came out. And what Lionel Hampton achieved on his first records was in fact crucial for the development of rhythm & blues, and ultimately all forms of popular music carrying a black influence – he introduced the screaming, tooting, honking saxophones. This galvanizing element first came to the wider public's attention in 1942, when Hamp's band recorded his version of the old Benny Goodman Sextet side from 1939, *Flying Home*.

In his 1942 band Hampton had two specialist tenor soloists, Jack McVea and Illinois Jacquet. It was Jacquet who took the solo on *Flying Home* which changed the voice of sax playing forever. His solo, after an authoritative, swinging start, moves into realms of hysteria (and a high-frequency range) previously undreamt of in jazz, or blues for that matter. This track, and others such as *Hamp's Boogie Woogie*, *Cobb's*

Lionel Hampton (above) *in Paris in 1956, and* (right) *as the frenetic bandleader and sometime drummer in the mid-forties. Hampton and his band specialized in ritualized mayhem: why have a ball when you can have a riot?*

Idea and *Air Mail Special*, set the style for Hampton, and sent an uncontrollable shiver of excitement through both the fans and other tenor players. After Jacquet left to join Cab Calloway as the tenor star, things got even more out of control, as his replacement, Arnett Cobb, with his huge Texas tone and flamboyant manner, worked the audience over himself. On particularly good nights, when the feature number came along, Cobb would start his solo at the front of the stage, work himself up into a state of screeching hysteria, then come down into the audience. Still playing, with the band rocking like maniacs on the stage, Cobb would lead willing members of the audience, conga-line style, strutting to the rhythm, out of the hall,

into the street, maybe round the block or across the road, then back inside. Once there, he would join the still-playing band and, with Hamp going crazy and the whole place beserk, bring the evening to a climax.

Cobb did this with Hamp for five years before going out on his own in 1947 as a leader of a small group. For a time in the late 1940s, Cobb and Illinois Jacquet had the two most popular black acts in the US, cutting best-sellers and playing long tours to sold-out signs in every town. But Hamp never ran out of red-hot

Left: *Louis Jordan, brilliant singer and alto saxophonist, instructs his Tympany Five in a new routine. Jordan's influence on all post-war popular music is vast and largely unrecognized.*

Below: *Great tenor saxophonists at a 1954 concert in England. Coleman Hawkins (centre) spars with Illinois Jacquet, who defined r&b sax playing.*

sax players: it was in his blood, and it became an indispensable part of his music. By the time Cobb went out on his own, the honkin' and screechin' tenor sax style had become an r&b genre. There were countless imitators, some good and some indescribably bad: most of them functioned out of small groups, and worked the small bars and clubs in the urban black areas, where they developed show-stopping routines to keep the customers coming back.

By the early fifties, rolling on the stage, lying on your back and kicking your legs in the air, or 'walking the bar', all while still playing hot tenor licks, had become common property and stock-in-trade for all r&b tenor sax players. With the hysterical approach devalued to the point of meaninglessness, rhythm and blues moved on, looking for newer, more contemporary ways of creating excitement. Then, in

1954, Bill Haley's group rolled around on the floor and played their instruments in impossibly contorted positions to a new generation of white teenagers who screamed and watched in fascinated amazement.

THE BLUES SHOUTERS

The other stream of music which originated with the swing bands was vocal blues with that big-band swing backing. One of the first in this field had been the Kansas City shouter, Jimmy Rushing, who had come to New York in 1937 with the Count Basie band. Rushing had been around a long time, originally joining up with Basie in Page's Blue Devils in 1929, and by the time the band started recording, was one of the main reasons for Basie's huge popularity with negro audiences.

Known as 'Mister Five-by-Five' because he was as broad as he was tall, Rushing had a gritty tenor voice as big as any auditorium the band played: he rarely needed a microphone to cut through the riffs of the band behind him. Additionally, he was a happy-go-lucky character, fond of jokes and stories and always ready to involve the audience in patter and hi-jinks. With this personality, his approach to the blues was a joyful, effervescent one, and his powerfully rhythmic voice, always on top of the beat or belting out long held blue notes over the riffing band, drove the numbers along.

By the early forties, Basie was increasingly playing with shuffle-beats, and experimenting with various types of boogie, instrumental and vocal, so that the band's music edged even closer to the down-home blues tradition. His repertoire had always been foursquare based in the blues, so this was a natural step. The band had quite an impact on the increasingly hard-edged music coming out of the urban ghettos, already being put on the right track by Louis Jordan's upbeat, wise-guy approach.

Equally big in impact, and over a longer period of time, was another Kansas City shouter, Joe Turner. Known as Big Joe Turner, so as not to be confused with the Baltimore-born pianist Joe Turner, he started out as a barman in the clubs of K.C. in the early thirties. Mary Lou Williams remembers him there: 'While Joe was serving drinks he would suddenly pick up the cue for a blues and sing it right where he stood, with Pete Johnson playing piano for him.'

In 1938, Turner appeared at John Hammond's 'Spirituals To Swing' concert at Carnegie Hall with his friend Pete Johnson, and they were one of the big hits of the show. Later that year, he

recorded his first side, *Roll 'Em, Pete*, accompanied by Johnson, and made an instant impact. The record's title had come from the fact that Johnson, a versatile pianist, would wait for someone to request boogie-woogie before he played it. People would come in the club and yell to him, 'Roll for me – come on, roll 'em, Pete, make 'em jump!' The combination of Turner's forceful and rhythmic blues shouting, and Johnson's boogie piano, was irresistible, and the two made many successful sides together.

Big Joe did not have a rough-house voice, or a particularly swaggering delivery, but he had fantastic drive, and his voice had a richness of tone which made it unmistakeable. He was also a fine balladeer. With the decline in popularity of boogie in the early forties, Turner's career took a long and gentle slide downhill. It was only at the close of the decade that he began recording prolifically again, and by this time his backing group was fully versed in rhythm and blues shuffles. In the opening years of the fifties, he recorded a string of epoch-making sides, including *Bump Miss Susie* and *Shake, Rattle and Roll*, and after that his career hardly faltered.

JAZZIN' THE BLUES

Lionel Hampton's Big Band was responsible for launching the career of another of the greatest post-war vocalists, Dinah Washington. Born Ruth Jones in 1924, she grew up singing both blues and gospel, and by the time she was 19, she had been noticed singing in a bar in Chicago by Hampton. That same night, Hampton hired her and gave her a new name – the one she stayed with until her early death in 1963. She sang blues for Hamp until

CHICAGO: **Two views of the home of postwar urban blues. Above is a typical night along Rush Street in 1945, scene of the best-known nightclubs. To the right is the more well-known face of the city: thrusting skyscrapers of the business centre. But Chicago blues in the forties could be hearly only in the lowest and toughest dives in the black section of the south side of town. It was a place of danger as well as art.**

1946, when she went out on her own. Having started out with gospel, she had a rare combination of scorching passion and extreme tenderness. Her voice had a full range, amazing flexibility, and a timbre which changed noticeably when she went from soft to super-loud. With an instrument like that, she was an extremely versatile singer who knew just how to connect those deep feelings to her audience, whether it was on record or live. During the second half of the forties, she had top r&b hits with *Baby Get Lost* and the classic blues *Trouble In Mind*.

By the beginning of the fifties, Dinah was unchallenged Queen of the Blues and r&b, but many people felt that she could be much more than that. Her voice

clearly had qualities that were not being fully used, and her unique phrasing could only benefit from being given a wider range of styles to work with. After much persuading and ventures into other minority styles of music, her company allowed her to record the pop ballad *What a Difference a Day Makes*. This massive 1959 hit gave her the worldwide audience she was to enjoy until her death from a sleeping pills mix-up in December 1963.

Like Lionel Hampton, bandleader Lucky Millinder (1900-1966) helped launch the careers of some great blues-tinged vocalists. Millinder had been in the business for about ten years when he landed a regular spot at the Savoy Ballroom in 1940 with his well-organized and jumpin'

big band. In 1944 he had two first-rate vocalists: Sister Rosetta Tharpe, a shouter with gospel in her soul and a voice guaranteed to warm up your apartment on cold winter days, and Wynonie 'Mr Blues' Harris. Rosetta Tharpe galvanised both band and audience everytime she sang, and was an important early exponent of gospel-based popular blues. She later withdrew completely from popular music, singing only for the Lord. Harris, born in 1915, was to be one of the most successful black vocalists of the following ten years. He stayed but a short while with Millinder, recording two hit singles for him, before going out on his own.

Harris was an arrogant and hard-living man, tall, well-built and handsome in a rogueish sort

of way. He had an energetic and convincing stage act, having trained as a dancer (he taught himself drums before becoming a singer), and was a particular hit with the females in the audience. His solo recordings during the rest of the decade showed strong jazz and blues influence, but the overall feel of the music was updated 'jump', especially when such superb instrumentalists as Illinois Jacquet, Jack McVea and Oscar Pettiford were the featured artists. Harris specialized in double-entendre lyrics, with hits such as *Good Rockin' Tonight* and *All She Wants To Do Is Rock*, capitalizing on the healthy appetite for 'up' songs with a rocking, jaunty beat, pushed ahead by a solid rhythm section and meaty arrangements, and in

this he followed in Big Joe Turner's footsteps. But his bawling vocal style was clearly his own, and for a few years, as the r&b sound took over completely in the black areas, he was the upbeat vocal king.

The other great blues shouter who came up through the big bands was Jimmy Witherspoon. Born in 1923 and vocalist with Jay McShann from 1944 to 1947, Witherspoon had that authentic gospel 'cry' in his voice which became his identifying mark – 'I have no musical training, but I did sing in the church choir in Gurdon, Arkansas, when I was a kid.' Witherspoon had an abiding love for both jazz and blues, and with his emotion-soaked baritone voice, he was a natural for combining the two in r&b. In 1949, he

recorded his theme song, the blues *Ain't Nobody's Business* which became the all-time longest-running single on the rhythm and blues charts and set Witherspoon's career direction for the next five years. However, as rock & roll took over, he found himself unable to move into the white market with his overtly black style, and suffered in obscurity on the chitlin circuit until, at the 1959 Monterey Jazz Festival, he delivered a blistering

set which gave him an international jazz audience overnight.

Harris, Jordan, Washington, Witherspoon and the other seminal r&b artists were picking up on the slowly improving social conditions of the negro population of America during the war years, and recording music that had spirit, optimism and loads of youthful energy. The war had forced the record companies and the entertainment industry in general to take the negro's needs

and desires more seriously than they ever had before. It was a matter of sheer economics: with so many white men gainfully employed overseas with the US Army, Navy or Air Force, with a war effort in full swing and with businesses looking to maximize profits, black labour filled the bill very happily in a great many unskilled, semi-skilled and even skilled jobs. Predictably, blacks were usually lower paid than their white counterparts. But although

nobody was getting rich apart from the big corporations, blacks in the industrial centres throughout the US suddenly had purchasing power, and one of the things they wanted, in quantity, was their own music – a music which talked about their lives or made them feel good.

The second wave of r&b came through as the War came to a close. This was the wave which included singers and instrumentalists who had much less con-

nection with the jazz and swing side of the business. People such as Amos Milburn, Roy Brown, Joe 'The Honeydripper' Liggins, Eddie 'Cleanhead' Vinson, Big Maybelle, Jesse Stone, Big Jay McNeely, Blow-Top Lynne and Earl Bostic all had big hits in the mid-to-late forties. They were the players able to communicate with the black public in the way it wanted, giving them a contemporary cross-section of gospel-touched scorchers; big-voiced, low-key singers with a solid groove; and the sort of updated instrumental boogie that was guaranteed to get anyone movin' and groovin'. Joe Liggins' big hit, *The Honeydripper*, had such an infectious beat that one restaurant owner who had a copy of it on his jukebox rang the juke servicers and insisted it was taken out of his box. It was continually being selected by customers, and the waitresses were jumping and bumping so much to it that things were getting totally out of hand!

Big Maybelle seemed at one point to be the natural successor to Bessie Smith, so strong was her voice and personality. She had the sort of vocal delivery that could strip paint, and her knowing lyrics, delivered with gospel and blues sincerity, proved a devastating combination. On a number like *One Monkey Don't Stop The Show*, her humour, her voice and her searing vitality cuts through like a laser beam. From her it was but a short step across to Little Richard: indeed, in Little Richard's first recording sessions, cut for RCA in 1951 when he was just 15, the vocal stylings of Maybelle, Wynonie Harris and Louis Jordan are never far away. Here

Richard's amazing voice is already fully developed, although it lacks the flame-thrower approach he was to specialize in when, along with New Orleans great Fats Domino, he became the greatest rock & roller of his generation.

One other man in particular made a major contribution to rhythm and blues, and to its success in first the black market, and then the larger white market beyond. Drummer, producer and talent scout Johnny Otis was Greek by parentage, but black by every other yardstick. He was born in 1921, and at an early age moved to the black suburb of Los Angeles, Watts. From that base he led a big band in the mid-forties, then disbanded in 1947, along with the bands of Count Basie, Jimmy Lunceford, Billy Eckstine, Woody Herman and others, as the big-band business came grinding to a halt. By the

Jimmy Witherspoon (above) *had a hit in 1949, after years of trying, with* 'Ain't Nobody's Business.' *In 1958 the Monterey Jazz Festival won him new fans.*

end of the forties he had established himself as an astute talent scout and ace producer on rhythm and blues sessions, recording such artists as Little Esther (later to take her full name of Esther Philips in a long and successful career), Big Mama Thornton (who had the original rhythm and blues hit version of *Hound Dog* years before Elvis), Etta James and Little Willie John.

Otis also produced many purely instrumental sessions for various labels, and helped define a whole movement in West Coast r&b during the early fifties. In 1953 he worked for Bob Shad at Mercury: 'Shad and I got Ben Webster out of Kansas City. We did some things with an r&b background, which he really loved. He had never worked with a twanging blues guitar before. We did four instrumentals, jazz and boogies.'

Johnny Otis had strong views on the takeover of rhythm and blues by rock & roll: 'Rock & roll was a direct outgrowth of r&b. It took over all the things that made

Wyonnie Harris – 'Mr Blues'. Harris was a massive star in the forties, but faded as the rock & roll era overtook black rhythm & blues in widespread appeal.

r&b different from big band swing: the after-beat on a steady four; the influence of boogie; the triplets on piano; eight-to-the-bar on the top-hat cymbal; and the shuffle pattern of dotted eighth and sixteenth notes.' He could have also added the utilization of a burning electric guitar, chorded or solo, but that was taken as much from post-war blues as from anywhere else. With the advent of rock & roll, there was nowhere for r&b as a genre to go anymore: even as great an artist as Ray Charles, the quintessence of quality r&b in the fifties, moved on, and by 1963 was putting his gospel-inspired touch to ballads and pop songs such as *Georgia* and *Crying Time*. This occurred after an early career which had moved from hesitant imitations of Nat King Cole and Wynonie Harris to, by the mid-fifties, a completely mature style which magically combined gospel and blues, often in a sophisticated jazz setting.

Big Maybelle (above) *could literally and figuratively stop the show: her voice and her physique were equally larger-than-life. Her appearance at the 1958 Newport Jazz Festival was a highlight of that event's history.*

Charles as a singer had that devastating 'cry' in his voice which is the mark of the very greatest singers, while his interpretive abilities and innate musicality brought to his public a flowering of gifts simply unparalleled in the blues and r&b scene.

THE ELECTRIC BLUES

As innumerable singers have reminded us, 'the blues never die,' and as the Second World War came to an end, blues was undergoing one of its periodic renewals from within. Probably the single most important ingre-

dient, beyond the talent of the players themselves, was the introduction of the amplified electric guitar. Perhaps the first to use it successfully in the blues was T-Bone Walker, a Texan who had been recording since 1929 and, along with Leadbelly, was a friend of Blind Lemon Jefferson. He was one of the first to see possibilities in the newly-invented electric guitar in the late thirties, and by 1942 made his first records featuring the instrument. He was years ahead of any other bluesman, and also had the inestimable advantage of possessing great talent. He gave the blues guitar much of its musical language, using bent tones, jazzy chords, choppy rhythms and fills and syncopated beats which settled quickly down into the Texas shuffle: a basic ingredient for millions of later blues performances. He was also somewhat more adventurous than many contemporary blues artists, moving into augmented chord patterns which interested jazz and blues players alike for their freshness.

As the post-war period developed, Walker and his Texas disciple, Gatemouth Brown, who was as much a showman as Walker but a much more aggressive guitarist, dominated the development patterns of electric blues. And their message was being heard loud and clear up in Chicago.

It is remarkable that Chicago, a centre for so much important blues and jazz over the past 70 years, had so few homegrown artists who broke through internationally. Most of them either moved there to get work and launch a career, or were brought there by white talent scouts who

T-Bone Walker, the widely influential blues singer and electric guitarist, in a publicity still from 1945. Walker had a style which was superficially relaxed, but in fact built up terrific power and tension.

had discovered them languishing on the treadmill of small-town southern US with no future to talk of. The three great postwar Chicago blues band leaders, Muddy Waters, Howlin' Wolf and Elmore James, all fall into that pattern.

Muddy Waters (born McKinley Morganfield in 1915, but known as Muddy Waters since childhood) certainly needed little encouragement to leave Clarksdale, Mississippi: 'I wanted to get out of Mississippi in the worst way ... I figured if anyone else was living in the city, I could make it there too.' Muddy soon adopted the electric guitar on his arrival in Chicago around 1943-44, and cut a few sides which disappeared without trace. After a few years of making ends meet the best way he could, Waters finally started cutting definitive tracks in 1951. In the following years, Muddy was to record a body of work which even today shocks the listener with its raw power and aggressive vocals. Songs like *Rollin' Stone*, *Hoochie Coochie Man*, *Mannish Boy*, *Got My Mojo Working* and the classic bragging song *I'm Ready*, would have to be in anybody's list of the greatest blues recordings. As Muddy sings:–

I'm drinkin' TNT, I'm smokin'
dynamite;
I hope some schoolboy start a
fight –
'Cause I'm ready, ready as a
man can be.
I'm ready for you; I hope you're
ready for me.

Waters has a style which is sharp as a knife-edge, carries no excess, sticks very closely to the classic 12-bar form, features his wonderful electric slide guitar, and often utilizes the shuffle rhythm. Solos are strictly rationed, and more often than not they are harmonica solos by greats such as Little Walter or Junior Wells. Muddy also had a backing band second to none, which included such great bluesmen as Otis Spann, James Cotton, Willie Dixon and Buddy Guy. His stage presence was electrifying: 'I like to think I could really master a stage . . . I never developed an act of any kind. I just had a natural feel for it.' That feel was, basically, sex appeal. His recorded legacy is a testament to a musician who has stuck to his chosen path with tremendous integrity and originality, within the tradition of the classic blues patterns.

His near contemporary, Howlin' Wolf, also trod his own path with few deviations and, if anything, created a more original body of work than Waters. Born Chester Burnett down in the Delta in 1910, he hung out with and learned from such key bluesmen as Charley Patton, Robert Johnson and Sonny Boy Williamson. This early experience as well as his long time in this world are reflected in his style. For Wolf was a modern primitive, using simple, hypnotic rhythms and stark guitar phrasing. Many of his songs have just the one chord, and build from a riff pattern into an intense, brooding edifice of power and menace. His patented howls and yelps, however, have a rather unexpected self-confessed source – the yodels of 'The Singing Brakeman', country pioneer Jimmie Rodgers.

Wolf, like Muddy Waters, concentrated in his lyrics on real life, real people and common situations. His approach was darker and more sinister, his attitude closer to amoral ecstasy. 'Blues is problems: singing about them doesn't make things easier. It just takes your mind off it. The problem is still there.' Songs like *Smokestack Lightnin'*, *Spoonful* and *Sittin' On Top Of The World* spell that attitude out in the starkest fashion, with Wolf's huge, biting and rugged voice dominating every other musical sound on his discs. His presence was mes-

merizing, and he exercised a spell unlike any other. Wolf died in 1976 after ill health and a debilitating car-crash, his reputation as a unique and great bluesman still intact.

Other artists operating out of Chicago had a similarly powerful influence on the development of modern blues. Some helped define what the electric blues guitar was all about while others became virtuosos on the harmonica, making it an indispensable element of any properly-constituted Chicago blues session. Elmore James, coming to attention in the early fifties with his classic reworking of Robert Johnson, *Dust My Broom*, set a virtuoso pattern for slide guitar that is still imitated the world over, while Little Walter, Sonny Boy Williamson II (Rice Miller), Junior Wells and James Cotton all took the harmonica into what many consider to be the realms of high art. Certainly, the sound they extracted from the little instrument, and the spectacle of them playing, swapping one fixed-pitch harp for another in between songs, was compelling in the extreme. Buddy Guy, for years the rock-hard guitarist behind Muddy Waters, developed his own career, in tandem with Junior Wells (shades of Sonny Tery-Brownie McGhee in the fast lane), until he lost his way in the proliferation of post-Hendrix rock-based blues guitar styles.

More commercially successful in the fifties and sixties than any other post-war Chicago bluesman was Jimmy Reed. Again, he came to Chicago from the south, and for most of the forties played the Chicago clubs with his buddy Eddie Taylor. In the fifties, however, he smoothed out his style from its rough beginnings, and began to have hits which crossed over into the white record-buying charts. By 1959 he was ready for success in a big

way, and quickly made his name with songs such as *Baby What You Want Me To Do* and *Big Boss Man*. Different again was Otis Rush, who was the first Chicagoan to use an electric bass, and often used a horn section to make his point. His singing was intense and haunting, evoking a melancholy which often lingers long after the performance is finished.

Out of Detroit came another primitive whose career has been astonishing and whose influence had not yet begun to fall away. This was John Lee Hooker (b.

1917). Like Muddy Waters, he was a migrant from Clarksdale, Mississippi, arriving in Detroit in 1943. Although he learned from such people as Tommy McLennan and Will Moore, Hooker is just as much an original as Howlin' Wolf. He is a sometimes overpowering performer, and when he is playing, it is to the exclusion of everything else, including the back-up musicians. Hooker is as happy accompanying himself as having any help, and plays like the old country players do: he changes when he feels like it, and not when the standard 12-bar

pattern dictates. He quite regularly ignores all chord changes and musical cadences, even when accompanying saxophonists, guitars and bassists stumble into conventional patterns in unthinking anticipation.

John Lee was a pioneer on the electric guitar not in the sense of being one of the first to use it, but in getting more out of it than anyone before him. In *Boogie Chillen*, recorded in 1948 and one of his first singles, one hears him literally flailing at his guitar, and making the amp work overtime.

That sharp-cutting, distorted sound, coupled with the driving rhythm which is a Hooker trademark, makes for wildly exciting music when John Lee is in form. He also has a magnificent singing voice, deep and rich, which seems to naturally carry a heartbeat of rhythm in it as he sings. By the sixties, Hooker was signed to a label which pushed him into the rock charts, and he succeeded in having a hit with *Boom Boom* while never for a moment deserting his fundamental style. His return to the wider shores of the music business in the 1990s has

again been accomplished without compromise, and it is a measure of his musical integrity that on a 1990 film soundtrack he plays with Miles Davis without moving an inch towards accommodating Miles' musical style. (The fact that Miles doesn't either makes it a rather bizarre meeting of the minds.)

Hooker's influence in blues circles was slight, but his impact on later rock and roll players was vast. His use of distortion, his hypnotic beat, his suggestiveness all became tools in the hands of

Above: Champion Jack Dupree, of New Orleans, has cut classic sides, alone or with small groups.

Above left: Chester Burnett – better-known as Howlin' Wolf – came to fame later than most, but entranced the listeners he attracted.

sixties guitarists, both white and black. Jimi Hendrix, easily the most gifted guitarist of the post-war period, was particularly indebted to him.

Equally as influential on rock and roll, although not nearly as large a figure in the blues, was Arthur 'Big Boy' Crudup. Another Mississippi man, born there in

MUDDY WATERS: Leaving his home in the Mississippi Delta, Waters turned to electrified blues in his late twenties and developed a pulsating, commanding style. Without ever losing the pure blues rhythms of his country roots, Waters shouted, roared, moaned and barked his way through a song. Because of his relatively late emergence, Waters was able to win the young white audiences of the r&b era. The sexuality of his performances exactly fitted the times; blacks and whites alike shared his rage to live.

Muddy Waters (right) *exuding charisma from every pore as he delivers another round of finely-judged, driving blues guitar. His early fifties band* (below) *included Otis Spann on piano, and Little Walter on harmonica.*

1905, with a large, ungainly body and an open, guileless face, Crudup came up through gospel and was 35 years old by the time he hit Chicago. In 1942 he was playing electric guitar and had evolved the loping rhythms that became his signature. Between 1942 and 1954, Crudup came up to RCA's studios in Chicago from Mississippi regularly for recording purposes. His sales were unspectacular but solid, and he made little money from the exciting guitar-and-vocal combinations, finally retiring in 1954. That same year, Elvis Presley did a cover version of a Crudup single, *That's All Right*, which was a smash hit on Sun records, and was later an international best-seller when reissued as a single on RCA Victor.

From that point onwards, Crudup's songs were covered by a bewildering number of rock performers. Crudup himself, a victim of unscrupulous music business manipulators, received no royalties for the use of his songs, and died poor in 1974. He got a plaque from Elvis in 1959 acknowledging his role in helping Elvis achieve his initial breakthrough, forming the young singer's style when he was still a young backwoods truck driver.

Willie Dixon is another man who never caught the public eye, but who has had an enormous impact on the development of post-war blues. Born in Vicksburg, Mississippi in 1915, and a colleague in the early days of such outstanding blues pianists as Memphis Slim and Roosevelt Sykes, Dixon began recording in the forties with a variety of players, and his bass-playing was in great demand. By the fifties he was session musician and producer on countless Chicago blues dates and a talent scout for Chess records. Although rarely a leader on his own dates, Dixon did manage a couple of first-class

albums, one in tandem with his friend Memphis Slim in 1960 which included his humorous vocal number *Shaky*, where he imitates a stammerer talking about the way he feels when he's with his girl.

Dixon's direct influence on the actual music-making, however, has come through his songs. His has been a golden touch, with hits such as *Big Boss Man* (co-written with Jimmy Reed), *Little Red Rooster*, *Hoochie Coochie Man*, *My Babe*, *Mannish Boy (I'm A Man)* and *I Just Want To Make Love To You*. Through these he helped the careers of all the key Chess label artists working out of Chicago and also brought the blues to a wider audience than anyone would have dreamed possible back in 1935 when he first moved to Chicago.

BLUES FOR TOMORROW

There may have been other players with the popularity of B.B. King, either briefly or over a relatively extended period of time – Sam 'Lightnin' Hopkins, Champion Jack Dupree, Bobby Bland, Joe Williams and Alan Toussaint come to mind. There have also been blues players such as J.B. Lenoir and Lowell Fulson who deserved to have the career span that B.B. has enjoyed. But very few people indeed would question King's right to the veneration he receives now after over three decades in the business of making great music. In those 30 years he has evolved a guitar sound and style which is instantly recog-

B.B. King with his famous guitar, Lucille, backstage at a concert in 1969. B.B. (the initials stand for 'Blues Boy', a nickname he used in his early days as a radio DJ) has for 35 years been at the top, with consummate skills as both singer and guitarist.

nizable, but more than that, it's also wonderfully lyrical, with beautifully balanced phrasing and great natural expressivity. His instrumental finesse is legendary. Equally impressive is his honey-toned light baritone voice, which can be harsh and caressing within the space of one phrase, and conjures a complete emotional range in the space of one song.

Born in 1925 in Mississippi, King was a Memphis disc jockey (where the initials B.B. came from, standing for his nickname 'Blues Boy') after the war, and also performed with gospel groups. In those days his influences were atypically broad, and along with favourites Blind Lemon Jefferson and T-Bone Walker, he confessed to being 'somewhat jazz-minded, too . . . I was crazy about Charlie Christian and Django Reinhardt.'

King's early career, starting in 1950 and continuing well into the sixties, had a definite rhythm and blues slant, and he had many r&b hit singles in these years, such as his version of Memphis Slim's *Everyday I Have The Blues* (also a fifties hit for Joe Williams and the Count Basie Band), *Please Love Me* and *Woke Up This Morning*. A change of record companies enabled a career re-think in the early sixties, and in 1964 King recorded *Live At The Regal*, which is so strong it is simply required listening for anyone with the faintest interest in post-war blues: it was the first time King had been recorded live, and the first in a long time which had him playing just his chosen repertoire with his own band. King has continued to broaden his horizons – his soul-influenced album, *Midnight Believer*, recorded with the help of members of The Crusaders at the end of the seventies, is a very superior effort, with his singing particularly well-caught – and even today continues to thrill audiences with

performances that are tellingly balanced between blues tradition and the sounds of today.

In the eighties, three players took over the job of taking the blues to the next generation, picking up from people like B.B., Freddie and Albert King. Z.Z. Hill, for example, was well versed in the blues tradition, having been recording since 1964, but it was only in the eighties, with his album *Down Home* that his subtle and modern arrangements of the old blues forms broke through to a larger market. Albert Collins, a guitarist and singer from Houston, Texas, was nearly 50 when he made his album *Copeland Special* in 1981, but it cut through to an eager audience, with its tough blues lines on guitar, stark and mean, and its fierce vocal style. Collins was perhaps a little old to become the darling of a new white audience for the blues, but a young bluesman, Robert Cray, was waiting in the wings.

Cray was born in 1953, which

partly explains why the dynamic guitarist from Georgia has produced albums such as *Strong Persuader* which not only satisfy the demands of tradition, but appeal to contemporary audiences, both black and white. His musical framework is simplicity itself, with guitars, bars and drums playing the familiar blues changes with stark urgency. What he brings to the contemporary blues scene is an ability to play classic blues patterns with a modern sound and with an urgency which fits the times, while avoiding any of the self-indulgent guitar heroics which sometimes led the previous generation astray. His stage presence is explosive. Cray has managed to bypass the modern-day trap for the bluesman of getting too close to rock guitar licks and techniques: that particular stylistic cul-de-sac was one of the prime reasons for the relative eclipse of modern blues in the seventies and early eighties.

Above: Otis Spann for years sat quietly and happily at the piano stool of the Muddy Waters band, but in the early 1960s began to make records under his own name. When he did, a compelling and beguiling blues vocalist and pianist was unveiled in his own right.

Above left: John Lee Hooker is a blues player of limited range and technique, but what he does within that range is unique. Hooker has a voice so rich and dramatic that he can make the most mundane lyrics sit up and beg for attention: similarly, his idiosyncratic guitar style has a drive and sometime savagery, despite its simplicity, which is riveting for the listener. Hooker has been vastly influential in the post-war period.

new things

'I'm not saying that everybody's going to have to play like Ornette Coleman. But they're going to have to stop copying Bird.'

Charles Mingus, *commenting on Ornette Coleman in 1960*

IN RETROSPECT, it is clear that the wholesale changes wrought in jazz in the 1940s by the bop movement were based on a subtle but crucial shift in viewpoints. With the inevitable exception of Duke Ellington and perhaps one or two others, jazz musicians prior to bop thought of themselves as musical entertainers in the broadest sense of that term. Their relationship to their public was the prime artistic relationship that they had, and they spent their working lives finding new, exciting and beautiful ways of communicating with and entertaining that public. They all had a fierce pride in

their instrumental prowess and craftsmanship, and the best of them had phenomenal dedication to their music. But their artistic sense of self was, in most cases, subsumed in the desire to excite, move, entertain and please others. In that sense, jazz was a folk art, and most of its practitioners were exceptionally skilled folk craftsmen. That is not to say that their music was primitive, naïve, lacking in structure, depth or meaning: by the time jazz came to be recorded commercially in the 1920s it was already sophisticated music, with these qualities, and others, formed in abundance.

Bop was different: its pivotal creative figures – Parker, Gillespie and Monk – had as their principal artistic relationship that between their music and themselves. It was a small step, and its import was perhaps more conceptual than tangible. But its implications have dominated and obsessed each successive generation of jazz musicians. With bop, jazz ceased, at its cutting edge, to be a folk art, and became a fine art; jazz had become self-referential, and this was one of the main reasons for the flurry of controversy at the time. As far as their listeners were concerned, the be-boppers expected the mountain to come to Mohammed, and in a sense they were right: bop eventually won itself a wide audience and became the prevalent contemporary style of progressive black music in the States.

What the boppers had also done, however, was put a sell-by date on their own inventions. One

Left: *Ornette Coleman's Quartet of 1971: Ed Blackwell, drums, Dewey Redman, tenor sax, Ornette Coleman, Charlie Haden, bass. This, with the substitution of trumpeter Don Cherry for Redman, was the same line-up which, ten years before, had scandalized the jazz world.*

concept, no matter how good, gets overtaken by another. In 1958, bop got overtaken, and by 1960 it was war, as the avant-garde and the old guard fought it out for prestige and popularity.

FIFTIES SUBTERRANEANS

The first shot was fired by a Texan alto sax player living in Los Angeles by the name of Ornette Coleman. Right from the beginning, Ornette annoyed the establishment: he played out of tune, his sound was wildly passionate, he did not believe in conventional tonality and he did not play anybody's music but his own (thereby stopping critics from playing their favourite game of

trace-the-influence). His unison playing with trumpet partner Don Cherry was inexact to say the least, and, crowning insult, he played a white plastic saxophone. He was also an utterly self-suffcient personality, articulate and polite, with a quiet but un-shakeable belief in what he was doing.

Many people, musicians especially, believed him to be a modern primitive. But if that was so, Ornette was only a primitive in the same sense that Picasso or Marisse were: all three used the techniques of so-called primitive art as a fully-considered choice out of all the available options.

Ornette had served a tough musical apprenticeship and was a well-versed musician. Born in 1930, he was, like Charlie Parker, predominantly self-taught, and

ORNETTE COLEMAN: After long years in the wilderness, Coleman's ideas about free form and performance in jazz were finally accepted by avante-garde enthusiasts in the late 1950s. In the following decade, Coleman's tenor saxophone playing drew inspired improvisations from some of the most technically gifted wind players of the era. His bands silenced many critics by achieving a harmony, blend and structure without losing his belief in improvisation.

studied alto saxophone before switching to tenor when he could not get work on the smaller horn. In the late forties, Texas was rhythm & blues territory, and he was kicked out of several bands for trying to incorporate progressive jazz ideas. On one such occasion, down in Mississippi, he recalled, 'I wanted to play jazz in the band, and tried to teach the other tenor a jazz number. He went out and told the director I was trying to make a bebopper out of him, and so I was let go.' On another occasion, in Baton Rouge, the saxophonist was called outside the dance on the pretext that someone wanted to talk to him. Once outside the hall, he was jumped by local rednecks who, shouting 'goddam it we don't like musicians', beat him up, and threw his horn off the top of the hill.

Ending up in L.A. in 1951 after being thrown off an r&b tour there ('The leader didn't understand what I was trying to do and it got

Above left: Ornette Coleman with London Symphony Orchestra conductor David Measham during rehearsals for Skies of America.

Right: Pianist Bill Evans, a *considerable influence on the majority of jazz pianists after 1960.*

so he was paying me not to play'), he worked an endless succession of demeaning day-jobs, while attempting to develop his own theories and crash into the L.A. jazz scene. For the next seven years he was a musical pariah, and people would actually walk off the bandstand if Ornette, now back on alto sax, tried to sit in. One night he got onstage with

Dexter Gordon's rhythm section when the tenor failed to show. When Gordon arrived, he walked straight up to Ornette and demanded he stop: 'Immediately. Right now. Take the tune out and get off the bandstand.' Reactions like that would have finished less determined men.

Gradually, however, Ornette met a sufficient number of adventurous young players to form a rehearsal band and, at long last, through a sympathetic introduction from established bass player Red Mitchell, landed a recording contract with Contemporary Records. Two years later, in autumn 1959, he was playing the Five Spot Cafe in New York, the same bar where Monk had made his phenomenal return to the scene with John Coltrane in 1957. What made Ornette especially controversial at this time were his theories about what he was actually doing, and why. He would say, 'When our group plays, before we set out to play, we do not have any idea what the end result will be. Each player is

free to contribute what he feels in the music at any given moment ... I don't tell the members of my group what to do. I want them to play what they hear in the piece for themselves. I let everyone express himself just as he wants to. The musicians have complete freedom, and so, of course, our final results depend entirely on the musicianship, emotional makeup and taste of the individual member.'

In a musical world where there were very clear hierarchies and pecking orders, and where the solo was sacrosanct, this philosophy was not only offensive, but subversive. Many thought it plain laughable. But was Coleman's music so weird? Ornette continued to play syncopated melodic ideas over a straight common-time beat; he did not wander into unusual time signatures, or dispense with metric pulse: in fact his music was emphatically rhythmic. But it was Ornette's sound, and what he did with it, that was the biggest single factor in his impact. Listening to it today, the pertinence of Ornette's own words cut through: 'You can always reach into the human sound of a voice on your horn if you're actually hearing and trying to express the warmth of a human voice. There are some intervals that carry that human quality if you play them in the right pitch.'

Ornette's sound on his instrument is immensely vocal, with virtually no vibrato: it is gutsy without being rasping, because there is a sweetness to it. He also has what in conventional mainsteam jazz would be called the 'Texas cry', only he pushes it further, distorts it more, and goes for the non-western pitches more often. It is those pitches which give the blues their source of endless renewal, and which gave Ornette much of his cutting edge. He felt very strongly about avoiding the normal structures of 20th

century popular music – chord changes, and verse-chorus-bridge-chorus-verse forms – and he could not see the point in playing other people's music, other writers' thoughts. 'Using changes already laid out gives you a place to start and lets the audience know what you're doing, I mean if they can whistle the song in your solo. But that means you're not playing all your own music.'

Eric Dolphy (1928-1964), a friend of Ornette's from his L.A. days, also arrived in New York in the winter of 1959-1960, and created similar mayhem when he joined Charles Mingus's group at a little club called The Showplace. A lover of music from childhood and a thoroughly trained musician, Dolphy was as wildly expressive on his three main instruments – alto sax, flute and bass clarinet – as Ornette. This, plus the fact that they both came to New York from L.A., caused some confusion at first, with many writers in particular claiming that Dolphy was from the Ornette Coleman 'school'. Dolphy, in fact, was a radical from a completely separate tradition: 'I think of my playing as tonal. I play notes that would not ordinarily be said to be in a given key, but I hear them as proper. I don't think I leave the changes; every note I play has some reference to the chords of the piece. And I try to get the instrument to more or less speak.'

Dolphy as a person was by all accounts a generous and courteous man, remarkably free from rancour or egotism. Tall, and of slender build with natural grace in his movements, he exuded an unusual quiet intensity. Charles

Multi-instrumentalist Eric Dolphy (right), *a vital exploratory force in the early sixties and a leading figure in the music until his death in 1964. Originally criticised as anti-art, Dolphy was to influence a generation to come.*

Mingus commented on this: 'A woman once told me about the effect of just looking at Eric from the audience. It was something about his eyes. The intelligence, the sense that he was absorbing everything around him.'

He was always ready, even eager, to give credit and thanks publicly to people he admired or who had helped him. He did this in his albums by titling his songs after them; 'G.W.' is for west coast bandleader and arranger Gerald Wilson ('I was helped greatly by Gerald Wilson'), 'Les' for trombonist Lester Robinson, 'The Baron' for Mingus (Mingus early in his career called himself 'Baron Mingus'), and 'Hat and Beard' for Monk, while he recorded Randy Weston's 'Sketch of Melba' as a tribute to the brilliant trombonist and arranger Melba Liston.

The gifted alto player Vi Redd remembers Dolphy's generosity; 'I was playing a job in El Monte and I broke my own mouthpiece while taking my horn out of the case. I hurriedly called Eric and he came all the way out from town to bring me one I could use.'

Dolphy stayed nearly a year with Mingus at The Showplace, while other musicians came and went in what Mingus called his 'Jazz Workshop.' In that time, his rhythmic fragmentation, harmonic radicalism and his vocalizing effects, especially on the bass clarinet, an instrument rarely heard in jazz up until then, turned New York's music establishment on its ear. As with Ornette, his alto sax tone was very different to anything previously heard, with a steel-hard richness come of thousands of hours practising and searching for his personal musical identity in sound. 'This human thing in instrumental playing has to do with trying to get as much human warmth and feeling into my work as I can. I want to say more on my horn than ever I could in ordinary speech.' This is literally true, because in Dolphy you can hear laughing, crying, humorous references to nursery rhymes, and a thousand other fragments of experience.

'He was a complete musician', commented Mingus. 'He could fit in anywhere. He was a fine lead alto in a big band. He could make it in a classical group. And, of course, he was entirely his own man when he soloed. He had mastered jazz.'

Some people apparently thought not, especially when Dolphy joined John Coltrane's quartet in late 1961, effectively making it a quintet. Conservative critics who should have known better accused the two saxophonists of 'deliberately destroying swing', being 'nihilistic' and 'anarchistic', and a cry that they were 'anti-jazz', whatever that meant, went up. Dolphy was especially ridiculed for imitating birdsong in his flute-playing, and being interested in classical Indian music. 'Why shouldn't I imitate birds? Sure it's deliberate; I've always liked birds and I like to sound like them.' It was a measure of the inordinate conservatism of the jazz establishment at that time that such issues even had to be addressed and defended.

Dolphy died while on tour in Berlin, in the summer of 1964, apparently from a heart condition brought on by an unsuspected diabetic condition. In the four brief years that he was on the wider musical stage, he developed at an extraordinary rate, moving from tinkering with the typical bop musical formats and rhythms to wholly free solo improvisations,

John Coltrane, 1965: the tenorist had in the years since he left Miles developed at an astonishing speed. In 1961 he enjoyed a wide success with My Favourite Things, *played on a soprano saxophone, which built a popularity which he never lost during his lifetime.*

starkly illuminating duets which abandon both metre and tune-solo-tune forms, and group performances of his challenging and provocative compositions which border on collective improvisation. His influence on the course of the avant-garde in the sixties and seventies was immense, because he had started fruitful explorations into so many different directions in music: explorations patently unfinished at his death. His impact continued into the eighties when many players returned to more mainsteam jazz concepts but retained much of Dolphy's approach.

His partner in 1961, John Coltrane (1926-1967), had an influence on contemporary jazz which could only be compared to Parker's in the late forties and early fifties. Coltrane was a tall, quiet man, rather shy and more interested in solving musical problems than in 'hanging out' or clowning. He was naturally cautious, exploring every option of his current musical thinking before taking a step onto the next plateau. But when he felt ready, he made the change, unhesitatingly and uncompromisingly. A member of Miles Davis's groundbreaking sextet and quintet of the late fifties, and the tenor soloist with Monk for four months in 1957, Coltrane was a musician who, by the time he went out on his own, was thoroughly schooled in the contemporary mainstream. He was two years older than Dolphy and had been playing professionally since leaving military service in 1946. Yet although he had done a stint with Dizzy Gillespie (1949-1951), and then with Johnny Hodges during the latter's four-year break from Ellington's band, he had done little recording and received little or no attention.

It was the stints with Davis and Monk which gave him an international reputation, and finally provided the impetus for forming his own group. Coltrane initially was making records no-one could object to, sticking within the confines of the music he had grown up with, and although some people found it hard to cope with his sound (a new one in jazz), which was pure, hard and incredibly intense, nobody questioned his musical motives. He even had a hit album in 1961 when his version of *My Favourite Things* was released, with him playing the soprano saxophone he had recently bought.

But Coltrane was, like Dolphy, a restless explorer, and an intense and voracious listener. He was one of the few jazz musicians – Ellington, Mingus and Coleman Hawkins are three others – who palpably evolved and changed during his public career, rather than finding an identifiable style and sticking to it for the remainder of his musical life. Both Coltrane and Dolphy were obsessed by music, and practised their instruments at every available opportunity: Dolphy often spent the entire time between sets at gigs practising while, on more than one occasion, Coltrane's wife would find him asleep on a couch in his practice room at home, the saxophone still in his mouth. Coltrane's departure from Miles was within a few months of Ornette's debut in New York. Although Coltrane certainly was not stylistically influenced by Coleman, he was fascinated by his music and theories. 'I've got to keep experimenting', he once commented. 'I feel that I'm just beginning. I have part of what I'm looking for in my grasp but not all.' By the time of Dolphy's arrival, Coltrane had found another vital component: drummer Elvin Jones.

Like Coltrane, Jones had been 'on the scene' a long while before he made his breakthrough. Partly because of the extreme difficulty of pulling together all the strands of the complex rhythmic style he was fashioning, and partly for extra-musical reasons, Jones had not achieved great prominence, even though during the fifties he had played or recorded with many of the decade's leading lights. Jones was the younger brother of pianist Hank and trumpeter Thad Jones, both univer-

SONNY ROLLINS: During the 1960s, Rollins *(left)* at first flirted with the avant-garde, even going so far as to hire Ornette's trumpeter Don Cherry for a few months in 1962, but by the middle of the decade had returned to his former repertoire – popular standards and off-beat tin-pan-alley material – if not his former style. Rollins had always delighted audiences with the sheer virtuosity with which phrases flowed from his saxophone. But he also lacked the drive to explore new frontiers. He reached an absolute peak of saxophone artistry before, in 1967, embarking on one of his periodic 'retirements' from the jazz scene. This one was somewhat longer than most and, when he came back four years later, both he and the music world had changed considerably.

sally admired musicians, but it was Elvin, during his more than five years with Coltrane, who took the risks and created something new. Steve Davis, who was Coltrane's bassist when Jones joined in the summer of 1960, recalled: 'That first night Elvin was in the band, he was playing so strong and so loud you could hear him outside the club and down the block. But Trane wanted it that way. He wanted a drummer who could kick, and Elvin was one of the strongest, wildest drummers in the world.'

Many times in the years that followed, live gigs featuring the quartet would often culminate in extended solos from Coltrane – quite frequently half an hour or more – accompanied by Jones alone, although 'accompanied' could never hope to express the dynamism of Jones' drumming in support of his leader's forays into new musical territories. They would be like two panthers, pacing each other, inspiring each other, and whipping the crowd into a state of frenzied disbelief about the incredible music they were hearing. By 1963-64, the Coltrane Quartet's appearances at clubs around the US, but especially in New York clubs like the

Village Vanguard and Birdland, had taken on a certain ritualistic quality: Coltrane averaged 20 to 30 minutes per song, and the incredible intensity that he could sustain for that period of time could mesmerize a crowd. Indeed, this other, overtly spiritual side of his achievement became increasingly pronounced in the three years before his death from liver cancer in July 1967. Although difficult to define or explain, too many people who heard him live or on record were swept up in a sense of quasi-religious experience for it all to have been an illusion. Only Coltrane could have recorded his great 1964 album, *A Love Supreme*, revealing his deeply-held belief in a divine being, and have moved even sceptics by the artistic beauty and musical unity attained through spiritual imperatives.

If 1960 was the year of Ornette, Dolphy and Coltrane, then 1961 was by common consent the year that pianist Cecil Taylor finally got noticed. It was still the case that nobody liked him very much, but suddenly his uncompromising music could be lumped in with what the revolutionary saxophone players were doing: he could be categorized as part of a new

movement, and so he no longer had to be ignored as an isolated creator of irritatingly different music. That was something he had been doing since around 1955, the year when he made his first album.

Taylor, born in New York in 1933, had a thorough musical education, and was playing as a sideman with swing musicians such as Johnny Hodges and Hot Lips Page before starting his own band. A short, wiry man with a face not dissimilar to Billy Strayhorn's, he has always been an independent thinker, and someone who, although a musician first, has broad intellectual interests. Like drummer Max Roach, he has studied both cultural and political history, and is incisively articulate about an artist's relationship to his society. In the fifties and sixties he had a great deal of time to study: by his own estimation, he probably worked only for something like 30 weeks in the four years between 1957 and 1961. The rest of the time he spent practising, working at menial day jobs when things got precarious, and involving himself in literary ventures. As he

once observed during this most difficult time, 'The hardest thing about being original is trying to stay alive.'

Taylor grew up in New York, and feels that his music reflects that: 'The energy that built those ugly buildings . . . and the tempo, and the people . . . well, they're here, but most of them have been beaten by the system. The most interesting ones are those who fill you with surprise, not necessarily charming, and it's hard to find those who are not destructive.' What was a continual surprise to Taylor during this time was the high level of antagonism he encountered from other musicians. It was not because he could not 'play the changes' in the way some suspected Ornette Coleman was not capable of, or that he was arrogant and impossible to deal with. His music was simply too intensely different; too hard. He had abandoned conventional bop and popular song chord changes in the mid-fifties, and by the end of that decade was fast approaching a similar freedom from metric rhythm. Added to this was the sheer speed and intensity with which he played, which at times could seem demoniacal, as well as his totally uncompromising stance in pursuing his own musical vision against all comers. Drummer Sunny Murray, who played throughout the fifties in a straight bop style but was later to join Taylor's band, remembered the first time he met the pianist: 'So one night (in 1956) I was in the Café Roué and I got up to sit in. The cats were never too happy to play with me, the bass players especially, and drummers would stand around and put me down.

Bandleader Charles Mingus retired after experiencing a veritable explosion of creativity between 1960 and 1966. He was sorely missed as jazz competed with pop culture.

So just as I got up to play, Cecil came in. I saw the musicians packing up their instruments, so I said, "What are you packing up your instruments for? You really don't dig playing with me that much?" And they said, "No Sunny, it's not you tonight, it's really not you!" And I said, "Well who is it then?" And they said, "It's that cat sitting over there in the corner. We're not going to play with *him*."'

Cecil Taylor has always maintained that, behind the theory, behind the incredible technical virtuosity and the seeming impenetrability, his greatest desire has been to communicate his visions. 'It is important, wholly important, to fulfil yourself. It is your life. If you are doing that then you are doing something for someone else, even if it's only one someone else. Even then, it's alright. That's my life. My particular battle is fighting for the cultural beauty spots of different peoples. In my case, of the negroes. I have made my contribution the way others have done and I want it recognised as such.'

Taylor fought a lonely battle for much of the sixties, slowly gathering around him a talented nucleus of willing young players such as Sunny Murray, Archie Shepp, Jimmy Lyons, Roswell Rudd, Alan Silva and Andrew Cyrille. He encouraged Murray in particular to make the rhythmic breakthroughs which were to lead directly to avant-garde jazz drummers of the mid-sixties abandoning metric pulse. This step, perhaps more than any other, drove an unbridgeable wedge between jazz generations, and produced direct accusations from all sides that what Taylor was doing may be improvisation – even if he was using clenched fists and elbows at times on the keyboard – but it had nothing to do any longer with jazz. Superficially, that could have been the

case, but a look at the roots of Taylor's music does not lead back to Bartok of Schoenberg: it goes back to Ellington, Monk and Morton, and beyond that, to blues and African music. He treats the piano percussively, as part of a non-western musical tradition.

Taylor once commented: 'One of the things that turned me off European music is that I'd get the scores by Boulez, Stockhausen, Pousseur and Ligeti and I would look at them and say "My, this is interesting." And I'd listen to the music and it didn't sound particularly good. I don't listen to artists who only want to create something that is interesting. To feel is perhaps the most terryifying thing in this society.'

Taylor's direct influence on other players at this stage was minimal, partly because his piano and compositional style was inimitable. His status was achieved solely through the forcefulness of his music. His example was one which was to be increasingly influential as the decade wore on.

ROLLINS ON THE BRIDGE

All four musicians – Ornette, Dolphy, Coltrane and Taylor – were seminal in forming the patterns of new music in the sixties. Each was pursuing freedom and personal self-fulfilment in music, down a unique path which led in a profoundly different direction to his colleagues. It was the second generation of players who would connect them up, and take ever more radical steps. Meanwhile, there were many musicians whose lives were being changed by the revolutions which were

Multi-instrumentalist Roland Kirk came to international attention through Charles Mingus, and stayed at the forefront of the music until his death in 1977.

shaking jazz. Sonny Rollins, the tenor saxophonist who had come to pre-eminence among saxophonists in the late fifties, had begun a two-year break from public playing in 1959. When he returned, both he and jazz had taken giant steps.

Rollins, like Monk, had a mysterious persona for most jazz fans, and although he did not consciously cultivate it, his changing tastes in clothing and haircuts alone kept everybody guessing: he would alternate between berets, cloth caps, mohawk haircuts, complete head-shaves, tweed jackets and ivy league suits. But most of all, he would just play tenor: the most virtuoso tenor anyone could remember. He unintentionally created publicity for himself when a jazz-loving

journalist, crossing New York's Williamsburg Bridge, heard a saxophone being played way up on the superstructure above the traffic, went to investigate and found Rollins, practising new ideas on his horn. To hipsters and writers, it was another example of the enigmatic Rollins' penchant for off-the-wall gestures. For Rollins, it had been a purely sociable gesture. 'There was this pregnant girl in a neighbouring apartment. I couldn't subject her to all that sound – and of course I couldn't do myself any good by inhibiting my practicing. I didn't know what pre-natal effects would result in the baby; but do you know, he's a beautiful, happy child.'

Many people saw the bridge – and the album called *The Bridge*, released in 1962 as Rollins' come-

back album – as a metaphor for a newly evolved style which successfully spanned the saxophonist's past and possible future. His reappearance with a new quartet at New York's Jazz Gallery and the subsequent tour had already served notice that this was a new Rollins. Jim Hall, the guitarist with the quartet, remembers the excitement of that time: 'He was so strong he could stop the whole group just by the way he played ... and taking a tune, playing a cadenza ... it was sort of like what Picasso did with a face: he'd just turn it every which way. So it was thrilling to hear him play – it was frightening ... except that the music was so good that it was fun to get involved in it.'

The following autumn Rollins hired Ornette Coleman's trumpe-

ter, Don Cherry (a singular honour, as Rollins had not shared the front line in many years). This in itself was a move which identified him with the experimentors in the early sixties. They played a season at The Village Gate with just a rhythm team of bass and drums, and Rollins' record company recorded three nights of music. Only one album has ever been released of this material, but it is an astonishing exhibition of total saxophone playing and intuitive group improvisation. There are only three selections on the whole album, all compositions which he had originally recorded years before, yet the inventiveness is at such a dizzying level that each contains a kaleidoscope of new ideas and approaches. Rollins moves through playfulness, aggression, loquacity and downright high spirits, dragging the quartet with him through every twist and turn.

As the sixties progressed, Rollins was to become increasingly puckish in his approach to improvisation, although at no stage was he to abandon the standard metric

rhythms and chordal basis of pre-Ornette jazz. The high point of his virtuosity was reached, ironically, in his only soundtrack album to date. In 1965 he was commissioned to provide the music for the British film *Alfie*. This unpromising initiative somehow caught fire with Rollins, and the resultant album found Sonny playing with a freedom and flexibility, especially when it comes to rhythm, that simply has to be heard to be believed.

As with all jazz greats, part of Rollins' achievement lies in his amazing manipulation of the instrument's sound. Freddie Hubbard, the trumpeter on the last album Sonny made before another retreat to re-group and re-think his career in 1967, commented at the time: 'Some of the quality of that tone is due to the strength of his body ... He always had a deep sound, and he learned how to perfect that depth of sound all over the instrument, from top to bottom. Many tenor players, when they play deep in the lower register, sound as if they're growling. Not Sonny.'

Another virtuoso who began the sixties with an unprecedented burst of creativity was Charles Mingus, who had been a vital and challenging group leader, bassist and composer for much of the fifties. This giant of a man, who was capable of provoking fist fights with his sidemen, critics or anyone else if the wrong mood descended on him, was a passionate and articulate spokesman for negro music and negro history, as well as an unquestioning fan of Duke Ellington since his youth. He remembered his first exposure to the Ellington band for the rest of his life. 'I never heard no music like that in church. I nearly jumped out of the bleachers. Someplace, something he did, I screamed.' Mingus had also been deeply moved by black church music and folk forms, and it was these two fountainheads which were to be

Chick Corea (above) *came to prominence as a gifted acoustic pianist before joining Miles Davis, at which point he swapped to electric keyboards. He was to experiment with virtually every modern jazz style.*

his inspirational sources for most of his greatest music, the stylistic impact of Charlie Parker notwithstanding.

By the beginning of the sixties, Mingus had successfully experimented with, among other things, pan-tonality, polyrhythms, soul- and blues-inspired pieces, poetry-and-jazz recitals, and writing extended works. In May 1960 he made an album called *Pre-Bird* which was made up entirely of pieces he had composed or conceived of prior to his mid-forties exposure to Charlie Parker. Parts of that album verge on 20th-century art music, while others reaffirm the Ellington link and the

tug of the gospel singers. Two months later, the bassist was directly involved in controversy when he and Max Roach, protesting at what they saw as the Newport Jazz Festival's betrayal of creative jazz by hiring acts like Chuck Berry, The Kingston Trio and The Four Freshmen, organized a rival Newport festival, held at a private house, Cliff Walk Manor.

The Cliff Walk event produced some exceptionally fine music, and also an atmosphere which saw musicians of every school and age combining to play music together. In an unpleasant irony, the main Festival was terminated

early by rioting on the sedate streets of Newport from drunken teenagers attracted by the very type of performers Mingus had objected to.

The bassist was to endure his own public debacle in 1962, on an occasion which should have been one of the great pinnacles of his career. He had signed a record deal which, among other things, promised to record *Epitaph*, a major orchestral work Mingus had been working on for many years. With the work of orchestrating what was over two hours' worth of music firstly interrupted by the preparations for a trio recording – with Duke Ellington

and Max Roach – and then jeopardized by *Epitaph's* recording date being advanced by five weeks, the project made a poor start. Added to this was the strange decision to make it an 'open recording session' at New York's Town Hall. When the evening for the event arrived, nothing was ready, and copyists were still racing around handing out newly-written manuscripts to the musicians in the orchestra. Nobody in the audience – critics included – seemed aware that they were watching a recording session, not a concert, and many were disgruntled at the re-takes of fragments of songs. By the end of the

Left: *Yusef Lateef (standing) is an unassuming woodwind player and composer who has thought more deeply about music than most, and whose contributions are uncommonly rewarding. He has also enjoyed success as a teacher.*

Left: *Brothers Nat and Julian 'Cannonball' Adderley played with Lateef, then led one of the finest modern-mainstream bands.*

Above: *Trumpeter Don Cherry developed into one of the most far-ranging musicians associated with jazz. By the end of the 1960s he was deeply involved in what has come to be known as 'world music' two decades later.*

evening, absolutely everybody was fed up, including the stage hands who, due to union rules in New York, lowered the safety curtain on the band as it staged its own impromptu jam session in an attempt to relieve their frustrations. The record which resulted from all this chaos was a chaos of its own, compounding the problems further. Mingus never attempted to record *Epitaph* again, and it was only finally realized in 1989 by a group of his previous collaborators led by Gunther Schuller.

Mingus continued to write major compositions and play internationally, achieving a great deal up to 1965, including in that year starting up his own record label after falling out with most of the people in the US recording business.

The following year he suffered a series of personal reversals which culminated in eviction from his New York apartment. Under immense strain and unable to deal with the pressures of running such a precarious lifestyle, Mingus became a recluse for the rest of the sixties, and a vital innovative voice from within the jazz mainstream was lost to the world at a crucial time.

Another jazz maverick, Roland Kirk (1936-1977), had been given a determined helping hand by Mingus, as well as by soul pianist Ramsey Lewis. Kirk had been on the national jazz scene since 1956 but had been utterly ignored. A 1960 album arranged through Lewis provoked controversy and gave Kirk a certain notoriety, but it was his involvement in a 1961 Mingus record, *Oh Yeah*, alongside another scorchingly good and undeservedly neglected tenor player, Booker Ervin, which demonstrated the power and vitality of Kirk's vision. And what a singular one it was, too. Kirk had, as a teenaged musician looking for new experiences, dreamed that he was playing three saxophones at once. The following day, in the basement of an old music shop, he found two ancient, long abandoned variants of the saxophone family, the manzello and the stritch. A few years later, he had evolved a unique way of simultaneously playing both instruments, plus a regular tenor saxophone.

This would have been an interesting but ultimately minor footnote to jazz history but for the fact that Kirk was no mild-mannered dabbler: he was a natural musician filled with such insatiable drive and energy that, in live performance, he was frequently an overwhelming experience. On record, at his best, he could approach similar listener overload levels. In addition, he communicated a rare understanding of, and appreciation for, the past greats of his own music. Kirk was aided in all this by his gifts as a showman. Like Ray Charles, another brilliant performer who was also blind, Kirk was able through sheer charisma to galvanize an audience by his mere appearance onstage. The sight of him then proceeding to play the three horns hung around his neck, a flute stuck in the tenor sax's bell, plus sundry other bells, whistles and alarms to punctuate proceedings, meant that few who saw him would ever forget the experience.

MAVERICKS IN THE MAINSTREAM

Kirk made many fine albums demonstrating his genius, but perhaps the pick of them were 1965's *Rip, Rig and Panic*, and *Volunteered Slavery* in 1969. Both demonstrate his incredible breadth of vision, with the former giving an occasional nod in the direction of the avant garde, while the latter has Kirk's unsurpassable versions of contemporary pop, including Burt Bacharach's *Say A Little Prayer For Me* into which at one point he brilliantly inserts two of the main themes from Coltrane's *A Love Supreme*.

While saxophonists hogged the limelight, trumpeters, for the most part, had a thin time of it in the sixties. Of the older school, Dizzy Gillespie was an exception, starting the decade with a brilliant and unaccountably forgotten series of orchestral and quintet albums which showed his clear determi-

133

Cecil Taylor in 1962, when still unable to make a living out of music full-time. After years of neglect and hostility, he brought his version to the wider music world.

nation not to be left behind by his friend and younger contemporary, Miles Davis. On such albums as *A Portrait of Duke Ellington*, *Gillespiana*, *Electrifying Evening*, *Perceptions*, *Something Old & Something New* and *New Continent*, Gillespie demonstrated the full extent of his latter-day ambitions by commissioning compositions and arrangements from brilliant contemporaries such as Clare Fischer, J.J. Johnson, Gil Fuller and Lalo Schifrin, as well as playing inspired and fully mature music on the small-group dates. There is more than a suspicion of jazz fashion in the current neglect of Gillespie's achievement after the early years of bop, as his sixties recordings demonstrate.

One trumpeter who should have made a deep impact on jazz history was Booker Little (1938-1961). Little came from Memphis (where he knew other musicians such as George Coleman and Charles Lloyd) and joined the Max Roach group in 1958, when he was just 20. By 1960 he was an established freelance in New York, and recorded four albums under his own name, each of them showing a phenomenal musical intelligence. His style was out of Clifford Brown, but he was no mere Browniephile: his harmonic conception was very advanced, and it is no surprise that he and Eric Dolphy developed an exceptionally fulfilling musical partnership. What was special about Little was his intense lyricism coupled to a glorious tone and a fiercely logical musical brain. On Dolphy's album *Far Cry*, Little solos with such simpatico

and passion that, although he is only on half the tracks, he is the album's focal point. Similarly, on the famed recordings of the Dolphy-Little quintet in autumn 1961 at The Five Spot, Little's internal musical balance is at times breathtaking. These latter recordings were made when he was already a very sick man. He died in October 1961 from uremia.

Other trumpeters inheriting the Clifford Brown legacy, such as Freddie Hubbard, Lee Morgan, Blue Mitchell, Carmell Jones and Donald Byrd all had mixed fortunes in the sixties. All, without exception, made excellent music during the decade, but only Lee Morgan made any real money. With the exception of Byrd, who ran his own groups and did a great deal of teaching (as well as studying with the great classical teacher Nadia Boulanger in Paris), the rest of them worked with

other leaders in the hard-bop area, while making records for independent labels like Blue Note and Riverside. Morgan, although he spent the mid-sixties working with Art Blakey's Jazz Messengers (for most of that decade a pretty unfashionable place to be), had a major hit album with *The Sidewinder* in 1963-4, and the title track also made some serious sales as a single. Morgan managed to resist the temptation to spend the rest of the sixties turning out warmed-over replicas of this initial hit, although he did increase the funk quota a little. He remained a supremely personal trumpet stylist who continued to extract musical gems from the post-bop stream long after most trumpeters had abandoned it for funk or fusion.

Stan Getz also demonstrated emphatically in the sixties that it was possible to experience massive popularity without sacrificing a whit of musical integrity. Admittedly, Getz had a head start on most popular people because he never played harsh, or even difficult, music. So when he started cutting records with Brazilian rhythms and the bossa nova craze caught on, Getz did not have to ease up on his style at all. After the initial *Jazz Samba* album with Charlie Byrd had sold half a million in the US alone, and the follow-up similarly, Getz recorded an album with Joao Gilberto and Antonio Carlos Jobim when the bossa nova craze was apparently dying down. This album was the best of the lot, with a group cohesion that borders on telepathic and one of those 'moods' which the very best album in any style takes on: Gilberto wrote in the liner notes 'In many ways, then, this is more than a record. It is friendship communicated by music.' The record went on to be the biggest seller of all bossa nova albums. It also saw the debut of Gilberto's wife, Astrud,

on *The Girl From Ipanema*.

Getz later reflected: 'Some of that music is the most relaxing I have ever played. It's beautiful and lends itself to what I want to do melodically. I can never think of it as "bossa nova". That seems like such a silly name for what is basically, beautiful, introspective music.' Also consummately artistic was the album with strings arranged by Eddie Sauter on a commission from Getz made two years previously. *Focus* was deeply unfashionable at the time of its release, and although it was a success with critics, the public passed it by until the bossa nova triumph stimulated interest in the Getz back-catalogue.

Sauter's method on the album was to write original pieces of music which were self-sufficient without the tenor, then have Getz come into the studio and play around what was already there. 'The string parts were so beautiful', remembered Getz years later, 'that I became inspired merely by listening to the tape ... The romanticism of those ballads – like *Summer Afternoon* – still gives me the chills.'

Getz has hardly spent the rest of his life merely living off the rewards of the bossa nova craze. He led a number of excellent groups for the rest of the decade, introducing or widening the public appreciation of such talents as vibist Gary Burton, drummer Roy Haynes and pianist Chick Corea. It was Corea who recorded with Getz on what is often thought to be his best overall recorded performance, *Sweet Rain*, a quartet date from 1967.

Another major attraction of the fifties and sixties, pianist Oscar Peterson, had all the technical expertise of Getz and the ability to swing so envied by his contemporaries: for many listeners he was, after Dave Brubeck, the personification of not merely modern jazz piano, but modern jazz itself. However, Peterson was an innately conservative musician whose conception and ideas changed little over the decades, a situation which finally rendered him isolated from the modern jazz mainstream.

Altoist Cannonball Adderley and tenorist Yusef Lateef were two intelligent eclectics who, after divergent experiences in the fifties, started the sixties together when Lateef joined Cannonball and his brother Nat in their successful small group between 1962 and 1964. By this stage Lateef had spent some time with Charles Mingus as well as African drummer Michael Olatunji, while the Adderleys had opened the decade with jazz hit albums and singles. This was partly due to the presence of the gifted pianist/composer Bobby Timmons in the

band: he contributed the hit compositions *This Here* and *Dat Dere*. But it was also due to Cannonball playing what he did best: funky, sophisticated jazz with a solid mainstream framework to it.

Adderley was often unfairly criticized for this by people who should have noticed that the altoist, an eloquent speaker and writer, was actually doing exactly what he wanted to do in music. He and his brother continued in the same style for the rest of the decade, occasionally bringing in a new face to refresh their repertoire. They rarely made a wrong move, hiring little-known Austrian expatriate Joe Zawinul to replace Timmons when he left, and the almost as obscure saxophonist/composer Charles Lloyd to replace Lateef. Both went on

to unprecedented breakthroughs with the young rock audience at a time when few jazz musicians outside of Coltrane and Davis had any base in the white youth market.

Lateef himself, meanwhile, challenged both Adderley brothers by his presence to some of their best work while he was in the band, both with his own big-toned and angular playing, and in his compositions, many of which utilized the unusual, and sometimes bizarre, ethnic instruments which Lateef had a penchant for. The tenorist also made a series of unusually stimulating albums under his own name during the sixties, one of which, *The Centaur & The Phoenix*, a mixture of large ensemble writing and intimate soloing at their best, deserves to be recognized for the classic it is.

Another erstwhile colleague of

Adderley, pianist Bill Evans, also had a busy decade. Evans, along with guitarist Wes Montgomery, vocalist Nancy Wilson and trumpeter Blue Mitchell, had Adderley to thank for his career break. Adderley had persuaded Riverside records to make Evans' first date as a leader. By the early sixties he had survived the verbal hyperbole of the initial years (one album was called *Everybody Digs Bill Evans* and had quotations from leading jazz musicians decorating the front cover to prove the point) and assembled a trio which evolved a genuine dialogue between all three players; piano, bass and drums. The bassist, Scott LaFaro (1936-1961), took instrumental dexterity to a new level in this group, interweaving constantly with both Evans and drummer Paul Motian,

thereby knitting the whole fabric of the music together. To gain the speed he wanted, he had to sacrifice a deal of sound on the instrument – something he was heavily criticized for at the time – but the freshness of his lines, and their melodic drama, more than made up for it. Killed in a car crash in 1961, his death was a crippling blow for Evans.

Their last album together, recorded live at the Village Vanguard just two weeks before the crash, is in many respects a pinnacle for Evans. He went on to record the extraordinary *Conversations With Myself* in 1963 where he used the then novel technique of multi-tracking himself on a group of songs, and formed another notable trio with Eddie Gomez filling the LaFaro role. However, although his restrained and sophisticated style was (and still is) hugely influential, Evans himself made no significant, lasting change to his approach before his death in 1980.

Wes Mongomery's death at the age of 45 in 1968 was also an incalculable loss to jazz. The first guitarist with a distinctive style which was not overtly indebted to Charlie Christian, he had revolutionized mainstream guitar playing with his easy, mellow style and rich, blues-laden melodies. Although his later work was weighed down with commercial arrangements, his own playing was never compromised, as can be heard every time he breaks through the ensembles with that distinctive, marvellously expressive melodic octave line which was his trademark.

Far left: Guitarist Wes Montgomery was one of three jazz-playing brothers (along with Monk and Buddy Montgomery), but he was the one to make the breakthrough into a wider public appreciation.

Left: John Tchicai, a European saxophonist with African roots, moved to New York in the mid-sixties and left a lasting impression.

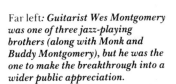

135

Meanwhile, by 1964 the second wave of the new music had arrived and was clamouring for attention. In October that year, the trumpeter and composer Bill Dixon (b. 1925) organized four days of avant-garde jazz in a little New York coffee house called the Cellar Café. Over 20 young players, black and white, appeared and played: few had been heard of at the time (only Jimmy Giuffre and Paul Bley were, however peripherally, part of the wider jazz world), and of the rest, only a portion of them ever became more widely known: Charles Moffatt, David Izenson, John Tchicai, Roswell Rudd, Mllford Graves, Guiseppi Logan, Dewey Johnson, and Alan Silva all had significant music to make in the next few years. There were also panel discussions attended by more widely-known figures such as Cecil Taylor, Archie Shepp, Steve Lacy, Rod Levitt, Andrew Hill and Sun Ra. The concerts were well attended, and the event gener-

ated a fair amount of publicity. Within a few months, Dixon had gone a step further and formed The Jazz Composers Guild.

He believed that such an organization was essential to the well-being of individual members who, on their own, could not hope to earn a living through their art. 'By now, it is obvious,' he said, 'that those of us whose work is not acceptable to the Establishment are not going to be financially acknowledged. As a result, it is very clear that musicians, in order to survive – create their music and maintain some semblance of sanity – will have to "do it themselves" In future.'

Although the Guild soon fell apart through the unsustainable pressures of individual poverty and group philosophies, but it gave artists a new sense of community and self-worth, particularly the negro members. As Dixon pointed out, avant-garde musicians in the US had it tough, and black avant-garde musicians

DETERMINED REVOLUTIONARIES: Albert Ayler, along with his brother Donald, ran a mid-decade band which played perhaps the most radical music to emerge from the black jazz tradition. His later stylistic confusions and eventual tragic demise detract nothing from the towering achievements of this most sophisticated of modern primitives. Ayler felt a deep, raging need to express his inner sense of a life force. In this, he was typical of a generation committed to the search for mental freedom, but lacking the patience and calm needed for such an ambitious vision. Ayler plumbed great depths of himself, but fell by the wayside when his genius was spent.

were the worst off of all. 'It must be remembered that white musicians elect to play jazz; their musical horizons are not bound by an enforced social tradition that relegates them to one area of musical expression. The negro plays jazz because . . . qualified or not, the other areas of musical expression are closed to him.'

This last point was made vividly clear when Art Davis, a bassist who had studied at both The Juilliard and Manhattan Schools of Music, attempted in the mid-sixties to find work in symphony orchestras such as The New York Philharmonic. Although an outstanding technician, and one of John Coltrane's favourite bassists, Davis failed to make any progress in a world which, though it accepted Andre Watts and Leontyne Prite, largely refused at that time to take seriously the idea of black musicians playing as regular members of symphony orchestras.

Albert Ayler (1936-1970) was never a contender for a symphony orchestra post. A tenor saxophonist, he was probably the most original, yet ultimately most tradition-oriented musician spawned by the new wave. As with so many jazz greats, his sound was immediately arresting; a great, cavernous wail which sounded at times as if it could knock a house over. Also arrest-

ing were his devastating forays into the so-called 'freak' sounds that the saxophone possesses. People had used these sounds before – *vide* the forties and fifties r&b scene – but had never based a whole musical style upon them, as Ayler was doing. The tenorist also dispensed with chordally-based improvisation, and metrically-based rhythms. Listening to his mature albums can be an electrifying experience: just coping with the energy level alone can be a full-time job for the uninitiated. Just plain weird, however, is his first album to attain wide distribution, called *My Name Is Albert Ayler* and recorded in 1963 in Europe. Here Ayler performs with a wholly competent European be-bop rhythm section and, when he is not playing, all proceeds as it should, like a suburban train calling at all stations on a sunny summer day.

When Ayler plays, however, the train is derailed and reduced to a wreck, and a thunderstorm erupts: he rarely attempts to hit the same pitch as the piano, his timekeeping is simply not covered by the same definition as the drummer's, and when he bothers with the harmonic backdrop of the songs he plays (simi-

Trumpeter Lester Bowie (left) *found in Chicago a congenial atmosphere for experimental music. By 1967 he was a founder member of the Art Ensemble of Chicago.*

lar repertoire, in fact, to mid-to-late fifties Miles Davis) it is usually to distort it. But mostly, he just goes his own way. On *Summertime*, with the normal jazz syncopation largely suspended and the pianist reduced to a very basic harmonic pattern, it all clicks into place, Ayler's tortured groans and squeaks dominating a moving performance.

By 1964, Ayler was settled in New York, had joined the Jazz Artists Guild and, for such a determined revolutionary, was recording on a decidedly regular basis. A concert with Cecil Taylor at Lincoln Gardens had brought his first critical notices and by 1965 he had teamed up with his trumpeter brother Donald, producing music which had moved on from its initial highly abstract style. Like Taylor, he had been playing with non-metric drummers such as Sunny Murray, so

Ayler's sudden introduction of unison themes which, in their simplicity and lack of all harmonic and rhythmic sophistication, had parallels only in New Orleans marching and Salvation Army bands, was quite a shock. But Ayler saw it as a natural progression: 'Sidney Bechet . . . was unbelievable . . . For me he represented the true spirit, the full force of life, that many of the older musicians had – like in New Orleans jazz – and which many musicians today don't have. I hope to bring that spirit back into the music we're playing.'

Albert and Don Ayler were also utterly committed to bringing what they regarded as holy and spiritual forces to the music they played: 'It's really free, spiritual music, not just free music . . . Many of the others are not playing together, and so they produce noise. It's screaming, it's neo-

avant-garde music . . . This music is good for the mind. It frees the mind. If you just listen, you find out more about yourself.'

By the end of 1967, Ayler had abandoned the careful juxtaposition of his early and later styles in his music, and was playing progressively more strictly controlled themes, leaving little room for embellishment. Shortly after that, he broke up his old band and recorded an album, *New Grass*, on which he gave a spoken introduction announcing an abandonment of his old music in favour of rhythm-and-blues based music, complete with vocals and guitar. For a man who had such a massive influence on the music (the influence went in both directions, to people younger than himself and to some of the more established players on the scene), his progressive musical isolation and the lack of con-

sequence at the time of his death in 1970 are a cause for regret to everyone who followed the music.

By the mid-sixties John Coltrane was actively encouraging a wide range of young radicals to pursue their musical goals. Following the path begun by Ornette Coleman's *Free Jazz* double-quartet album of 1960, where eight musicians (2 reeds, 2 trumpets, 2 bassists, 2 drummers) alternated between collective improvisation and soloist-led sections, Coltrane gathered 2 trumpeters (one of whom, Freddie Hubbard, was also on *Free Jazz*), 2 alto saxes, 3 tenor saxes, 2 bassists, 1 pianist and 1 drummer (he had intended 2 drummers but one pulled out before the date) to record a single piece of music the length of an l.p., *Ascension*. Like Ornette, Coltrane arranged for collective and solo improvisational passages. Unlike Ornette,

he had musicians in the studio who were prepared not just to converse on their instruments, but scream and shout. Altoist Marion Brown later commented, 'We did two takes, and both had that kind of thing in them that makes people scream. The people who were in the studio *were* screaming. I don't know how the engineers kept the screams out of the record.'

Coltrane's two fellow tenor sax players on the date, Archie Shepp and Pharoah Sanders, both played out of their skins that day. Soon after *Ascension* Sanders became a full-time member of Coltrane's band, both on the road and in the studio. Born in 1940, Pharoah had made an impact in New York by combining a clear Coltrane influence and overtone techniques which were indebted to nobody. His music, as Coltrane publicly recognized, was several steps

further out from Coltrane's own style, so Sanders was in a very real way acting as a goad to the older man. Nowhere is this more explicit than on the opening track of Coltrane's subsequent album *Meditations*, titled *The Father And The Son And the Holy Ghost* where, after a long and turbulent solo, Coltrane builds to a cathartic climax, only for Sanders to come in and immediately soar several octaves – and several steps in intensity – above his mentor in an astonishing solo. Albert Ayler claimed after Coltrane's death that the older man had indicated that he perceived himself musically as the father, Sanders as the son, and Ayler as the holy ghost of the new music scene.

Archie Shepp was stylistically much less indebted to Coltrane although Trane was a consistent and liberal supplier of help to him. His talents lay not just in improvisation, but also in composition, arrangement and, in allied fields, drama and poetry. Shepp had a sound which was like an updated Ben Webster: rich, throaty, blustering, with a wide vein of roman-

ticism. He had made his New York debut in 1960 with Cecil Taylor, had a fine but short-lived quartet with Bill Dixon in 1962, and co-led the New York Contemporary Five with Don Cherry and altoist John Tchicai. He was also a founder member of the Jazz Composers Guild. Although the avant-gardists were notably articulate compared with many of their forebears, Shepp was perhaps the most articulate of them all, and certainly one of the most outspoken: his article in a 1965 *Down-Beat* magazine, called 'An Artist Speaks Bluntly', addressed issues of race, politics and sociology in a way seldom previously heard in white living-rooms in the America of the day, and in an uncompromising manner that no other musician had done previously.

On the music side, the saxophonist created a body of high-quality and varied work which, in retrospect, is clearly within the traditions evolved by Dameron, Ellington, Mingus and George Russell, as well as being touched by Coleman and Coltrane. He often experimented with form in

Vibist Bobby Hutcherson (far left) *was involved in persuasive new music aggregations in the 1960s – including Eric Dolphy, Archie Shepp and Jackie McLean – before leading a quintet with saxophonist Harold Land. Roscoe Mitchell* (above) *was a leading spirit in the Chicago new music scene of the 1960s. Saxophonist Pharoah Sanders* (right) *became associated with Coltrane, acting as an inspiration to him much as Eric Dolphy had done.*

his compositions, and constantly strove for a new type of balance between soloists (collective and otherwise) and written material. For every piece of music which contains turbulence and chance, there is another expressing other complex emotions rarely touched by the rest of the avant-garde. By 1969 his live concerts were consciously theatrical as well as musical events, and in the studio he was creating a series of masterpieces with various octets and nonets such as *For Losers*, *Mama Too Tight* and *Kwanza*, which still stand as a highwater mark for much of the sixties. Similarly, a series of albums resulting from broadcast collective sessions in Paris in the same year demon-

strates Shepp's ability to create valid large-scale works from even the slightest material.

The New York Art Quartet was a short-lived group, comprising four vastly talented players – including two of Shepp's erstwhile sidemen. Altoist John Tchicai, trombonist Roswell Rudd, bassist Lewis Worrell and drummer Milford Graves eschewed the grab for the throat that other New York avant-gardists were aiming for, and produced a small but brilliant body of work, relying heavily on collective improvisation of a rare intuitive level. The band was the harbinger of collective musical approaches and philosophies which leading avant groups of the seventies such as The Art

Ensemble of Chicago would develop.

While the farther reaches of the avant-garde were getting a great deal of media attention, if not a great deal of work, there was another loose grouping of individuals whose playing slotted them uneasily, between the established players and the hi-flyers. The two vibraphonists Bobby Hutcherson and Gary Burton both appeared initially around 1962-3, the first new voices on the instrument since Red Norvo and Milt Jackson in the mid-forties. The two players had very different approaches and interests, and as their music developed during the decade, those differences became evident. Burton proved himself as a player when working as a sideman for Stan Getz between 1964-66, where his classical and folk inspirations first became noticed. He was instrumental in the four-mallet technique becoming standard for vibes players in the course of the decade, while also being innovative in many other areas of sheer sound, even getting notes to bend downwards by as much as a semitone. This last technique significantly increased the vocalization of the instrument.

When Burton formed his own quartet in 1967, it had a decidedly rock bent, and from the first it had guitar (Larry Coryell, later to be John McLaughlin's friend and rival) rather than piano as the second frontline instrument. As the decade came to a close, his popularity among the people who liked 'progressive' rock enabled him to direct their attention to some truly worthwhile jazz. In this he was running a similar course to tenorist Charles Lloyd, who was often denigrated at the time for 'playing to the crowds' but who had a first-rate quartet (with young Keith Jarrett on piano and Jack DeJohnette on drums) and managed to bring the denizens of Fillmore West and many more besides some outstanding modern jazz at a time when everyone else was deserting the music for more bankable sounds.

Among many achievements, Burton commissioned *A Genuine Tong Funeral* from composer Carla Bley, using his own popularity to bring about the creation of a major modern large ensemble piece: this 'dark opera without words', when recorded in 1969 by Burton, proved a vital breakthrough for a composer who, up until that point, had received little exposure and next to no critical attention.

Bobby Hutcherson arrived in New York from L.A. in 1961 having just turned 20 years of age. A

flawless technique and an enviable natural gift led him quickly into playing and recording with major moderns such as Jackie McLean, Eric Dolphy and guitarist Grant Green. His clear, open sound and quick musical imagination made him a standout sideman with many groups, and led to his presence on a number of classic albums, including Dolphy's last studio date *Out To Lunch* plus Jackie McLean's *One Step Beyond* and *Destination – Out!*. Hutcherson, a relaxed, open personality with a larger than usual awareness of the musicians he works with, subsequently began a career as leader of his own record dates, and in 1967 took the next step by forming his own group, co-led with L.A. colleague Harold Land. For five years, this group created a varied and exciting body of work with imaginatively arranged material which was largely ignored at the time, as it adhered closer to pre-avant-garde concepts than found favour with the critics.

Pianist Andrew Hill had a similar problem in that he had talent to spare and a playing and composing style which had no obvious indebtednesses. He thus sat uneasily between both the avant-garde and the boppers. Hill had played with Roland Kirk at the start of the sixties, and landed a record deal in 1963. Between then and the end of the decade, Hill recorded a string of albums (many unreleased at the time, some still unreleased) which had critics raving, musicians admiring, and public largely avoiding. Just why, nobody has ever seemed to work out. His 1964 date *Point Of Departure*, featuring Eric Dolphy and Kenny Dorham, contained impressive composi-

Gary Burton was, with Bobby Hutcherson, the first vibist to emerge in 20 years who was not a pale imitation of the great Milt Jackson.

tions which were a million miles away from the old bop idea of tune-improvisation-repeat tune. Each piece had a completely conceived path to tread, expressing specific points concerning Hill at the time. Other albums are equally impressive, such as *Judgement!* (with Hutcherson and Elvin Jones) and *Compulsion* (an overpoweringly rhythmic session foreshadowing much of the world-music concerns of the eighties). Hill never performed live a great deal, and he dropped out of sight as his record label slowly went cold on him.

Jackie McLean, a sax player who came to the fore with Mingus and Blakey in the fifties, went through a major stylistic change in the early sixties before, in the

last few years of the decade, taking himself off the scene. 'Freedom in jazz', he once said, 'is like a complete new field, new grazing grounds for all the cattle that want to go out and eat some new grass. All those who want to keep picking over the same grass, let them stay there. But those who want to move out into new grazing grounds – it's there. If they want to – if they feel like it.' McLean, a player who gradually evolved a style and sound which is instantly recognizable, had moved from his days as a Charlie Parker imitator to a stage where his music carried total conviction every time he played. He also put together some sensationally talented bands in 1962-67. Young players who made important

breakthroughs in his band include Bobby Hutcherson, the drummer Tony Williams, (only just 17 and still to join Miles Davis), pianists Larry Willis and Lamont Johnson, and the trombonist-composer Grachan Moncur III.

The sixties also saw a significant rebirth of a distinctive Chicago jazz style. It started with the pianist and composer Richard Abrams (b.1930) when he established a rehearsal band in 1961 called, appropriately, The Experimental Band, and which included reedman Roscoe Mitchell. Abrams saw the need to organize resources carefully if experimental music – and its creators – were to survive. By 1965 that organization had been established: it was the Association for the Advance-

ment of Creative Musicians (AACM), and it played a pivotal role in doing what its title suggested it would, stressing the value of the whole over individual parts.

The Chicago style is marked by a very clear commitment on the part of individual musicians to collective creativity. Violinist Leroy Jenkins, at this time playing with altoist Anthony Braxton, commented: 'This is a group music. Like Richard Abrams says, the era of the individual is gone.'

On the first albums by such key artists as Roscoe Mitchell, Joseph Jarman and Lester Bowie, this sense of group identity is very strong, as is the sense of mission and purpose. Joseph Jarman summed it up this way: 'Until I

Saxophonist Joseph Jarman was, with pianist Richard Abrams, the other leading avante-garde player and composer in the Chicago of the sixties. Late in 1967, he joined the fledgling Art Ensemble of Chicago.

had the first meeting with Richard Abrams, I was "like all the rest" of the "hip" ghetto niggers: I was cool, I took dope, I smoked pot, etc. I did not care for the life that I had been given . . . [with them] I found the first something with meaning, reason for doing. That band and the people there was the most important thing that ever happened to me.'

The Chicago players' experiments with sound, structure and real collectivism was one of the most important and lasting contributions to the latter-day development of jazz. By late 1967, four of the leading players, Joseph Jarman, Roscoe Mitchell, Lester Bowie and Malachi Favors, had joined together to form the Art Ensemble of Chicago. Their first concerts and albums together were stupendous feats of creativity and exploration, set against a background of silence and 'little instruments'. Their consequent creative journey was to take them

through the next two decades.

Miles Davis's creative voyage through the sixties, his last period as a player of acoustic music, was aided immeasurably by his formation in 1963 of a completely new group after a period of indecision and artistic stagnation. The rhythm section was Tony Williams on drums, Ron Carter on bass and Herbie Hancock on piano. Of these players, only Hancock was known to the general public prior to joining Davis through his work with Eric Dolphy and his hit record *Watermelon Man*. The dynamism and flexibility of this young group was unlike anything Miles had experienced in the past, and in Tony Williams he had a drummer capable of playing anything – anything at all – and making it work brilliantly. In fact it is possible to listen to some of Miles' records, such as *Live In Europe*, *Miles Smiles* and *Filles de Kilimanjaro*, and close off from everything but the drums, yet still

feel invigorated at the end of each album.

On tenor, Miles started with a fine ex-colleague of Max Roach and Booker Little, George Coleman. The Memphis-born sax player had a fertile melodic imagination, bags of technique and tonal beauty surpassed only at that time by Stan Getz. He was not a fashionable player, however, and so his contribution has often been overlooked. Indeed, on a classic such as the 1964 live album, *My Funny Valentine*, the fact that his solos are consistently absorbing and not a let-down after the burningly intense communications of Miles at the top of his form, is a tribute to his very personal gifts. Coleman also appeared on sideman Herbie Hancock's classic date, *Maiden Voyage*, a peak in the post-bop style.

When Coleman left the band, Wayne Shorter joined. As a soloist, but more as a composer,

Shorter was the foil Davis needed to keep pushing himself into new musical fields. There is little doubt that the trumpeter felt under great pressure from the exploits of the avant garde and his old sidemen such as Coltrane, Rollins and Adderley: by the mid-sixties, each in his own way had overtaken their old employer. Coltrane had gone significantly further into unknown musical territory, Rollins had pushed absolute improvisation to a point of virtuosity Davis could not hope to match, and Adderley had met with unprecedented success pursuing his 'roots' jazz with a strong soul inflection. Davis responded by increasing abstraction, and indeed created a fine body of albums which, if they had been by

As the decade came to a close, Miles Davis picked up the gauntlet flung down by rock and the New Wave. He is pictured here in 1969 with Dave Holland and Jack deJohnette broadening horizons in Berlin.

somebody new to the scene, would have caused astonishment and delight.

But Miles remained dissatisfied for a number of reasons. He was no longer the man in the vanguard, nor was he the best-seller he had been just five years before, and he genuinely disliked the direction the younger players were taking. The solution to his problems came at the end of the decade, when he progressively adapted the electric sounds, and finally the rhythms, of popular music. In 1968, as his great acoustic quintet broke up, he brought in Chick Corea, a pianist working as sideman in a number of New York-based groups, to play Fender Rhodes piano, and Jack de Johnette on drums. Within a year, he was recording *In A Silent Way* and *Bitches Brew* with guitarist John McLaughlin and a bevy of electronic keyboardists including Joe Zawinul. On the 'live' front, he was playing rock festivals. Miles was coming out of the sixties back on top of the heap.

But jazz was no longer the popular force it had been, as impresario Norman Granz noted: 'As far as recordings are concerned, there may be more recording going on, but it seems to me that the number of men making the sessions remains almost stationary. You go to a Patti Page date or Ella Fitzgerald date with Marty Paich arrangements, or some other guy's date with a different arranger, and you see the same cats every time.

In the end you've got 500 cats in three cities who do all the recording, and obviously you can't expect the level of recording to go up in Dubuque.'

Finally, in the decade which saw the first genuine signs of significant jazz being created on a wide scale outside of the USA, from Oslo to Sydney, the jazz community also suffered the loss of the following key musicians: John Coltrane, Eric Dolphy, Booker Little, Albert Ayler, Paul Chambers, Coleman Hawkins, Pee Wee Russell, Jack Teagarden, Charles Clark, Dinah Washington, Christopher Gaddy, Herbie Nichols, Bud Powell, Johnny Hodges, Billy Strayhorn, Scott LaFaro, Doug Watkins, Booker Ervin, Wes Montgomery and Rex Stewart.

Pianist and composer Andrew Hill made unforgettable albums between 1963 and 1968, playing with the likes of Joe Henderson, Eric Dolphy, Bobby Hutcherson, Elvin Jones, Richard Davis, Freddie Hubbard and, on one occasion, a string quartet. His artistic quality has rarely been matched by his popular acclaim, however, so he has remained a fascinating but neglected artist of the finest quality.

after the storm

'I'm sure that if the people who controlled the media exposed jazz and all the other arts, the people would go for it. But they don't want to because once people start thinking, they'll do more and more of it. Jazz is a true thing, and it's got to be surrounded by truth. And they don't want to get into truth – not when they can do something else and make just as much money.'

– Lee Morgan, 1970

JAZZ WAS IN AN embattled position as the seventies dawned. The avant-garde players were still generally regarded as renegades who were busily chasing each other up cul-de-sacs; the newly emergent fusion bands from the Miles Davis circle such as Weather Report, Mahavishnu Orchestra and Davis himself, left many saying 'yes, it's good but is it jazz?'; the so-called 'soul brigade' led by musicians such as Les McCann, Ramsey Lewis and Eddie Harris were moving ever closer to out-and-out instrumental funk, while the updated swing and post-bop mainstream were suffering neglect. They were so out of fashion it hurt. In such circumstances, it is hardly surprising to find that musicians such as Sonny Rollins and Charles Mingus simply retired from the fray for a number of years.

Right: Wynton Marsalis (with Dizzy Gillespie looking on), the bastion of jazz tradition in the modern age. After two decades of turbulent advance in jazz, the retrospective movement among young players was spearheaded by figures such as trumpeter Marsalis and his brother, Branford. Branford Marsalis (Far right) first came to attention in his brother Wynton's band, and in the later eighties emerged as the more original and exploratory of the two musicians.

Considering the crisis of confidence jazz was going through, the amount of records with solid jazz content that were made at this time is little short of amazing: some people clearly still had faith. But there was such a bewildering array of directions to head in, and so few which made any real money, that even the musicians got confused. Adding to this confusion was the explosion of electronic technology and its availability to contemporary musicians at prices the individual could afford. Rock musicians had shown a remarkable capacity for embracing technology as soon as it became available, and doing something worthwhile with it in pretty short order. Jazz musicians were innately more conservative, having invested a lifetime in developing a personal sound and technique on the traditional acoustic instruments. They spent most of the late sixties toying with innovations like the Fender Rhodes electric piano and the Varitone electric saxophone, and not getting very far. At the same time, Jimi Hendrix was trashing amplifiers every night of the week and recording masterpieces of electrically-induced sound such as *Are You Experienced?, 1983 – A Merman I Should Be* and *Voodoo Chile*.

It is tempting to say that in the sixties jazz simply lost too many of its visionary leaders at a time when it needed them more than ever. Few would dispute that jazz would have had a different history in the seventies had John Coltrane lived past 1967. As it was, the Coltrane school quickly lost impetus and direction, as had the Parker school in the fifties.

Unfortunately, no-one could devise a way of furthering what Coltrane had taken so far himself. Even ex-colleagues and sidemen such as McCoy, Tyner, Elvin Jones and Pharoah Sanders by the mid-seventies found themselves unable to proceed any further down the path they had been sent in, and a period of re-appraisal was in order. By the time Sanders, in particular, re-emerged in the early eighties with a revised vision, jazz had moved on.

RE-DEFINING JAZZ: MILES' *BITCHES BREW*

As the new decade began, most of the noise, heat and action was coalescing around Miles Davis and a number of ex-employees. Miles had brought subtle rock inflections into his studio work as early as 1968, though his stage act stayed fixed very much in his repertoire of the fifties and sixties. At home his listening habits had veered almost completely towards the new soul, funk and rock of the time, and he was particularly taken by Sly Stone, James Brown and Jimi Hendrix. In 1969 he made two albums which were to transform and re-define what was seen to be the cutting edge of jazz. *In A Silent Way* did things in a new way, although in mood and ambience it was not wholly detached from its prede-cessors, and in terms of Miles's own playing had clear overtones of his albums with Gil Evans. Miles had no fewer than three keyboardists, all playing elec-tronic instruments, plus one elec-tric guitarist creating a constantly changing musical backdrop for his solos. The guitarist was Englishman John McLaughlin, who had been brought over to New York by drummer Tony Williams to join his new band, Lifetime.

If that album signalled a change, then the follow-up, *Bitches Brew*, a double-lp, acted like a catalyst for the whole jazz scene, just as Ornette Coleman had ten years earlier: like it or hate

In the early 1970s, Miles Davis was the pacesetter in the realms of jazz-rock and so-called 'fusion': he pointed out the directions and others followed.

it, everyone concerned with the music, from fans to musicians to night-club owners and critics, had to take it on board. The album was also exceptionally success-ful, selling far in excess of any-thing Miles had done in years. On it, Davis had created what amounted to a new, electronically-driven soundscape, delivered ad-lib by three keyboardists, a guitarist, soprano saxophonist and bass clarinet, in addition to acoustic and electric bass, and drums. Bass and drums stuck mostly to simple rock-like beats and ostantino patterns (repeated melodic/rhythmic phrases). The

rest of the group were given specific background areas to fill in, and in that way Davis built up the sound pictures, almost in the style of an action painter. Over the top of the whole melange was his bitingly strong trumpet, play-ing with a conviction not heard on records since the mid-sixties.

His long-time producer, Teo Macero, described how Davis worked in the studio: 'When they're in that studio it's like God coming – oh, oh, here he comes. They stop talking, they don't fool around, they tend to business and they listen, and when he stops, they stop. When he tells the drummer what to play, the drum-mer plays. When he tells the guitar players to play, they play and they play until he stops them. This is a fact, this is not hearsay, I've seen it . . . He is the teacher

. . . He's the God that they look up to and they never disagreed, to my knowledge, in the studio. If they did, they got a goddam drumstick over their head and I've seen that happen, too.'

Miles capitalized on the break-through to the larger young rock audience by playing at places like Fillmore East and Fillmore West, as well as festivals such as the Isle of Wight and Atlanta. His follow-up album, *A Tribute to Jack Johnson*, was the closest he ever came to out-and-out funk. Made to accompany a documen-tary on the legendary boxer, the first black heavyweight champion of the world in 1908, it included the drummer Billy Cobham, soon to become a mainstay with John McLaughlin, and ex-Stevie Won-der bassist Michael Henderson. Miles himself wrote the liner notes

– 'Johnson portrayed Freedom – it rang just as loud as the bell proclaiming him Champion. He was a fast-living man, he liked women – lots of them and most of them white. He had flashy cars because that was his thing. That's right, the big ones and the fast ones . . . His flamboyancy was more than obvious. And no doubt mighty Whitey felt "No Black man should have all this." But he did and he'd flaunt it.'

Much of this could have been Miles speaking about himself. The trumpeter had always lived hard and fast, and on more than one occasion his body had suffered, either through car crashes, pain-ful operations on his troublesome hips, or drug abuse. In fact, although Miles continued to tour and produce challenging new albums with an ever-changing array of new young talent, by 1975 he was physically, mentally and creatively in need of a rest. By then he had done more than enough to ignite a few artistic fires in his ex-associates. It was to be 1981 before he played in public or released an album of new material. When he did, it was as someone trying to catch up with interim developments. To this date, while running some excellent groups and hiring peo-ple of the ability of Al Foster, John Scofield and Bob Berg, Miles has not created music which, like so much of what he did previously, cut through the current musical trends and into a new one.

Within a short time of the suc-cess of *Bitches Brew*, a number of groups had formed composed of ex-Davis men. Tony Williams and John McLaughlin formed Lifetime with organist Larry Young; Joe Zawinul and Wayne Shorter formed Weather Report; Chick Corea formed Return to Forever; and Herbie Hancock formed his Sextet. After the breakup of the original Lifetime, McLaughlin formed the Mahavishnu Orchestra while Williams had fitful success with a number of different line-ups.

Williams' Lifetime band had recorded its first album, *Emergency*, prior to Miles' *Bitches Brew*: like most of his albums it was a frustrating combination of gob-smacking brilliance and ill-advised indulgence. The band made two albums before breaking up (one with ex-Cream member Jack Bruce), plus a series of concerts where their highly-amplified all-out attack, allied to the drummer's penchant for mind-bendingly complex and subtle rhythmic veerings, left audiences in silent dismay. Williams had the right idea – but the wrong approach and unlucky timing. Before the band could properly re-focus its energies within a more populist style, McLaughlin had left, and the unique frisson between the two was lost for good. It was to be the mid-eighties before Williams, then back in the acoustic jazz bag, could consistently deliver the goods with his own band again.

McLaughlin, on the other hand, was both man-of-the-moment and man with a mission. He formed the Mahavishnu Orchestra, an all-electric band with guitar, violin, keyboards, bass and drums, and produced high-energy music, often based on ostantino patterns and modal harmony with a thunderous rhythmic drive underneath it. He also openly displayed a link with Indian mysticism (the band's name made that clear enough) and developed an onstage persona which made him a revered, almost godlike figure to his fans.

Not surprisingly, the music the band produced was fairly humourless, but it certainly kicked like a mule, and McLaughlin was adamant that he was making no compromises: 'It's my sole conviction that the listening audience is totally underrated and patronised by music business people who project their own limitations on the general listening public.' The wide popularity of his band with Billy Cobham, Jan Hammer and Jerry Goodman

seemed to bear him out.

McLaughlin was a fearsomely impressive technician, but he had the other necessary quality to make his music of lasting value – a burning commitment to human expression. 'Music is born out of the inner sounds within a soul; all the music that was ever heard came from the inner silence in every musician. The musician has to hear it first, and if you cultivate the art of listening, then sooner or later you're bound to be able to execute it . . . Technical competence is only to accurately express these things that you have inside.'

The guitarist broke up his first band in 1973 and formed an 11-piece Mahavishnu Orchestra which featured, among others, the European violinist Jean-Luc Ponty who had previously starred with Frank Zappa. Since then, he has pursued a varied and stimulating career, often spending long periods concentrating on the acoustic guitar. Some of his ventures, especially the ones with other guitar virtuosi such as Al

DiMeola, Paco De Lucia, and Larry Coryell, are strictly for the enjoyment of other guitarists, but he has such an inner compulsion to communicate in his music that there is always something in his own playing which will set him apart from the rest.

HANCOCK, COREA & JARRETT – PIANO ENDS HERE

The path for Miles' other ex-colleagues was never quite so wayward. Herbie Hancock, for example, has managed an admirable balance between what amounts to two virtually separate careers, one in the charts and the other with his older listening audience. Hancock had, since the beginning of his career, been an extremely intelligent and versatile musician, interested in working in many musical areas. In 1963, when Miles gave public notice of his dislike of Eric Dolphy's music, and everybody was tut-tutting

about the then-burgeoning 'soul' jazz of Ramsey Lewis, Les McCann and the organists Jimmy Smith and Jack McDuff, Hancock worked with both Dolphy's and Davis's bands, and had a soul-drenched hit with his song from 1962, *Watermelon Man*.

When it came to life after Miles, Hancock was happy to aim at both ends of the market again. His Sextet of 1971-73 had some remarkable musicians in it, including former avant-garde reed player Benny Maupin, trombonist Julian Priester, bassist Buster Williams, trumpeter Eddie Henderson and drummer Billy Hart. Two of the three albums the band made had large funk elements in some degree or another, but they were used always within a jazz approach to the music; Hancock was still feeling his way into new popular styles and into an ever-deepening understanding of electronic keyboards and synthesizers. The last album the band made before it split up, *Crossings*, is a classic of the electrified jazz genre, a hugely imaginative effort from the entire band, and a wonderful synthesis of all the cross-currents of popular black music of the day. But more than that, it also encompassed the entire space and depth of Hancock's musical imagination and his ability to organize sound. Nevertheless, the album sold poorly, and the Sextet was disbanded because, said Hancock, 'I ran out of money. I could get gigs, but they wouldn't pay enough for the expenses.'

Hancock's next band had only Maupin from the previous outfit, and a more determinedly pop style. Their first album was *Headhunters*, which had a reworking of *Watermelon Man* on it. It quickly became the biggest-selling album ever by a jazz outfit. At that point, with Hancock still exploring the instrinsic qualities of synthesizers and electronic

Left: *Billy Cobham, explosive drummer in guitarist John McLaughlin's Mahavishnu Orchestra, later a fusion star of his own.*

Above: *Al DiMeola played with Chick Corea's Return to Forever, then recorded technocratic albums.*

sounds, many of his old fans gave up hope that he would ever play unequivocal jazz again. In 1977, Hancock recalled one particularly ironic situation: 'There's a writer who used to write for *Crawdaddy*. When I first met him, he was a rock & roller, and I had my far-out Sextet band, and he didn't know what the music was about. I did a whole number on him about how to really listen to music, and the responsibility of this and that. And he gained a lot of respect for me. And then, when I started getting into funk, he turned on me!'

By the late seventies Hancock was feeling the need to play acoustic piano again, and even return to the type of music he had created in the Davis group of the sixties. Through contact with his old colleagues, the idea came that it would be good to play a season of such music together, music which they saw as not having dated at all in the intervening years. Ron Carter, the group's bassist, said: 'It might be a change for some of the guys in the band to play this music again, from a physical standpoint, but not from an emotional or mental point of view. The forms may date back ten years, but that doesn't mean the music isn't contemporary.' With Freddie Hubbard subbing for Miles, the V.S.O.P. Quintet toured extensively and cut a number of records.

Buoyed by the public succes of this reunion, Hancock became more adventurous, and in 1978 initiated a series of two-piano concerts with Chick Corea which were again welcomed by the large public following of both artists, and the resultant albums, although perhaps musically imperfect, were very popular. The same year he reneged on an old oath never to record a solo acoustic album, and the result was a stunning distillation of Hancock's originality and unique musical insights both as a com-

poser and as an interpreter of others' music. Hancock has a harmonic ear as sophisticated as Bill Evans, and greatly more rhythmic variety and subtlety than the older pianist. His range of expression as demonstrated on the solo album is also significantly wider.

In the eighties, Hancock continued to alternate between V.S.O.P. (the 1981 tour had a young Wynton Marsalis on trumpet in place of Hubbard) and his increasingly funky groups. It is an indication of his musical stature that Hancock has been so singularly successful in both acoustic and electric music; indeed, an examination of his chart-orientated material reveals an astonishing attention to musical detail and consistently attractive melodic, rhythmic and harmonic shapes.

His partner in the 1978 two-piano tours, Chick Corea, was born in Massachusetts in 1941, and in the early sixties played with a number of Latin Jazz bands. An articulate, highly intelligent man and a thoroughly schooled musician, Corea worked successfully with Stan Getz in 1967, and with Miles Davis for the rest of the sixties before forming a radical trio, Circle, with Chicago avant-gardist Anthony Braxton and ex-Miles bassist Dave Holland. This band made some critically acclaimed concerts and albums before Corea left to form a band, Return to Forever, which achieved what he termed 'a better balance between technique and communication'. In a simultaneous development, Corea made two devastatingly beautiful and original solo piano albums for ECM, simply called *Piano Improvisations Vols 1 & 2*, made up exclusively of his own compositions. With these two discs, Corea produced both improvisation and writing of a very high order, with a fresh and

HERBIE HANCOCK: A pianist trained in the conservatory tradition, Hancock was one of the versatile, younger musicians taken on board by Miles Davis in the early 1960s. After this expert apprenticeship at the top of his trade, Hancock went on to become a leading exponent of jazz mixed with newer forms such as funk. Hancock was never a purist or diehard about jazz traditions. He became fascinated by technical innovations in sound provided by electronics. By the late 1970s, however, he and some of his former colleagues from the Miles Davis days longed to return to their roots. They felt that music still had force. Audiences and record producers agreed. From then onwards, Hancock was both an acoustic and funk performer, appealing both to mainstream jazz audiences and the newer, pop-oriented fans. His careful attention to melody and nuances of sound helped both strands of his career to thrive in the following decade.

In the 1970s keyboardist Herbie Hancock (left) *went one better than his mentor, Miles Davis, and had consistent chart success with his 'Headhunters' band and album. Ex-Miles bassist Ron Carter, seen here with Hancock* (above left), *also had considerable success as a recording artist with CTI.*

Below: *Hancock was the driving force behind a mid-seventies return to acoustic jazz for all the members of the great 1960s Miles Davis Quintet – minus Miles. Freddie Hubbard fulfilled Davis's trumpeting role. Hancock* (right) *continued to balance electric and acoustic careers for the next decade.*

arresting approach to the rhythmic and harmonic conventions of post-bop jazz and a decidedly tasty Latin influence in the sinuous and elusive rhythms and melodies of pieces such as *Sometime Ago* and *Song for Sally*.

This gracefulness and lack of the need to force his music in order to make it exciting or attractive became one of the most winning characteristics of Corea's electric excursions during the seventies. A reflection of the changing times in which jazz was now making its way is the fact that in 1971 Corea became a student of Scientology, and has remained ever since. Similarly, as Corea's fame and stature grew, he began to record his compositions written within the modern classical idiom – solo piano pieces, string quartets and other works for different chamber combinations. Such diversification

would have been unthinkable for a jazz musician even 15 years previously (Charlie Parker's ill-fated efforts with a string section come immediately to mind), and was not merely a measure of the depth of Corea's own musical ability, but also of the radically shifting cultural perception of what constituted being a contemporary jazz musician.

This development is paralleled in the other outstanding keyboard talent of the past 20 years, Keith Jarrett (b. 1945). Both he and Corea have recorded items from the standard classical repertoire – Mozart concertos, Bach's Well-Tempored Klavier and received glowing reviews for their interpretations. Forty years prior to this, Art Tatum, one of the most gifted pianists of his generation had never progressed publicly with classical music beyond making dramatic little arrangements of

throwaway salon pieces by Dvorak and Massenet. Had Tatum ever had the desire, it is certain that no one would have wanted to record him playing the repertoire covered by Jarrett and Corea.

Jarrett was a child prodigy, studying the piano from the age of three and performing as a leader by the time he was 18. He was a member of Art Blakey's Jazz Messengers in 1965 before joining the ground-breaking Charles Lloyd Quartet in 1966. This was a crucial experience for Jarrett, as it brought him directly into contact with the new audience that Lloyd had reached in the late sixties – the white college kids and hippies who were willing to take on jazz provided the musicians did not wear dark suits and ties and look like their parents. Extensions of that audience on a worldwide basis gave

Jarrett his unprecedented popularity as a solo piano performer in the 1970s, with best-selling jazz albums such as *Facing You*, *The Köln Concert* and others.

However, it was not merely Jarrett's youth or the way he dressed which won him this audience. He seemed to have a limitless ability to supply fresh and affecting melodic and harmonic improvisational ideas, a flawless technique which could respond to any musical situation, and a penchant for wildly infectious rhythms, often contained in left hand ostantino patterns, which could grab an audience by the throat and keep them entranced for upwards of half an hour at a time.

Jarrett, moreover, was more than just a solo pianist, despite the release of a welter of unaccompanied recitals on disc in the seventies and eighties, and even a 10-disc set of solo recordings taken from an early eighties Japanese concert tour. Although he steadfastly refused to get involved in electronic keyboards – he had played them as a sideman for Miles Davis at the beginning of the seventies and did not want to do it again – he ran a long-standing and highly suc-

cessful group, built around the trio nucleus of himself, bassist Charlie Haden and ex-Bill Evans drummer Paul Motian. These three had been making outstanding albums since 1968, and through the seventies and eighties they continued to diversify and deepen their impact with the assistance of two different saxophone partners, the American Dewey Redman and the Norwegian Jan Garbarek.

Jarrett is an outspoken and decisive personality, very sure of his specific abilities. Once when talking about his time in the Miles Davis band, he commented: 'The main reason I joined the band was that I didn't like the band. I liked what Miles was playing very much and I hated the rest of the band playing together . . . I heard what sounded to me like four ego trips, like each one was trying not to play what the others were playing . . . It was like seeing a diseased organism on the stage.' This confidence in his own perceptions closely parallels Davis's own, and invests all his musical ventures (whether group improvisations, solo concerts or recitals of his own compositions) with an authority which can be irresistable when his mood is right, and

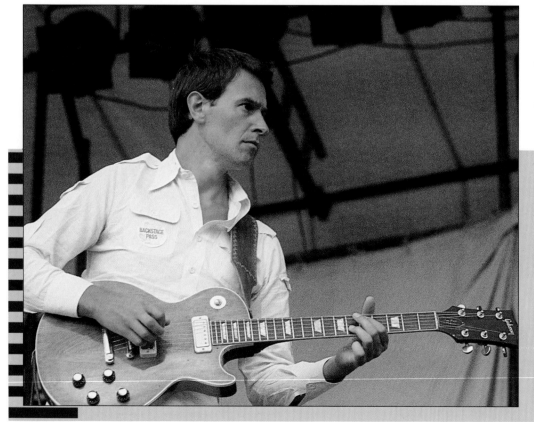

NEW DIRECTIONS: **John McLaughlin *(left)* was the electric guitarist who also became a messiah, guru and musical seer to young audiences for much of the 1970s: in the middle of the decade he changed direction and pursued acoustic guitar music with his new line-up. His band also aspired to some of the ideals of Eastern music. Weather Report *(right)* also grew restless with familiar patterns, but branched out with a different approach, looking into the fabric and structures of rock sounds and jazz harmonies, balancing strong compositional ideas with high flights of extemporised imagination.**

which helps sustain the drama of performance even when he is at his least inspired.

HEAVY WEATHER

One final offshoot from the Davis menagerie was the group Weather Report. The fact that it was formed two years after Tony Williams' abortive efforts with Lifetime, and a year after McLaughlin had got his Mahavishnu Orchestra off the ground, may has something to do with its longevity. The original line-up was Joe Zawinul, Wayne Shorter, Miroslav Vitous, Alphonse Mouzon and Airto Moreira. Zawinul had spent nearly a decade with Cannonball Adderley's hugely popular band, and had written more than one hit for them: his single, *Mercy, Mercy, Mercy* had won the Adderley group a Grammy award. He and Shorter, fresh from Miles's aggregation, were ready to experiment a little, and in particular break out of the jazz straightjacket. From the beginning they were involved in Latin and other polyrhythmic ethnic musics, and the way they would be incorporated into their electrically-oriented improvisa-

tions and song structures. Their first albums, and the concerts that accompanied them, were dominated by vast soundscapes punctuated with complex rhythmic patterns and snaking, angular improvisation. As time went on, and the musical climate changed in favour of rhythms more closely wedded to dance, Weather Report simplified its concepts, chopping and changing members over the years in the process. They had a breakthrough in 1976 with the song *Birdland*, which was a cover version hit for Manhattan Transfer and which gave the group instant media accessibility.

This is something they were clearly not averse to, especially after the arrival of charismatic bassist Jaco Pastorius, a man with strong ties to the contemporary rock field. As Zawinul once said, 'Most jazz artists have such hard lives that they always project the hardness of their life. We want to uplift people. We want to make them feel good. And we don't have to sell out to do it.'

The band continued to enjoy a high critical and public acceptance, but its arteries were beginning to harden by the early eighties, and Zawinul's dominance within the musical thinking led to

a closing down of options rather than a continued expansion. By 1985 Wayne Shorter, the only other remaining original Weather Reporter, had left. This necessitated a change of name to Weather Update, but by then everybody had the report, and the update was something of a superfluity.

Seventies fusion – and eighties fusion, come to that – was not the exclusive province of Miles Davis and his ex-employees, however. Many bands arose from loose groupings of musicians who had served an apprenticeship in struggling jazz units, then gone into lucrative studio work and formed fusion bands as blowing units to relax in. The popularity which came their way was often an unlooked-for bonus: certainly the Brecker Brothers, Tom Scott, the Mangiones, and many other such bands were not primarily formed with the idea of cynically manipulating the music market to make a few bucks; often, the music their own bands made was a blessed chance at playing with more freedom than they managed to establish elsewhere in their professional lives.

But perhaps one unfortunate side-effect of these bands was that high-tech flashiness and sheer musical competence were perceived by public and musicians alike as more attractive goals to pursue than the basic human expressions which such techniques are meant to serve. In this sense, such bands as The Crusaders, Eddie Harris and Donald Byrd's funk outfits had a great deal more to offer the unprejudiced listener in the following decade.

Still, not everybody had been convinced that electrifying jazz meant pursuing the middle market. At the beginning of the seventies, pianist Paul Bley (a founder member of the Jazz Composer's Guild in 1964 and a

striking avant-garde piano stylist) and composer Annette Peacock acquired some synthesizers, played a few concerts either side of the Atlantic and made a handful of records which showed that a radical application of such equipment could produce memorable results. Both musicians had previously been connected with an abstract lyricism, divorced from a constant metric time flow and heavily dependent on space and silence. Bley once explained his reasons for this: 'The thing I wanted to do was show that you can make beautiful music regardless of the materials or the equipment you're using. I felt the same way in the early avant-garde, when everybody sounded like a room full of screaming cats.'

Bley certainly stuck to this dictum in his electronic forays, but Peacock, his partner at the time, was often intent more on conveying sheer intensity of feeling, either through vocals or through

Larry Coryell (above) *came out of the Gary Burton Quartet, and was a challenger to McLaughlin as the hottest guitar in the West; today, Coryell makes superb music without competing.*

sound manipulation. Ironically, it was her stark lyricism which had been the seed of much of Bley's achievement in the sixties. Within a short space of time, they were to go their separate ways, Bley back to acoustic music, and Peacock further towards a redefinition of what radical rock could constitute.

Another key sixties innovator, Sun Ra and his Solar Arkestra, began in the seventies to use electronic equipment, and coincidentally build up a sizeable worldwide following. He had spent most of the fifties and sixties in obscurity in Chicago and New York, with only a smattering of hardy musical explorers recognizing what he and his band had to offer. Realizing early on that the only possible way forward was to

implement a self-reliance programme, Ra over a period of time
gathered around him a very
close-knit community of musicians which would be dedicated
to his music, his theories and his
goals. He also set up his own
label, Saturn, and released his
own records – in very limited
editions, but at least the music
was disseminated to those outside
Chicago who wanted to hear it.

By the mid sixties, Ra was
enjoying an influence in the progressive jazz world which belied
his obscurity to the average jazz
fan. He had relocated, along with
his entire Arkestra, to New York,
and was holding down a regular
weekly engagement in Slugs', a
Harlem venue. He had also nurtured some key avant-garde
('free') players, among them for a
period Pharoah Sanders, and had
been a direct influence on John
Coltrane's musical thinking in his
explorations beyond conventional late fifties jazz forms. One
of Ra's crucial developments was
to successfully direct a large
ensemble through a whole evening without the band once referring to written guidelines. This
adherence to complete collective
improvisation, with frequent
abandoning of metric rhythm,
recognizable themes and unison
playing, had a significant impact
on the free players of the sixties
and seventies. The extraordinary
thing about Ra at his best was
that a wonderful order and peace
was evident in his band's playing,
due to his sure but subtle direction as the music was being
created. But this did not prevent
him and his musicians from being
miserably poor: 'I want to be the
only thing I could be without
anybody stopping me in America
– that is to be a failure . . . I never
wanted to be a part of planet
Earth, and I did everything not to
be a part of it. I never wanted their
money or fame, and anything I do
for this planet is because the

Creator of the universe is
making me do it.'

As the seventies wore on, Ra
began to reach a much wider
audience as it dawned on promoters that his Arkestra's stage presence, in the age of hippy festivals and all sorts of weird
exhibits, was the real thing. He
also began to enthusiastically
embrace electronics, and later
again, perform music from the
jazz tradition such as Fletcher
Henderson's, Duke Ellington's
and Jelly Roll Morton's. This
helped pull him into the orbit of a
large and enthusiastic worldwide
audience who both loved the
stage show and were excited by
the music. Ra's is certainly one of
the longest-lived ensembles in
jazz history, and his achievement
has been immense in two
respects: in the earlier part of his
career, he often led the way in
developing effective free jazz
techniques for large ensembles,
and latterly he has been able to
persuade a large number of people that difficult music can be fun
and a whole lot more besides,
when approached in the right
way. For those two things alone,
Ra is a great man.

Unlike Ra, Archie Shepp had
enjoyed wide exposure in the
sixties, and had taken his music
to many countries and many people. At the dawn of the seventies
he created a series of surpassingly brilliant albums which, due
to a deteriorating relationship
with his main record company
were largely forgotten in the
stampede for fresh musical and
commercial pastures. A thorough
re-examination of them finds
Shepp capable of a deeply human
drama and pathos in his music,

*Tony Williams (pictured here in the
sixties) had so much talent as a
percussionist that he could be
overwhelming. His own career has
been erratic, and today he has come
full circle, playing music similar to
that which first brought him to the
public's attention in 1963.*

Chick Corea, like Herbie Hancock, had success in balancing two parallel careers, one with electronic instruments and one with acoustic, and has managed to retain his musical credibility. Corea has also ventured into classical composition.

and at times his organization of written material reminds the listener of Mingus at his chaotic and cathartic best. *Un Croque Monsieur (Poem: for Losers)*, a long and sprawling composition, has a very simple form, and two long solos from Shepp on soprano saxophone separated by a completely scored five minute interval. But his playing, at a time when virtually everyone imitated Coltrane, was uniquely expressive, and his written accompaniments produced meaningful backdrops to those solos. The central section utilized his large ensemble in a series of slow-moving harmonic passages and

vocals from Chinalin Sharpe in the heartburnt Billie Holiday tradition, producing a truly moving experience, beautifully controlled and sustained.

Shepp's career in the seventies, however, slowly lost momentum: he took a fine quintet with him to the Montreux Festival in Switzerland in 1975, where he played a new mixture of original material and established jazz classics such as *Lush Life*, but within a couple of years he was no longer leading his own ensembles, and therefore lost a valuable permanent platform on which to develop his music. He was justly praised for his playing on two duet albums with pianist Horace Parlan, one from 1978 and one from 1981, which concentrated on negro spirituals and traditional songs, and continued to occasionally pull together powerful performances within a post-bop

traditionalism (including a reunion with Parlan in 1988). But his days as an innovator at the cutting edge of the music were gone, and his opportunity to consolidate his achievements had slipped away.

FREE JAZZ: METHOD AND MADNESS

Of the group which formed around composers Carla Bley and Michael Mantler – which at one time or another included such diverse talents as Paul Motian, Gato Barbieri, Larry Coryell, Pharoah Sanders, Roswell Rudd, Don Cherry, Dewey Redman, Perry

Keith Jarrett (right) *is a musician able to sustain solo piano improvisations for periods of a half-hour, hour or even for a whole evening while keeping the audience entranced.*

Robinson and Howard Johnson – it was perhaps bassist Charlie Haden (often in association with Carla Bley) who produced the most memorable musical statements. This he did twice from within this loose association of talents – once in 1969 with *Liberation Music Orchestra*, and again in 1983 with *The Ballad of the Fallen* – and many times from outside, with musicians as different in spirit and style as Ornette Coleman, Keith Jarrett and 'New And Old Dreams', a quartet which included Don Cherry, Dewey Redman and Ed Blackwell, all veterans of various Ornette groups. Haden long ago developed his musicianship to the point where everything was stripped to its essentials, and had deep spiritual and emotional layers of meaning. His work under his own name has often been political in a broad sense: both albums mentioned above dealt with the issues of freedom and anti-fascism. The Liberation Orchestra album was built around Haden's discovery of Spanish popular music at the time of the Civil War of 1936-37, and built from those melodies and freedom songs into music depicting struggles against perceived oppres-

sors in other countries, including his own America.

His 1983 album, *The Ballad of the Fallen*, dealt with the folk and popular music of Latin America and, in particular, El Salvador, which at the time was being torn to pieces under a military junta. Haden, a sincere and committed man, has stated, 'The music ... is dedicated to creating a better world; a world without war and killing, without racism, without poverty and exploitation; a world where men of all governments realise the vital importance of life and strive to protect rather than destroy it.' His political philosophy may be regarded as naïve, and his goals unattainable, but the music created from these aspirations is noble, greatly moving, and imbued with a simple human warmth and compassion which, aside from its purely formal qualities, makes it a very powerful brew indeed. It is perhaps a shame that on many of her personal projects, Carla Bley was unable to sustain a similar width of creative vision.

The avant-garde continued to make headway in the seventies and eighties, even though it was no longer as newsworthy as in the previous decade. Enduringly

creative bands such as the trio Air, the World Saxophone Quartet, The George Adams-Don Pullen Quartet, the David Murray Octet and the Steve Lacy Group all began life in the 1970s, and every one of these influential groups tackled head-on the problem of facing up to tradition.

Pullen and Adams had both enjoyed long periods of employment in the latter-day groups of Charles Mingus, and it was with Mingus's drummer of 20 years' standing, Dannie Richmond, that they went out under their own names. Adams had previously enjoyed international exposure as the rollicking tenor player with the Gil Evans Orchestra (he had played in r&b groups in the sixties) and, after Mingus, he spent three years with ex-Coltrane pianist McCoy Tyner's steamrollering small group. Don Pullen started his career in the sixties as a free jazz player who was even further left of centre than Cecil Taylor: his duets with seminal free drummer Milford Graves, which were released in 1967 on a label started by the two musicians themselves

(following Sun Ra's lead), became something of a rallying point for free jazz in the late sixties. However, Pullen had to earn a living by playing r&b, as Adams did. By 1973 he had fallen into Charles Mingus's orbit, and played in his group for three years: this exposure, and the opportunity to play in a consistently challenging creative ensemble, readied Pullen for a career of eclecticism and gradual public acceptance. By the time he got together with Adams, both men were well prepared to lead a group.

If the Adams-Pullen Quartet represented an attempt to embrace a wide number of jazz styles from within the tradition itself, the music of saxophonist/composer David Murray represented the mavericks and outsiders. He had first made a splash in the late seventies as a member of guitarist James Blood Ulmer's Music Revolution Ensemble. Ulmer had himself emerged earlier in the decade as part of Ornette Coleman's electrified group playing what Coleman

called 'harmolodic' music, often with a steady funk beat. By the end of the seventies, Murray was leading different groups and recording under his own name across a range of styles, from relatively structured music with themes and orderly developments through to totally free blasting and honking, like Albert Ayler. What set him apart from thousands of other Ayler imitators was his sheer strength as a wind player, and the incredible gusto and sense of purpose he brought to bear on such wildly impromptu performances. Murray was not following patterns laid down by other pioneers: he was retreading the past in order to make his own discoveries.

During the course of the eighties, Murray played and composed in an extraordinarily diverse set of contexts, including the groups of Sunny Murray, Jack DeJohnette, Cecil Taylor and The World Saxophone Quartet. This last-named band had been started in an accidental way when, in 1976, four saxophonists, Murray, Julius Hemphill, Hamiet Bluiett and

Oliver Lake, performed live at a New Orleans festival. They enjoyed the results so much that they jettisoned the pick-up rhythm section hired for the first concert, and went out into the uncharted seas (for jazz musicians) of acapella wind playing, both scored and improvised.

They were such a success that the band has regularly toured and recorded ever since, and has continued to diversify its musical approach: in the late eighties it has had resounding musical and popular successes with its refreshing and thought-provoking arrangements of many jazz standards, including the work of Ellington and Strayhorn. Murray, meanwhile, has continued his flourishing career away from the Quartet, making a brilliant name for himself as a bandleader and composer as well as the most stimulating saxophonist of his generation. Aside from sheer talent, part of the secret of his success in a field littered with stillborn ambitions is his surreal sense of humour and his general avoidance of both the Miles Davis

Saxophonists from two generations: Archie Shepp (above left) and David Murray (above), both important innovators in their prime, with Shepp consolidating in the seventies and eighties, and Murray thrusting ahead into new territories. Murray has worked in many formations, including The World Saxophone Quartet.

and John Coltrane legacies. As Keith Jarrett once noted, 'Coltrane's influence after he died was very negative, mostly because he couldn't control it any more. He didn't intend there to be a big gap, he intended that there be more space for everyone to do what they should do. That's what his music represents to me, that there is a much greater potential for a human being and an instrument. That and the fact that people are so attached to Miles is very unhealthy. It seems like people don't know any more what's good in their own playing.'

Murray, with his roots in Sonny Rollins, Ayler, Webster and other less obvious heroes, avoided that pitfall as he developed his Octet, his Quartet and his role with the W.S.Q. With their roots similarly in

The Ensemble have attained many peaks over their 23 years together, and have always managed to renew their creative flow just as the well seemed to have run dry and they seemed in danger of parodying themselves. Recycling the whole history of the music through their distorting lens, the band has continually offered new and intriguing insights into both the past and the present state of jazz (what they call 'Great Black Music'), and suggestions as to the way ahead. In a parallel development of the eighties, trumpeter Lester Bowie has also established himself as a single, and made serious inroads into popular consciousness with his Brass Fantasy band, which has both toured and recorded. This band was a logical extension from the ensembles and ideas of his mid-seventies album, *Rope-A-Dope*, named in honour of heavyweight champion Muhammed Ali's avowed style of winning boxing matches. Its riotous version of old popular songs like *Personality (he's got – PERSO-NALITY)* makes Sun Ra sound like a dry academic, and Bowie's onstage image, in his white doctor's coat and with his urbane 'cool', has ensured a significant cult following for himself and the band which spreads a long way past the hard core of jazz devotees. And it is this very embracing of disparate musics and styles by his audiences which Bowie is most eager to sustain.

Compared to the richness and diversity of these players, the studied assimilation of former jazz styles and languages by the young trumpet virtuoso Wynton Marsalis communicates a lack of vitality and an over-emphasis on detail. Marsalis, himself from a jazz-playing New Orleans family, was playing beautifully-controlled and musically sophisticated solos while still a teenager with Art Blakey's Jazz Messengers

For many years since his emergence in the 1950s, Sun Ra (above) has stood for iconoclasm and other worldly presentations. In fact, Ra has a strong sense of jazz history. He is partnered (left) by saxophonist Marshall Allen.

the byways rather than the highways of jazz, the Art Ensemble of Chicago also played a major role in free jazz in the seventies and eighties, both in their example to others of how to play 'complete music' – by drawing on all available styles and sources, and synthesizing something startlingly new – and in their remarkable pooling of four great talents over such a long period of time. The band came out of the Chicago tradition which stressed the equal value of diversity, drama and humour in music.

153

Above: *Carla Bley first established herself in the mid-sixties as a composer of fascinating songs. Soon, she was composing fully realized orchestral scores.*

Left: Branford Marsalis in 1987, playing in his brother's band: he is a saxophonist who is as much at home with Sting as he is with Miles Davis, or simply running his own band.

between 1980 and 1982. He continued to develop an updated mainstream approach as a viable musical alternative to free jazz and fusion, feeling that these two forms had done much to bury jazz in the seventies. Whatever the truth of that belief, Marsalis had an amazingly swift and all-embracing impact, and within 12 months of releasing his first album as leader and starting his own band, he was the most talked-of, written-about and interviewed jazz musician of the decade. Possessing an unshakeable technique and a thorough musical grounding, Marsalis also pursues a singularly distinguished career as a trumpet soloist within the classical repertoire, recording award-winning and best-selling versions of a range of classical, baroque and modern concertos, transcriptions and brass pieces.

With a career which is still so young, it would be foolhardy to attempt to guess Marsalis's future paths. He clearly has an abundance of talent, a sincere interest in the jazz and classical traditions and the determination to succeed. Perhaps the years to come will see a broadening of his talent and a consequent flowering of a more passionate originality. Certainly his older brother, saxophonist Branford Marsalis, has exhibited more of both these qualities since his appearance on the international scene in his brother's group in the early eighties.

The US jazz scene in the eighties has continued to be enlivened by mavericks and unlikely winners-through. Four such players, as diverse in their personalities and contributions as one could wish for, are pianist JoAnne Brackeen, trombonist Ray Anderson (a phenomenal technician who always stresses the human and approachable side of music), and the guitarists John Scofield and Bill Frisell. The Canadian

pianist Brackeen, who first came to prominence playing with Stan Getz in the mid-seventies, is an incredibly gifted player with such authoritative force in her articulation and choice of notes that hearing her live can be an exhilarating if overwhelming experience. She has that most enviable of gifts, the ability to invoke a constant stream of delightful ideas while playing at any speed, across any harmonic progression, and in any musical company. She also has the dexterity to always be able to play what her inner ear and feelings dictate. Few people hear as much as she clearly does, and even fewer can play it: of the pianists who have emerged since, only Mulgrew Miller, Geri Allen and Marcus Roberts come close.

Both Bill Frisell and John Scofield blossomed as guitarists in the 1980s, though they came from rather different circumstances. Scofield, although active in bands since the early seventies, and recording as a leader for nearly as long, only really encountered a wider audience after a four-year

stint with Miles Davis between 1982 and 1985. Miles commented, 'I liked the subtleties of John Scofield's playing ... The blues was John's thing, along with a good jazz touch, so I felt comfortable playing the blues with him.'

Scofield certainly was a masterful blues player, displaying the essential prerequisite of that genre – total rhythmic ease, and a sense of all the time in the world to deliver a phrase. But he was more than that, because his sophisticated ear enabled him to take any harmonic route to his desired end. By the close of the eighties, Scofield had matured into a stylist very much at peace with his own talent, and able to harness his outstanding technique to a unique sense of musical order which makes him a subtle and fascinating musician.

Bill Frisell came through the schools of guitarist Jim Hall and drummer Paul Motian, and during the eighties has helped make the previously unbridgeable gulf between avant rock and modern jazz seem conquerable. Frisell uses huge sculpted sound shapes, reverb, echo and a combination of note articulation which makes his music seem to fade in and out of its own accord.

However, Frisell is not merely some neo-impressionist New Age oik who wandered into the wrong practice room by mistake: he can mount a convincing attack on the material at hand, especially when accompanied by someone of the calibre of drummer Ronald Shannon Jackson, making intriguingly tangential responses to every musical situation.

The other major phenomenon in the past 20 years has been the

rapid emergence of major jazz talents outside the US. Up to the late sixties, the mediocrity of foreign musicians, especially foreign rhythm sections, was a standing joke among touring American stars. This attitude had a modicum of truth in it, especially when so much of what European, Africans, Australians, Latin Americans and others were producing was notably derivative. The exceptions such as Django Reinhardt, bassist Niels-Henning Orsted Pedersen, pianist and bandleader Dollar Brand (later known as Abdullah Ibrahim), the West Indian saxophonist Joe Harriott, trumpeter Shake Keane, German trombonist Albert Mangelsdorff and Australian vibist, composer and all-round "guru' John Sangster only reinforced the point. And for every player well within the mainstream traditions, such as saxophonists Arne Domnerus, Tubby Hayes and Ronnie Scott (all of whom enjoyed solid reputations in America), there were hundreds of leaden and uninspired copyists.

EUROPE: OLD WORLD & NEW FRONTIER

The free jazz movement of the sixties opened the door for European musicians in particular to find their own voices, and such talented and original players as Gunter Hampel, Peter Brotzman, Willem Breuker, Evan Parker, John Stevens, Derek Bailey, Han Bennink, Kenny Wheeler and John Surman all made the giant leap into fiercely individual music with a deeply satisfying aesthetic attached. Some players opted for the intensity of the Ayler-led free players, but with a peculiarly Teutonic twist, while others pursued more intimate and conversational modes of expression. John Surman, to take an example,

managed a fascinating musical amalgam of neo-US *avant* and the spatial and architectural elements more often associated with European art music.

This healthy flowering of talent was given an incalculable boost by the establishment, in Munich, of the record label ECM by Manfred Eicher, who favoured a full, atmospheric sound, with plenty of space around each instrument to achieve high aural definition.

Under Eicher's careful direction, several European talents emerged on the ECM label in the seventies and eighties, while a number of hitherto undervalued Stateside musicians such as Ralph Towner, Keith Jarrett, Chick Corea, Gary Burton, Jack deJohnette, Paul Motian and Bennie Maupin made important and ground-breaking albums for the label. Ex-Miles Davis bassist, Englishman Dave Holland, was an early beneficiary of the label's attention, and later on John Surman developed both his compositional and multi-instrumental powers on a series of elusively beautiful albums. Another bassist, the German Eberhard Weber, was responsible for the first ECM 'breakthrough' album when his *Colours of Chloe* set the tone for a whole wave of ambient music over attractive ostantino patterns, some of which came dangerously close to pretty colour patterns rather than emotionally or intellectually engaging music. But, more than any others, it was Jarrett, guitarist Pat Metheny and saxophonist Jan Garbarek which made ECM's future safe and set the style for good.

Jarrett's best-selling solo con-

Wynton Marsalis, group leader and jazz spokesman: at the beginning of the 1980s, he seemed the obvious candidate to lead jazz into the future. Today, no-one is so sure. That uncertainty can only be a good thing for such a changeable, will-o-the-wisp entity as jazz.

certs, Metheny's widely popular and influential group, which toured the world in the seventies and eighties and set the tone for meaningful group interplay in the netherworld of pop/jazz fusion without the high-decibel overkill of the early fusion bands, and Garbarek's spare, rich playing in somewhat bleak musical landscapes, all proved vastly impressive with listeners, critics and musicians alike. Each player represented the triumph of personal vision and integrity over more venal and short-term pursuits. Also pleasing was the fact that all three players stayed with ECM for many years and developed increasingly adventurous approaches: the exact reverse of most career patterns. Metheny later developed a curious but rewarding twin career by making more pop-oriented albums for the US WEA record label, investing much subtle quality in the ostensibly bland musical surroundings, while occasionally letting loose on a scorching avant-garde date such as *Song X*, made with Ornette Coleman.

Today, European musicians playing within the jazz tradition are quite proud of their independence from the US scene and their different cultural identiy. But it was through the pioneering efforts of the players from the sixties and seventies, on labels such as ECM, Enja, Soul Note and ICP, that these young musicians enjoy that status. The rapid evolution of a new generation of highly talented players in Great Britain, for example – such as Andy Sheppard, Courtney Pine, Jason Rebello, Tommy Smith, Clark Tracy, Loose Tubes, Django Bates and Roadside Picnic – is directly attributable to the extraordinary dedication and talent, as well as sheer bloody-minded perseverance, of an earlier and much less fashionable set of unsung European pioneers.

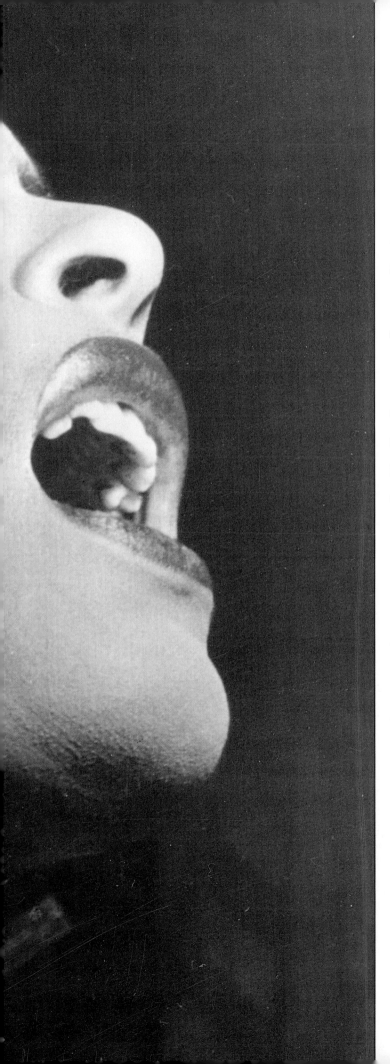

the vocalists

'I had two separate reviews from the same concert – top reviewers. One said I looked great but I didn't fulfill my capacity; in other words, I didn't sing that good, but I sure looked good. The other one said I didn't look too hot but, boy, could I sing.'

– Sheila Jordan

IN JAZZ HISTORY, the major vocalists of any one period have, on the whole, reflected the prevailing instrumental styles of the time. While it has been the role of seminal personalities on each instrument, or prescient bandleaders and their arrangers, to advance the technical and stylistic basis of the music from New Orleans onwards, there has been little incentive for singers to do a great deal more than interpret the popular songs of the day. A singer is born with a sound – the voice – and while the range and versatility of the voice can be worked on, and a technique acquired, the essence of that personal sound is unchanging. The singer is also primarily concerned with delivering the melody and the sense of the lyrics in an affecting and, if possible, moving way. The style of presentation can be modified – singing with or without a vibrato, for example, or using different types of phrasing – but the basic aims of the vocalist are constant.

Left: *Billie Holiday: the voice of jazz.*

Popular music in this century has been dominated by the voice, while jazz has seen a non-vocal hegemony. It is, therefore, hardly surprising that most vocalists generally accepted as jazz singers have to strike an often uneasy balance between the sometimes conflicting demands of the two worlds. Vocal improvisation in the popular music business is about as welcome as Joe Stalin at the Leon Trotsky Remembrance Tea Party, while the average pop singers of the day, from Rudy Vallee through to Madonna, approach their material from an entirely different tradition – that of Tin Pan Alley. However, someone with jazz credentials has to move forward in a way which will satisfy both the demands of Tin Pan Alley and the need to create vocal music of lasting value in a manner which demonstrates real interpretive ability, a feel for the rhythm of jazz, a soul which is drenched in the blues (even if the songs being sung are a million miles from the blues), and a voice which can open the listener up. The difference between singing within the blues and jazz tradition and singing out of Tin Pan Alley is the difference between telling people the truth and keeping them happy.

LOUIS: THE FOUNTAINHEAD

The vocal innovators in jazz have, by and large, been great intrumentalists as well, and the first such artist was Louis Armstrong. Up to the advent of Louis' voice on records, there was no jazz vocal tradition: one either sang Tin Pan Alley or one sang 'race' (i.e. blues). Armstrong, with his first vocals on record in February 1926, created a genre, but went further than that: on the song *Heebie Jeebies*, he invented a type of wordless vocalising clearly in imitation of instrumental improvisation which was to revolutionize popular singing and indelibly mark all subsequent jazz vocal styles. Louis had all the qualities with which to bring this off: his voice, a gruff, blues-based shout in his early years, lent itself to use as an extra instrument, while his delivery of song lyrics had all the unerring phrasing ability that so distinguished his trumpet playing. Louis also had the priceless ability for unfettered communication of his enormously engaging spirit and enthusiasm.

For many years, Armstrong's singing was looked upon by critics of the music as being of distinctly secondary importance to his trumpet playing: his contribution as a vocalist was grossly undervalued. But in the 1950s, after close to three decades at the top of his profession, Louis began to receive his due recognition as a complete musician and performer. The timbre of his voice had gradually changed over the years, and he had brought an increasing simplicity of phrasing to his vocals, as in his trumpet-playing. What Armstrong was doing was reducing his approach to its essence, and taking the best parts along with him, just as he had on the trumpet. It is no chance thing that, in the 1950s and 1960s, Armstrong found far greater public success from people in every walk of life than ever before.

Louis' utter vocal ease, personal warmth and impeccable phrasing can be heard in his duets with Ella Fitzgerald, where Louis briefly escapes his normal concert repertoire of New Orleans classics and tackles popular songs by composers such as Gershwin, Kern, Porter and others. Singing such familar material as this, his uniquely beautiful tone, overflowing with

emotion in a wonderfully controlled fashion, makes a lasting impression.

One other great instrumentalist of the late twenties and early thirties, trombonist Jack Teagarden, also had an incalculable impact on jazz vocals. Teagarden was certainly the first great trombone stylist in jazz, with an effortless technique, a sound as smooth and mellow as the finest whisky, and a lazy, easy-going way of phrasing a melody and subsequent paraphrases which sounded like an intimate conversation with an old friend. His singing was the musical equivalent of a big, lazy smile, and it brought him wide fame, with a

All-Stars was a version of *Rockin' Chair* where his straight-man vocals, in a lazy Texan drawl, fitted Louis' bantering replies like an old glove.

The swing era saw the continuing expansion of the number of vocalist-instrumentalists, cast mostly in the Armstrong mould – people such as Wingy Manone,

The rise of the big band jazz vocalist was in some ways anticipated by Duke Ellington who, by 1927, had already recorded the first wordless vocal (by Adelaide Hall) to a jazz melody on *Creole Love Call*. In February 1931, he hired Ivie Anderson, a cultivated and vivacious young woman who was just 23, although she was an

gracefulness of phrasing and rhythmic ease meant that ballads stayed afloat rather than sagged in the middle, and swing numbers swung from the vocalist down, rather than having the lyrics dragged along by the band. Anderson was a strikingly beautiful woman who had many hits with Ellington, including a version of *Stormy Weather* which became almost as famous as the original by Ethel Waters; the first and best recording in 1932 of Duke's *It Don't Mean a Thing (If It Ain't Got That Swing)*; a wholly convincing blues performance in 1941 of *Rocks In My Bed*; and one of the truly great ballad performances in *I Got It Bad (And That Ain't Good)* from the same year. On a track such as this she combined the technical confidence of Ella and the emotional impact of Billie Holiday.

In 1929 Paul Whiteman took on a new female vocalist, Mildred Bailey, to supplement his 'Rhythm Boys' vocal team of Bing Crosby and Bailey's brother, Al Rinker. She proved to be not only a lot more than a novelty attraction, but also the first white singer to fully grasp and subsequently project the message of negro jazz and blues. Bucklin Moon described her as a singer with complete stylistic integrity: 'she never made a song that didn't have her name on it indelibly.' Her voice was light, warm and very expressive, while her diction and phrasing were impeccable. Unfortunately, Bailey was never a particularly happy woman and always deeply dissatisfied with her looks: she was naturally given to plumpness, and fretted about it constantly. Her longstanding marriage to vibraphone player Red Norvo, and the group they led subsequent to her Whiteman days, foundered in 1939. Between then and her death in 1951, through heart failure, she performed as a solo artist with backing trio.

Bailey was a superb vocalist

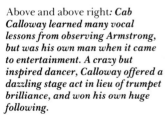

Above and above right: Cab Calloway learned many vocal lessons from observing Armstrong, but was his own man when it came to entertainment. A crazy but inspired dancer, Calloway offered a dazzling stage act in lieu of trumpet brilliance, and won his own huge following.

Left: Louis Armstrong, the first great vocalist in the history of the music. Without Louis, there would be no jazz vocal tradition.

version of *Basin Street Blues* making his name. The song would be associated with his honeyed baritone voice for the rest of his life.

In 1947, after a long spell leading his own big band, Teagarden joined the newly-formed Louis Armstrong All-Stars, a small-group brought together after the demise of Louis' own large ensemble. Among other highlights of Big T's four years in the

Oran 'Hot Lips' Page and even Fats Waller. Waller's humour was certainly his own, but his style can be traced right back to Louis's. There are also significant traces of Armstrong's and Teagarden's approach in the mature singing style of Bing Crosby, who had started as a singer with the Paul Whiteman band. Crosby's younger brother, Bob, led a white Dixieland band, rooted in New Orleans jazz, in the 1930s.

experienced revue artiste by this time. Although Ellington had an uncanny ability to pick undistinguished singers for his band, Ivie Anderson was something special. It is clear that Duke recognized this too, because she stayed with the band right up until 1942, when poor health finally forced her to pursue a less strenuous lifestyle. Her voice was unusually clear and full without her ever resorting to yelling, or 'belting it'; her natural

with much to communicate, and in her music perhaps became the person she wanted to be in real life. Her life was something else again, however. A person capable of intense jealousies, she was particularly envious of Billie Holiday's talent, and at one time, in a rather ill-conceived act of vindictiveness, hired Holiday's out-of-work mother as a cook and maid, only to call her the laziest and most slovenly she had ever had. Inevitably, the cook's daughter's name would be denigrated as well. Sadie Holiday left after a very brief employment.

Another singer capable of having a devastating impact on the listener was Lee Wiley. Like Bailey, she had mixed white and American-Indian parentage. But her voice and her career were quite different. While Bailey had a clear, high voice, Wiley had a smoky contralto which, used with a well-controlled vibrato and often set in intimate small-group surroundings, communicated an overpowering sense of the singer addressing you, and only you, in the whole world. A fan once described the effect: 'She makes you hurt more and more with the remembrance of other never-to-be-recaptured nights. Lee Wiley can do that to you – damn her! But damn her gently . . .'

Wiley sang in a number of bands, but made her breakthrough as a lead with small combos such as guitarist Eddie Condon's. The co-composer of the hit *Anytime, Anyday, Anywhere*, she ran a short-lived band with an equally short-lived husband, pianist Jess Stacy, in the mid-forties. Stacy afterwards referred to this time as 'The Wiley

Mildred Bailey was a singer of real class during her heyday in the thirties and forties. She had unfailing verve and charm, and could supply the message in a song as few others could.

Incident'. Her semi-permanent retirement from the music business came at the end of the forties when she married a millionaire. For the four years before her death in 1975, she revived her recording career to the delight of her now middle-aged fans, and added to what was a relatively small recorded legacy for such a major singer.

Cab Calloway was a bandleader and vocalist who learned in equal measure from Louis Armstrong and Duke Ellington. He discovered much about being a front-man and bandleader from playing opposite Duke at the Cotton Club, while he quite consciously adopted Armstrong's scatting technique, making it in time his own as he adapted it to the natural qualities of his own voice. Calloway became an enormous star in the early thirties, and his popularity has rarely been eclipsed since then. Though he specialized in novelty numbers such as *Minnie The Moocher*, *The Lady With The Fan* and *Kickin' The Gong Around*, he was a fine all-round entertainer with a rather bizarre dancing style which could best be described as 'frenetique', a rich light baritone voice which he could use superbly in straight singing when he wanted to, and a band which was never less than excellent. He and Fats Waller both developed their highly individual styles of scat singing in the first years of the thirties, and this was undoubtedly a key element in their enormous public success, which extended far beyond the jazz world.

Many other singers, most of them women, came to the attention of the public through the success of the big bands in the late thirties: some lasted only as long as the bands did, while others went on to bigger things. A few stayed with the music all the way through. Louise Tobin, Martha Tilton and Helen Ward had starring roles with Benny Goodman's orchestra in its prime, and Ward also sang effectively with Goodman's Quartet and Trio.

Jo Stafford and Kay did a similar thing for Tommy Dorsey, Bob Crosby and Glenn Miller. Rosemary Clooney and Lena Horne both started their careers in the jazz world, then graduated to movies and the broader sphere of showbiz. Peggy Lee started with Goodman as well, and for the entire length of her career retained a definite jazz character in her singing, however far her later outlook and repertoire took her away from the jazz mainstream. Helen Humes, a sweet-voiced singer with a naturally happy-go-lucky approach to her craft, progressed from small groups in the early thirties, to replacing Billie Holiday in the Count Basie band in 1938. She stayed on until 1941, providing a lyrical and sweet-voiced foil to the hard-driving blues shouting of 'Little' Jimmy Rushing, the band's resident Kansas City bluesman. Ironically, after leaving Basie, Humes was to become best known for her pioneering r&b vocal work in the mid-forties, although 20 years later she was making jazz records again as the nostalgia market grew, offering appreciation and profit.

Frankie: the man who changed the direction of popular music as surely as had Benny Goodman ten years previously, Sinatra delivered a whole new style to popular balladry, supplying a real alternative to Crosby imitations and straight-on blues bawling. His technical control, and power of dramatic pitch, turned him into a legend.

Two women dominated jazz vocals in the years up to the end of World War 2: Billie Holiday and Ella Fitzgerald (their initial entries into the world of jazz are sketched in Chapter 3). John Hammond, the producer who 'discovered' Holiday, felt Billie was the greatest jazz singer of all, but a difficult person to deal with.

THE INCOMPARABLES: BILLIE HOLIDAY & ELLA FITZGERALD

Holiday had her own reasons for being difficult. An independent-minded person, she had a very tough start in life, with a broken family being just for openers. Carmen McRae said of her in later years, 'As far as I'm concerned, she's her own worst enemy. She's a queer woman. She has temperament. I guess she was born with it – I mean I don't think it's because she's a star. She's been very unhappy for a long time now ... I think all her troubles have stemmed from her unhappiness. I'll say this about her – she sings the way she is. That's really Lady when you hear her on a record.' Basie trumpeter Buck Clayton, however, remembered her differently: 'Billie was great to work with as she was game to do anything that we would do. She would shoot dice with us, joke with us ... we all liked Billie.'

Though the relationship was always platonic, Holiday became particularly close to Lester Young when they were both in the Basie band together in 1937: it was the saxophonist who named her 'Lady Day', while Billie gave Lester the title 'President', or Pres, because to her he was simply the best.

After Basie, Billie became the featured vocalist with Artie Shaw's enormously successful

band. Although Shaw did all he could to protect her, she suffered a stream of humiliations through the blatant racism of the audiences and venue managements on the band's tours. Holiday finally quit and went out on her own. She was to remain a solo headliner for the rest of her career.

Billie's other major problems were twofold: men and drugs. In the forties, both got on top of her in a big way: by the mid-forties she had a major heroin habit, and her husband of the time, trumpeter Joe Guy, was the worst possible influence on her, like most of her men were. In 1947 she was arrested twice for narcotic offences, and served the majority of a 12-month sentence. Her Cabaret Card, the passport to work in New York, was also withdrawn. For the rest of her life, Holiday fought to establish some form of equilibrium in her life, and at one point tried to break her dope habit with large quantities of booze. But she was on a path of irreversible physical decline, as pictures in the mid- to late fifties show. She died in 1959, within months of her friend Lester Young.

The music she made speaks to us like no other's. In it, she communicates herself totally, with no cupidity, no self-consciousness: we hear the depths of her soul open up on every track, whatever the subject of the lyrics. In the process, she opens us up too. This, her gift, is the rarest in all forms of music.

Ella Fitzgerald has also been a consummate musician and artist throughout her long career, and has managed to avoid many of the personal pitfalls Holiday fitfully embraced. Ella's life was by no means easy, having been orphaned at the age of 15, but she had the character to absorb such blows and continue to grow as a human being. The fact that she also continued her artistic growth through over 30 years of singing is a testament not only to her staying power but also to her dedication to her art.

Fitzgerald's career was astutely built from the late forties onwards by her manager and agent, Norman Granz, and she became a pivotal part of his hugely popular 'Jazz At the Philharmonic' tours, which by the end of the fifties had become worldwide events. In addition to her own set with her trio, she would invariably join in on the jam session with greats such as Coleman Hawkins, Dizzy Gillespie, Lester Young, Oscar Peterson and others, scatting through the grand finale, and bringing the house down with her musicianship and onstage charisma.

But Ella's lasting achievement will undoubtedly be the marvellous series of *Songbooks* she recorded for Granz's company, Verve, in the mid-to-late fifties. She did double-lps of composers Cole Porter, Gershwin, Rogers & Hart and Irving Berlin, and a special 4-lp set of Duke Ellington, on which she is accompanied for the majority of it by Ellington and his orchestra. The phenomenal standard of interpretation and sheer vocal beauty is so consistent that even the most phlegmatic listener must wonder how she could possibly do it. The answer probably lies in guitarist Barney Kessel's eloquent

LADY DAY: Billie Holiday *(above)* **first wore a swatch of gardenias in her hair when she appeared at Café Society in New York in 1938. It was to become her trademark throughout the forties, as can be seen** *(left)* **when she joined company with Art Tatum (piano), Big Sid Catlett (drums) and Oscar Pettiford (bass) at the Esquire Jazz Concert in 1944. By the mid-fifties** *(right)* **the years of alcohol and drugs, on which she squandered her earnings, were taking their toll. Yet she was always a great performer and a superb musician. Her accompanist for many years, Bobby Tucker, once said, 'Man, it was a thrill to play for her. She had the greatest conception of a beat I ever heard. It just didn't matter what kind of song she was signin' . . . you could take a metronome and she'd be right there.'**

description of her: 'Singing is her whole life. I remember when we were on tour in Europe with JATP and she and I would get together and have little jam sessions in restaurants and on buses. She would make up lyrics and improvise and sing in the style of other singers and do everything possible with her voice. There is just no limit to her imagination or her interest in singing.'

1940s: FRANKIE AND MR B.

In the forties, a new generation of singers came on the scene, and while women such as Anita O'Day, Betty Carter and Sarah Vaughan did not supersede Ella or Billie, the new influx of male singers swept away the likes of the old swing-style big-band crooners such as Glen Miller's singers, Ray Eberle and Tex Benecke. The black singer with Earl Hines for many years, Billy Eckstine, went on to front his own band and met with unprecedented success, while a skinny white guy called Sinatra, after a stint as the heart throb with Tommy Dorsey's outfit, finally went solo and became the biggest thing since Al Jolson. Both men would dominate big-band male singing styles between them for the next 20 years.

While Sinatra has never regarded himself as a jazz singer, only a jazz-influenced singer, he has explicitly acknowledged a profound debt to Billie Holiday on more than one occasion. Sinatra's sense of rhythmic placement, his ability to vary the given melody to make it better than before, and his unabashed pleasure in swinging, makes this non-jazz singer a damn sight more enjoyable to listen to than many self-professed jazz vocalists. And, regardless of his own per-

THE INCOMPARABLE ELLA: Ella Fitzgerald has for over 50 years graced the music world. She is blessed with a voice of almost unique flexibility, range and beauty. It is a voice made to communicate the pure joy of singing. She is seen here (left) at a late forties concert with her short-lived husband, bassist Ray Brown; (below) in a publicity shot of the early forties; (below right) as a teenager with Chick Webb; (right) as a jamming scat singer with Oscar Peterson, Roy Eldridge and Max Roach.

Nat 'King' Cole graduated from being just a fine jazz pianist to being everybody's favourite romantic balladeer. He is coupled (above) *with an equally romantic Eartha Kitt, while* (right) *he presents to his TV audience the image that echoed around the world.*

sonal ups and downs, his total sincerity in singing a song's lyrics comes across to every honest listener. It is no accident that one of his biggest fans was Lester Young.

Sinatra's greatest follower in the forties was Mel Tormé, and for a short while the younger man rivalled the older in popularity. Tormé's career was faltering by the end of the decade, and he never made the crossover into films that Frankie did. However, in the seventies and eighties, he made a series of vocal records in a recognizable jazz vein, utilizing his fine technique and vocal ebullience to the full.

Billy Eckstine had everything that Sinatra had, only more. If there was any area of Sinatra's singing which could perhaps be improved upon, it was his actual vocal tone. Eckstine had an instrument which could only be listened to in awe: such strength and beauty of tone has rarely been surpassed. Eckstine also had impeccable modern tastes in music, and his big band at one time or another in the forties housed virtually every bop musician worth recording, including Bird and Diz. He recorded pop ballads of the day to keep the money rolling in, but on the road he encouraged his band to play whatever way-out be-bop they wanted. Very few black singers in the years to come remained untouched by Eckstine, especially in his legato approach to a ballad, with a wide, lazy vibrato tail-off to a note making the most of that fine, rich tone. From Joe Williams to Johnny Hartman, the influence was there to be heard.

Eckstine's influence was even discernible in a vocalist who eventually eclipsed him in terms of fame, Nat Cole. Nat started out as a first-rate jazz pianist, cutting some early forties sessions with Lester Young which remain among the best things either men did. Pianist Billy Taylor remembered only good things about his piano playing: 'Nat had that personal thing of his. Art Tatum could cut him up and down anyway you go but Nat had his own thing . . . Nat was one of the greatest pianists for doing things with the blues.' Cole developed from a pianist to a vocalist who accompanied himself on the piano, and from a blues-based vocalist to one who could sing anything at all, but who specialized in ballads. His voice was his greatest ally, closely followed by infallible timing and the same ability to communicate Billie Holiday had. That Nat 'King' Cole chose to do it outside the jazz mainstream, crossing over into the massed ranks of hit-parade lovers, hardly lessens his artistry: it just makes it different. He continued to play jazz piano for the rest of his life, even after his massive hit *Mona Lisa*, but for the most part only in the privacy of his own home.

THE NEW WOMAN

The 1940s was a golden era for female vocalists, with great talents such as Carmen McRae, Sarah Vaughan, Anita O'Day, Betty Carter and June Christy all making their debuts in that decade. O'Day was initially moulded from her experience in such swing bands as Gene Krupa and from her exposure to the black vocalists of her day: she was a naturally gifted improviser, and although she had a small voice and no particular range, her personality shone brilliantly through everything she did, even when confronted with the massed ranks of Stan Kenton's orchestra in the mid-forties. A heroin addict for long stretches of time, she missed years when she could have been developing her career. 'A business like ours can make us easy marks', she once commented. 'Look at me. I was a kid still in my teens when I was singing around those Chicago spots. Then, next thing I knew I'm up there in front of a band, with a trumpet rocking the joint . . . and kids screaming. All that wartime excitement. Then the post-war slump, with its big let-down.'

During the fifties she made a string of worthwhile albums for Norman Granz, and appeared at the Newport Jazz Festival in 1958, making a sensational musical comeback at a time when her personal fortunes were at a low ebb. However, she stuck with the music, even in the teeth of her addiction, and finally came out of the other side more than ten years later, a mature woman and fully-rounded singer. Mary Ann McCall, skilled and sensitive vocalist with Woody Herman and an admirer of Billie Holiday, never got that far: the top vocalist with the public in 1950, she ruined her life and career for a decade with heroin abuse.

The great female singers to emerge in the forties and fifties, Carmen McRae and Sarah Vaughan, were like two sides of a coin. McRae took Billie Holiday as her model, concentrating her considerable powers on refining and deepening her interpretations of songs, lyrically and musically. A pianist who had endless admiration for the new musicians she

heard around the Harlem scene such as Gillespie, Monk and Parker, she was at one time married to the drummer Kenny Clarke, and sang with many top bands, but never came into her own until the fifties, when her incomparable gift for painting the complete picture of a song's lyrics became fully grown. She has commented, 'No matter what song I sing the lyrics have to be meaningful and believable – unless, of course, you're doing up-tempo tunes. Then nobody listens to the words.'

Sarah Vaughan, on the other hand, had such a stupendous vocal technique, and such unlimited imagination with which to employ it, that at times she was in danger of losing the import of the song. She has always said that she thinks in terms of an instrument, and that melody lines which would sound equally valid on a saxophone or trumpet come naturally to her inner ear. From the beginning, after a triumph at an Apollo Amateur Night in 1942, she had fallen in with the be-boppers by taking Billy Eckstine's advice and joining the Earl Hines band as second vocalist, at a time when the Hines band was full of young rebels. She also went with Eckstine when he formed his own band, thrilled to be playing with such great musicians – 'I thought Bird and Diz were the end. I was singing more off key than on. I think their playing influenced my singing. Horn always influenced me more than voices.'

Vaughan also used key bop arrangers on her own dates, including Tadd Dameron. In fact Dameron was instrumental in Sarah developing her vocal tech-

Three all-time giants in the vocal world: l to r *Mel Tormé, Sarah Vaughan and Billy Eckstine, singing for the war effort in the mid-forties. All had to come to terms with rapidly-changing fads and tastes.*

nique beyond what others had done before: 'Breath control was the most important thing if you had the other things', he once said. 'I would work with . . . Sarah and Billy, and tell them to think this way – sound the note, then bring it out, then let it slide back.'

Vaughan eventually carved such a reputation that she could go out as a solo, and in the fifties she created two parallel careers for herself – one as a successful popular singer, and one as an out-and-out jazz singer, willing

and able to jam with the likes of Clifford Brown, Cannonball Adderley and others. By this stage she became known as 'The Divine One' and 'Sassy', and her cascading inventions across the melodies and lyrics of the songs she sang were an innovation unmatched by any singer of the period. Admired by musicians and public alike, she was a clear product of the new music of the forties.

Of the others who established reputations in that decade, the

fine voice and interpretive ability of Betty Carter, and the cheek, whimsy and sheer joie-de-vivre, as well as the unique vocal timbre of Nellie Lutcher stand out. Lutcher enjoyed tremendous popularity as the forties came to a close. Lutcher had a unique sound, an engagingly coy delivery, a lively rhythmic attack in her voice and at the piano, and a fine line in self-penned songs. She is one of the very few who have successfully balanced verbal humour and outstanding

musicianship. Slim Gaillard managed the same difficult feat although Gaillard took the earthy humour that was Lutcher's stock in trade as a mere starting-point for insane and inspired ramblings into anarchic vocalese which occasionally bordered on a benevolent existentialism. What is more profound than *Opera In Vout*, or *Avocado Seed Soup Symphony*? Or as black in its humour as *Dunkin' Bagels*?

FIFTIES MODERN

The fifties saw few new male vocalists successfully emerge, although Joe Williams, a big-boned and big-toned urban blues singer who had been around for most of the previous decade, finally achieved his international breakthrough with his recording for Count Basie of an old Memphis Slim number, *Everyday (I Have The Blues)*. However, three others who first made a splash in this decade revealed not only a new modernity in vocal outlook, but also gave an indication as to how self-conscious and inward-looking jazz was becoming in the wake of the bop and cool movements. Eddie Jefferson, King Pleasure and Jon Hendricks all, at some time during the fifties, put on record vocal transcriptions of previous instrumental hit solos. Jefferson was probably the first to do it, and King Pleasure had a minor hit himself with his version of *Parker's Mood*, the famous slow blues by Charlie Parker. But it was probably Jon Hendricks who had the most lasting impact and took the technique further than anyone had previously.

Carmen McRae, a singer of rare depth, elegance and style, came to the fore in the 1940s and was adored by fellow-musicians ever after. Although she took Billie Holiday as her model, she developed her own unique style.

This is more than partly due to his forming in the late fifties the influential vocal trio, Lambert, Hendricks and Ross (later Lambert, Hendricks and Bavan), made up of himself, tenor Dave Lambert and Scottish singer Annie Ross. Some aspects of their work were derived directly from the three-part harmony groups of the swing era such as the Boswell Sisters, The Andrew Sisters, The Mills Brothers and The Ink Spots. But Hendricks radically rethought this tradition. Taking whole arrangements, plus perhaps the main three solos, from an instrumental hit, the group would sing their way, first in three-part harmony, then later in individual 'solos', right through the pieces with just a rhythm section accompaniment to keep them afloat. It was an extraordinary achievement at the time, although today, with studio multitracking of one voice a commonplace, the effect is nowhere near as striking. Still, when at their best, the panache, humour and excitement they could generate makes them worthy of remembrance, and their hits such as *Yeah-Yeah!* and *Jumpin' At The Woodside* are still played today. The group disbanded in 1964 and never re-formed. Dave Lambert died in 1966 in a freak pedestrian accident involving a reversing lorry.

The fifties saw a number of richly talented and very individualistic female singers come to the fore, even in the teeth of increasingly tired big-band arrangements, stale repertoire and the advent of rock & roll. Abbey Lincoln, Morgana King, Lorez Alexander and Dakota Staton all made their debut in this time, and all but Lincoln continued to use the updated big-band arrangements and large-voiced interpretations of thirties and forties standards well into the sixties. Lincoln, however, came quickly to detest this early phase

of her career: 'They put me into a Marilyn Monroe-type dress and they coached me in dramatics, classical singing, and diction. I was told to "sound like a negro" when I spoke and I sang the titillating standards and phony folk tunes.'

What Lincoln discovered through people such as her husband-to-be Max Roach was that it was not only possible, but desirable, to discover her pride in what she was, as a woman and as a black. She made a decision around 1960 that she 'would not again sing anything that wasn't meaningful to me.' Accordingly, as the new decade started, she made an album, *We Insist*, with Max Roach and singer and songwriter Oscar Brown Jr, which had a startling impact on its audience. Its overt politicization and confrontation of issues such as slavery, the state of Africa (especially South Africa), and the demand for freedom within the US, was unprecedented in its way. More than that, the music used to convey these feelings and viewpoints was of an extraordinarily high quality. On *Straight Ahead*, Lincoln's follow-up album, and the first as a leader since her cabaret days, these issues were once again targeted, with the singer taking the spotlight throughout. Her dark, rich voice and amazing emotive strength made her themes a reality for an audience which had never had to confront such issues head-on before, and in that way these albums were seminal, just as Max Roach's follow-up, *Percussion Bitter Sweet*, was, both in the power of Lincoln's performance and her intermingling with fine playing from musicians such as Eric Dolphy and Booker Little.

Lincoln, in fact, went on to expand and deepen her role in the rediscovery of the black cultural heritage, ancient and modern, even in 1975 accepting African

names conferred on by her politicians in Guinea and Zaire in recognition of her work. She continues to work today in a refreshingly direct and honest, intelligent manner, not allowing musical or cultural fashions to sway her from her path. This can also be said, for different reasons, of two other fine singers coming to the fore in the sixties, Jeannie Lee and Cleo Laine, both of whom developed incredible vocal dexterity, sophisticated harmonic usage and vividly imaginative arrangements of original material.

Two more fine singers who brought great integrity to their musicianship, and always tried for innovative ways to bring fresh sensation to their listeners, were Sheila Jordan and Helen Merrill. Of the two, Jordan has proved to be the more radical, not just in terms of repertoire but also in terms of what she is prepared to do with it. Very sophisticated harmonically, she manages striking arrangements and bold rewriting of familiar material, or simply writes her own material. Every performance from her is

stimulating and thought-provoking. Her version of *You Are My Sunshine* on a George Russell album in 1961 set everyone on their ear for the almost surrealistic approach from both Russell and herself. Her risk-taking with the melody-line went back to her study of Charlie Parker's music: 'I became so familiar with his music that when I'd hear him play in a club, I'd know when he substituted another bridge or used altered chords. I could tell what the tune was even though he'd give it another name and put a

Sarah Vaughan in England, 1954, accompanied by Joe Benjamin, bass, Coleman Hawkins and Illinois Jacquet, saxophones. Vaughan was the most musician-like of all postwar vocalists, with a phenomenal technique at her disposal.

line to it, because I could hear his chord changes.' After these lessons in musicianship, Jordan was able, when improvising, to 'take liberties with tunes, with melodies, holding them together.' Jordan in the 1960s formed a superb modern quartet with Steve Kuhn which continued to redefine the legitimate musical areas for vocal involvement, while in the eighties she has moved into an even more intimate setting in duet with double bassist Harvey Swartz. Her intelligence and daring have kept her as a vital force.

INDIVIDUALISTS AND ECCENTRICS

Helen Merrill also employs a formidable musical intelligence, but not in such a radical way: her forte is in careful re-evaluation of a song's lyrics and in the strength of its melody line. Her approach has won her many new fans among contemporary musicians.

Neither Nina Simone nor the impish Blossom Dearie took many musical risks, and both singers have inhabited the margins of jazz rather than the mainstream. But both are great individualists in their vocal styles and piano accompaniment, and both create an insane loyalty in their fans. The songwriter and singer Blossom Dearie has an absurdly little-girl voice which profoundly irritates some people, and which rarely comes above a whisper. However, her delivery can be extremely intense, and her honesty can devastate. On a song such as *It Amazes Me*, the

Left: Nina Simone, 1967, in concert. Simone began her career in the late fifties with a deft mixture of old standards, her own arrangements of classical music and a smattering of folk songs. During the sixties she diversified into Kurt Weill and pop repertoire.

unknowing wonder of an ordinary girl in love is so overpowering that the song becomes truly moving. Blossom has also proved to be a dedicated artist, having set up her own record label in the late 1970s in order to continue her career in exactly the way she saw fit.

Nina Simone was born in 1933 and by the age of four was learning the piano. Soon after that she began singing in the local church, and also came under the spell of the great black classical singer, Marian Anderson. As a teenager she continued to study music, and eventually did two years at Juilliard Music School in New York. The importance of this early combination of gospel and classical training can be seen all the way through her subsequent career.

By her mid-twenties, she had begun playing in clubs and attracted sufficient praise to get herself signed to a record company. Her rise after that was meteoric: her first album in 1957 had a version of *I Love You, Porgy* which remains today a classic in the field. Sid Mark, a DJ in Philadelphia where Simone was based, recalled the initial struggle with the record company to get that track released: 'The radio audience, responding with a tremendous volume of phone calls, insisted – or rather demanded – that we replay one track – *Porgy* – we did, time and time again. With Nina's permission, I called the record company to report what had happened . . . the voice at the other end then retorted those now famous words . . . "Forget it, kid – it's a local rumble." Needless to say, the "local rumble" sold well over a million.'

With this sort of success so early in her professional career, Simone was coping with unusually heavy pressure to cater to the demands of her vast new audience. It is a measure of her integrity as an artist that the

music she made in the next five years was remarkably consistent, both stylistically and qualitatively. With just one exception (a big-band album), she stuck to her small group arrangements, continued to play the piano and take extended solos when she felt like it, dabbled in her updating of the classics, and chose her repertoire with no thought to its commercial potential.

Simone possesses a voice which is quite shocking in its darkly evocative ability; similarly, her facial features are arrestingly expressive, while her onstage personality can by turns enthuse a crowd into wild appreciation and cow it into horrified silence. There is a deep disturbance in the Simone voice, especially in the ballads, where songs which were written as Tin Pan Alley fodder or spur-of-the-moment show tunes become frighteningly intense scenarios of a tormented, lonely soul. The only parallel in jazz would be the unbearably intense ballads of Bud Powell's later period, when the pianist seemed to be emptying whole seas of emotions into the tiny, frail melodies he was heaping dark harmonies upon.

By the latter part of the sixties, Simone had moved away from jazz as the mass audience base for straight jazz singers at first crumbled, then collapsed. Since then, she has managed to sustain a career which straddles repertoire from both, while never really focusing her enormous talent in a way which would perhaps make her a leader and innovator rather than a stylist.

Latin American music was another strain of music which had a big impact on instrumental jazz in the sixties, then went on to produce gifted vocalists whose work, however marginal, helped

create a lasting body of music. Astrud Gilberto was the first, recording almost accidentally with her then-husband, Joao, and Stan Getz.

BLAME IT ON THE BOSSA NOVA!

She found herself no longer a singing housewife but an internationally acclaimed artist backed by huge orchestras, strings, trumpets and other impediments. Somehow, her naivety helped her to survive and win the day as she tackled progressively newer repertoire, but by the seventies

June Christy, along with Anita O'Day Stan Kenton's best and most distinctive singer, Christy developed her own large personal following which stayed with her long after she quit Kenton.

she had disappeared from the scene, only to re-emerge in the 1980s essentially unchanged, and as affecting as ever. Flora Purim came to the attention of the jazz public when the Latin influence in jazz was not constricted to a particular rhythmic fad, but was more widespread, and so her mixture of wordless vocals and beautifully poised lyrical singing, often with groups as sophisticated as Chick Corea's and Airto Moreira's, was accepted at face value.

THE MODERN SCENE

Similarly, Urszula Dudziak came to the US from her native Poland with her husband Michal Urbaniak in 1974, and after thorough musical training in classical theory and practice. Both Dudziak and Urbaniak, like the Brazilians, were bringing a new slant to jazz, but from a very different tradition – that of the formal music of the old world. Their new angle in modern sounds, her stratospheric vocals, which often involved heavy use of synthesizers (as had Annette Peacock's a number of years earlier), built up a substantial and loyal following.

The careers of both Ray Charles and Bobby McFerrin, though quite different in their courses, demonstrate the amazing diversity of style and content to be found in modern jazz vocals. Both men are consummate technicians with a truly overwhelming ability to control and project their voice into virtually any musical style or situation they choose to involve themselves in – as opposed to, say, Harry Connick Jnr, who is more or less an updated crooner in the Tormé-Sinatra mould. Charles was an innovative singer, combining the sounds of the church and the blues, and a fine pianist who was quite at home making records with his friends Quincy Jones or Milt Jackson. But his vocal conception, and his musical personality are simply too vast to be fitted into a category labelled 'jazz'. His incredible versatility, his ability to sing virtually any-

thing and make it a moving experience for the listener, and his restless desire to communicate to as many people as possible, kept him well clear of the jazz fraternity. Yet he regularly played the Newport Jazz Festival, always had jazz musicians in his touring bands, and used all the jazz elements of vocalizing, including the ability to reinvent the original melodic and rhythmic patterns of a song and so present it to the listener as a wholly new experience.

Bobby McFerrin's career is at a much earlier stage of development than Ray Charles', but he has already moved completely away from the conventional idea of a jazz vocalist. He takes 'the voice as an instrument' to its logical conclusion, and uses his own voice to create wonderful abstract patterns of human tones. At one time, he was heavily committed to spontaneous live and unaccompanied performances which were breathtaking in their audacity and thrilling in their musical content. Today, he has developed this approach immensely, and uses the recording studio to overdub his own voice, in all registers and with a bewil-

The Genius', 'Brother' Ray Charles has had an incalculable effect on popular music since the mid fifties. Not content with r&b and soul success, Charles had his biggest hits in country music.

dering array of different timbres, to create whole vocal orchestras. This is an impressive achievement, and McFerrin's projects are all filled with his optimism, sense of fun and frequently devilish sense of humour: all qualities which, added to his deeply serious approach to the actual craft and logistics of singing and performing, become more sharply focused in person at a concert. It remains to be seen whether he has the staying power of a Ray Charles or Nina Simone; however, he seems much too creative an individual to simply fade away into insignificance.

Perhaps the current generation will need to bear in mind the cautionary tale of an afternoon on the band bus of an old Jazz At The Philharmonic tour, somewhere deep in Europe. A young horn player, bored and frustrated with the length of the journey and the lack of anything to do except doze, play cards or drink, was

Far left: Dave Lambert, Annie Ross and Jon Hendricks were the most popular vocal trio in jazz at the close of the fifties. With Yolande Bavan in for Annie Ross, their popularity continued into the 1960s. Left: Astrud Gilberto attained fame almost by accident, but has proved remarkably resilient over the years.

walking up and down the aisle between the seats, playing his instrument, and blowing all the weirdest, most uncomfortable-sounding things he could think of. Everybody ignored him until, finally, he walked up to where Lester Young was sitting, put the bell of his horn to Pres's ear, and let rip with a volley of frenzied runs. At last he relented, and with a glint in his eye, he asked Young what he thought of his playing. Young looked up at him, those lidded eyes masking a world of meaning, and in his quiet, lazy, jaded voice, said: 'OK, but can you tell me a *story*?'

Bobby McFerrin – 'The Voice' – a vocalist of extraordinary power and natural talent. McFerrin has moved into previously unexplored territory, by using his own voice to create abstract patterns of sound.

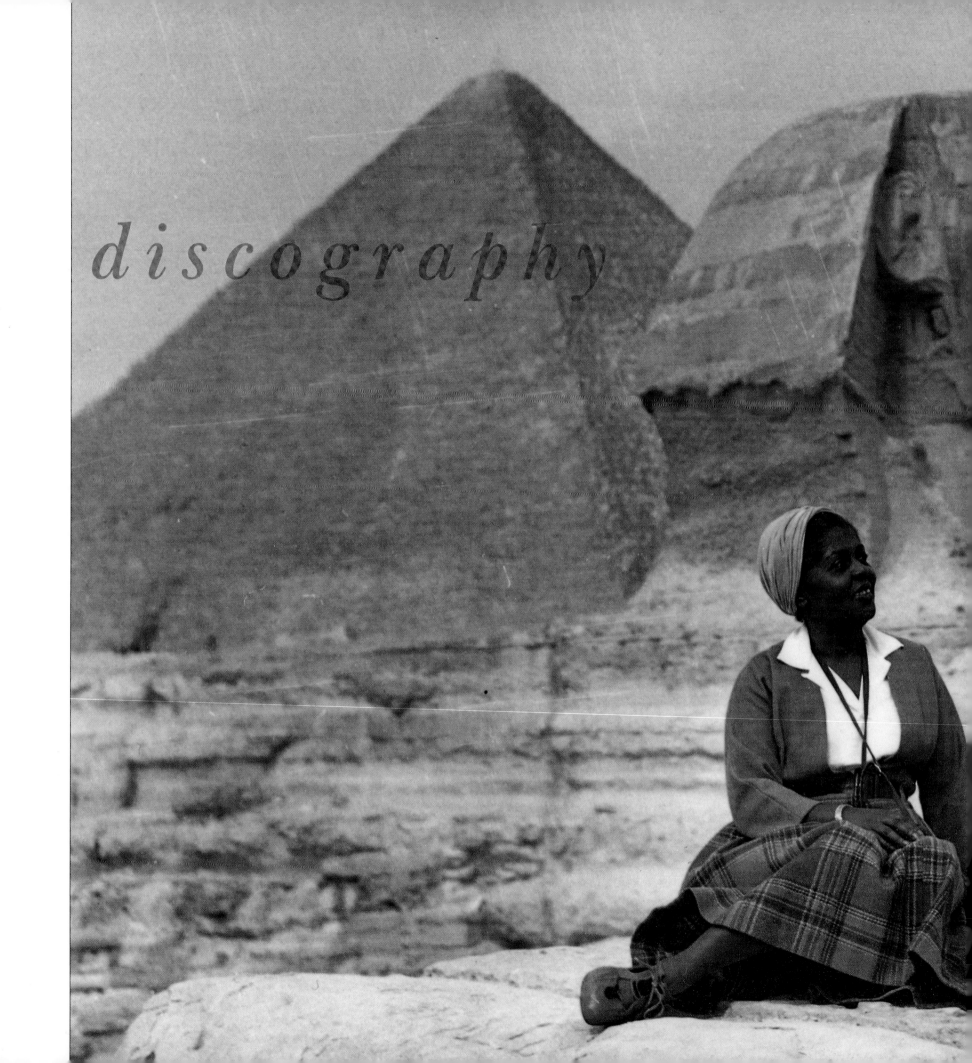

discography

Chapter One

Sidney Bechet:	*The Bluebird Sessions (RCA Bluebird)*
	Sidney Bechet, Vols 1/2 (Blue Note)
	Petite Fleur (Vogue)
Bunk Johnson:	*And His Superior Jazz Band*
	(Contemporary)
Scott Joplin:	*Ragtime Classics (Dick Hyman – RCA)*
Freddie Keppard:	*1924 (with Armstrong, Cook, Red Onion*
	Jazz Babies) (Swaggie)
George Lewis:	*At Herbert Otto's Party (Jazzology)*
Jelly Roll Morton:	*The Complete Bluebird Recordings (RCA/*
	Bluebird)
	Library of Congress 1938 Vols 1-8
	(Swaggie)
	New Orleans Memories 1939 (Commodore)
	Last Band Dates 1940 (Commodore)
King Oliver:	*Oliver's Creole Band 1923 – The Okeh Sides*
	(EMI)
	Oliver's Creole Band 1923 – Gennett Sides
	(CJM)
	The New York Years (1928/30) (RCA
	Bluebird)
Original Dixieland Jazz Band:	*Sensation! (ASV Living Era)*
Kid Ory:	*At Club Hangover Vols 1-6 (Storyville)*
	1944-45 (Arhoolie)
Young Tuxedo Brass:	*Young Tuxedo Brass (Atlantic)*

Chapter Two

Henry 'Red' Allen:	*Meets Kid Ory (Verve)*
Louis Armstrong:	*Hot Fives and Sevens 1925-28 (CBS/*
	Swaggie)
	VSOP Vols 1-6 (CBS)
	& His Orchestra 1929-31 (Swaggie)
	Town Hall Concert 1947 (RCA)
	Soundtrack to 'New Orleans' (Hep)
	Satch Plays Fats (CBS)
	Plays W.C. Handy (CBS)
Bix Beiderbecke:	*Bix & His Gang 1927-28 (Swaggie)*
	Bix & Tram (Swaggie)
	Golden Age of (EMI/MFP)
Hoagy Carmichael:	*Stardust & Much More (RCA Bluebird)*
Eddie Condon:	*Chicago Style (VJM)*
	Town Hall Concerts (Jazzology)
	The Rhythmakers 1932 (VJM)
Johnny Dodds:	*Blue Clarinet Stomp (RCA Bluebird)*
Duke Ellington:	*Early Ellington (RCA Bluebird)*
	Hot From The Cotton Club (EMI)
	Rockin' In Rhythm (Living Era)
Fletcher Henderson:	*A Study In Frustration (CBS)*
Eddie Lang:	*Jazz Guitar Virtuoso (Yazoo)*
McKinney's Cotton Pickers:	*(RCA Bluebird)*
Jimmy Noone:	*Apex Club Orchestra Vols 1-4 (Swaggie)*
Muggsy Spanier:	*Hot Horn 1944 (Commodore)*

Jack Teagarden:	*King of the Blues Trombone (Columbia)*
	That's A Serious Thing (RCA Bluebird)
Stride Pianists:	*Harlem Piano (Good Time Jazz)*
	Harlem Stride Piano Solos (Swaggie)

Chapter Three

Charlie Barnet:	*Clap Hands, Here Comes Charlie (RCA*
	Bluebird)
Count Basie:	*Swingin' The Blues (Affinity)*
	Swingin' At The Daisy Chain (Affinity)
	Count Basie Vols 1-6 (1936-1943) (CBS)
	Good Mornin' Blues (Affinity)
Bunny Berigan:	*I Can't Get Started (RCA Bluebird)*
Cab Calloway:	*Cab & Co (RCA)*
Benny Carter:	*Symphony In Riffs (ASV Living Era)*
Roy Eldridge:	*Roy (CBS)*
	Roy Eldridge 1935-40 (Tax)
Duke Ellington:	*The Small Groups 1934-1939 (CBS)*
	Braggin' In Brass (Tax)
	Brunswick Sessions 1932-35 (Jazz
	Information)
	The Blanton-Webster Band (1940-43)
	(RCA Bluebird)
	Black, Brown & Beige (1944-46) (RCA
	Bluebird)
	Carnegie Hall Concert, January 1943
	(Fantasy)
Tommy Dorsey:	*The Sentimental Fella (RCA)*
Benny Goodman:	*The Complete Small Combinations (RCA)*
	Carnegie Hall Concert 1938 (CBS)
	Rehearsal Sessions 1940 (Jazz Document)
Gene Krupa:	*Let Me Off Uptown (CBS)*
Lionel Hampton:	*Complete Vols 1/2 (RCA)*
Coleman Hawkins:	*Body & Soul (RCA)*
	Hawk In Europe 1934-37 (Living Era)
	Hollywood Stampede (Capitol)
Jimmie Lunceford:	*The Complete (Vols 1-4) (CBS)*
Bennie Moten:	*Moten Stomp (RCA Bluebird)*
Django Reinhardt:	*Golden Age of (EMI)*
	1910-1953 (EMI Manhattan)
Artie Shaw:	*Begin The Beguine (RCA Bluebird)*
Art Tatum:	*The Solo Piano Masterpieces (Pablo)*
Fats Waller:	*The Joint Is Jumpin' (RCA Bluebird)*
	1940-1943 (RCA Bluebird)
Chick Webb:	*In The Groove (Affinity)*
	Stompin' At The Savoy (Collector's Classics)
Teddy Wilson/Billie Holiday:	*The Essential Billie Holiday Vols 1-4(CBS)*
Lester Young:	*At His Very Best (Keynote Sessions) (Philips)*
	Story Vols 1-5 (CBS)
	Savoy Masters (Savoy)

Chapter Four

Albert Ammons	*Boogie Woogie Classics (Blue Note)*

Previous page: Two of the wonders of the world: Louis Armstrong plays his trumpet in front of the Pyramids.

Blind Blake	*Ragtime Guitar's Foremost Fingerpicker (Yazoo)*
Big Bill Broonzy:	*Young Big Bill (Yazoo)*
	Last Sessions Vols 1-3 (Verve)
Ida Cox:	*Vols 1 & 2 (Fountain)*
Blind Boy Fuller:	*1935-40 (Arhoolie)*
Jesse Fuller:	*Frisco Blues (Arhoolie)*
Alberta Hunter	*Classic Alberta Hunter (Stash)*
Mississippi John Hurt:	*1928 Sessions (Yazoo)*
Skip James:	*I'm So Glad (Vanguard)*
	Complete 1931 Sessions (Yazoo)
Blind Lemon Jefferson:	*Vols 1-3 (Roots)*
	King Of The Country Blues (Yazoo)
Robert Johnson:	*The Complete (CBS)*
Pete Johnson:	*Boogie Woogie Classics (Blue Note)*
Blind Willie Johnson:	*Praise God I'm Satisfied (Yazoo)*
Tommy Johnson:	*Complete (Wolf)*
Leadbelly:	*Last Sessions Vols 1-4 (Folkways)*
Furry Lewis:	*In His Prime 1927-29 (Yazoo)*
	Back On My Feet Again (Prestige)
Meade Lux Lewis:	*Complete Blue Note Sessions (Mosaic)*
Charley Patton:	*Founder of The Delta Blues (Yazoo)*
Ma Rainey:	*Ma Rainey's Black Bottom (Yazoo)*
Tampa Red:	*Guitar Wizard (Arhoolie/Blues Classics)*
Bessie Smith:	*Any Woman's Blues (CBS)*
	The Empress (CBS)
	Empty Bed Blues (CBS)
	Nobody's Blues But Mine (CBS)
	World's Greatest Blues Singer (CBS)
Son House:	*Son House (CBS)*
Frank Stokes:	*Creator of the Memphis Blues (Yazoo)*
Bukka White:	*Sky Songs Vols 1 & 2 (Arhoolie)*
	Aberdeen Mississippi Blues (Travelin' Man)
Robert Wilkins:	*The Original Rolling Stone (Yazoo)*

Chapter Five

Graeme Bell:	*And His Australian Jazz Band (Swaggie)*
Charlie Christian:	*Solo Flight (CBS/Columbia)*
	At Minton's 1941 (Vogue)
Kenny Clarke:	*Meets The Detroit Jazzmen (Savoy)*
Tadd Dameron:	*Fontainebleau (Prestige)*
	Mating Call (Prestige)
Billy Eckstine:	*Mr B & The Band (Savoy)*
Dizzy Gillespie:	*Dizziest (RCA Bluebird)*
	Groovin' High (Discovery)
	One Night At Birdland (With Parker) (CBS)
	Pleyel Concert 1953 (Vogue)
	Jazz At Massey Hall 1953 (Fantasy)
Dexter Gordon:	*Long Tall Dexter (Savoy)*
	The Chase (with Wardell Gray) (Spotlight)
Woody Herman:	*The Thundering Herds (CBS)*
Stan Kenton:	*Greatest Hits (Capitol)*
	In Hi-Fi (Capitol)
	1945-47 (Hindsight)
Dodo Marmarosa:	*Dodo's Dance (Spotlite)*

Thelonious Monk:	*Genius of Modern Music Vols 1 & 2 (Blue Note)*
Fats Navarro:	*Fabulous Fats Navarro Vols 1 & 2 (Blue Note)*
	Fat Girl (Savoy)
Charlie Parker:	*The Savoy Masters (Savoy)*
	The Dial Masters (Spotlite)
	Bird At The Roost Vols 1-4 (Savoy)
	Charlie Parker (Prestige)
	On Verve (Verve)
	JATP: Bird & Pres 1949
	Yardbird In Lotusland (Spotlite)
Bud Powell:	*Jazz Giant (Verve)*
	The Genius of (Verve)
	The Amazing Bud Powell Vols 1-5 (Blue Note)
	Bud Powell Trio (Roulette)
Sonny Stitt:	*Stitt-Powell-J.J. Johnson (Savoy)*
Lennie Tristano:	*Lennie Tristano (Atlantic)*

Chapter Six

Cannonball Adderley:	*Cannonball & Coltrane (Mercury)*
	Somethin' Else! (Blue Note)
Chet Baker:	*Chet (Riverside)*
	Once Upon A Summertime (Fantasy)
Count Basie:	*Dance Session Vols 1 & 2 (Verve)*
	The Atomic Mr Basie (Roulette)
	Count Basie Swings, Joe Williams Sings (Verve)
Art Blakey:	*Jazz Messengers At The Cafe Bohemia (Blue Note)*
	Moanin' (Blue Note)
	Caravan (Riverside)
	A Night At Birdland (Blue Note)
	Free For All (Blue Note)
Ruby Braff:	*Hustlin' & Bustlin' (Black Lion)*
Clifford Brown:	*Brownie: The Complete Emarcy Sessions (Emarcy)*
	Memorial Album (Blue Note)
	Clifford Brown/Max Roach In Concert (GNP)
Dave Brubeck:	*At Oberlin (Fantasy)*
	Jazz Goes To College
	Jazz: Red Hot & Cool
	Time Out
Serge Chaloff:	*Fable Of Mabel (Black Lion)*
	Blue Serge (Capitol/Affinity)
John Coltrane:	*Lush Life (Prestige)*
	Soultrane (Prestige)
	Traneing In (Prestige)
	Giant Steps (Atlantic)
Miles Davis:	*Complete Prestige Sessions (Prestige)*
	Round About Midnight (CBS)
	Milestones (CBS)
	Miles Ahead (with Gil Evans) (CBS)

Porgy & Bess (with Gil Evans) (CBS)
1958 Miles (CBS)
Kind of Blue (CBS)
Sketches of Spain (CBS)
& Coltrane in Sweden 1960 (Dragon)
Someday My Prince Will Come (CBS)

Duke Ellington:
Masterpieces (CBS)
At Newport 1956 (CBS)
Such Sweet Thunder (CBS)

Gil Evans: Big Stuff (Prestige)
Tal Farlow: Autumn In New York (Verve)
Erroll Garner: Misty (Mercury)
Afternoon Of An Elf (Mercury)
Concert By The Sea (CBS)

Stan Getz: Complete Storyville Sessions (Roulette)
At The Opera House (with J.J. Johnson)
At The Shrine (Verve)
The Steamer (Verve)

Dizzy Gillespie: At Newport 1957 (Verve)
Trumpet Kings (with Roy Eldridge) (Verve)
An Electrifying Evening With (Verve)
Portrait of Duke Ellington (Verve)

Wardell Gray: Wardell Gray (Spotlite)
Johnny Griffin: A Blowing Session (Blue Note)
Bobby Hackett: Gotham Jazz Scene (Capitol)
Chico Hamilton: Gongs East! (Warner Bros)
Milt Jackson: Bean Bags (with Coleman Hawkins)
(Atlantic)
Bags Meets Wes (Riverside)
Memories of Thelonious Sphere Monk
(Pablo)

Ahmad Jamal: But Not For Me (Vogue/Argo)
Portfolio (Vogue/Argo)

J.J. Johnson: Say When (RCA Bluebird)
Lee Konitz: At Storyville (Black Lion)
Sax Of A Kind – Konitz In Sweden (Dragon)

Shelly Manne: At The Blackhawk Vols 1-4
2,3,4 (Impulse)

Charles Mingus: The Clown
Pithecanthropus Erectus
Blues & Roots

Modern Jazz Quartet: Django (Prestige)
No Sun In Venice (Atlantic)
Odds Against Tomorrow (United Artists/
EMI)

Thelonious Monk: Monk's Music (Riverside)
Brilliant Corners (Riverside)
The Unique (Riverside)

Wes Montgomery: Full House (Riverside)
Dynamic Duo (with Jimmy Smith) (Verve)

Gerry Mulligan: Reunion (with Chet Baker) (Pacific/EMI)
Meets Thelonious Monk (Riverside)
Two of a Mind (with Paul Desmond)
(RCA Bluebird)

Art Pepper: Meets The Rhythm Section (Contemporary)
Smack Up! (Contemporary)

Oscar Peterson: In Concert (Verve)
Trio Plus One (Clark Terry) (Mercury)
Shorty Rogers: Short Stops (RCA Bluebird)
Sonny Rollins: Saxophone Colossus (Prestige)
Worktime (Prestige)
A Night At The Village Vanguard
(Blue Note)
George Russell: The Jazz Workshop (RCA Bluebird)
Jazz In The Space Age (Riverside)
Stratusphunk (Riverside)
Horace Silver: Best of Horace Silver Vols 1 & 2 (Blue Note)
Zoot Sims: Morning Fun (with Bob Brookmeyer)
(Black Lion)
Jimmy Smith: Crazy Baby! (Blue Note)
Plays Fats Waller (Blue Note)
Organ Grinder Swing (Verve)
Cal Tjader: Concert By The Sea (Fantasy)
Ben Webster: Meets Coleman Hawkins (Verve)
Meets Gerry Mulligan (Verve)
Lester Young: And The Oscar Peterson Trio (Verve)

Chapter Seven

Earl Bostic: Blows A Fuse (Charly)
Pete Brown: All-Stars at Newport 1957 (Verve)
Roy Brown: Boogie At Midnight (Charly)
Ray Charles: The Right Time (Atlantic)
Live! (Atlantic)
Greatest Country & Western Hits (Castle)
Albert Collins: Ice Pickin' (Alligator)
Arnett Cobb: Complete Apollo Sessions (Vogue)
Robert Cray: Strong Persuader (Mercury)
Arthur 'Big Boy' Crudup: Crudup's Rockin' Blues (RCA)
Willie Dixon: Chess Masters (Chess)
Champion Jack Dupree: Blues From The Gutter (Atlantic)
Buddy Guy: Chess Masters (Chess)
Lionel Hampton: Apollo Concert 1945 (Mercury)
Leapin' With Lionel (Affinity)
Wynonie Harris: Mr Blues Is Coming To Town (Route 66)
Z.Z. Hill: Down Home (Malaco)
John Lee Hooker: Boogie Chillun (Charly)
No Friend Around (Charly)
Lightnin' Hopkins: Lightnin' In New York (Candid)
Illinois Jacquet: Fabulous Apollo Sessions (Vogue)
With Jazz At The Philharmonic 1944
(Verve)
Elmore James: Best of (Ace)
Etta James: R&B Dyanmite (Ace)
Louis Jordan: Golden Greats (MCA)
Jivin' With Jordan (Charly)
Albert King: Laundromat Blues (Edsel)
B.B. King: Live At The Regal (MCA)
Now Appearing At Ole Miss (MCA)
Midnight Believer (MCA)
Best of the Memphis Masters (Ace)
J.B. Lenoir: Chess Masters (Chess)

Joe Liggins:	*The Honeydripper (Jukebox Lil)*		*A Love Supreme (Impulse)*
Fred McDowell:	*Keep Your Lamp Trimmed (Arhoolie)*		*Ascension (Impulse)*
Big Jay McNeely:	*Roadhouse Boogie (Saxophonograph)*		*Meditations (Impulse)*
Jack McVea:	*Open The Door, Richard (Jukebox Lil)*		*Live At The Village Vanguard Again*
Big Maybelle:	*The Okeh Sessions (Charly)*		*(Impulse)*
Amos Milburn:	*Chicken Shack Boogie (EMI Fr)*		*Expression (Impulse)*
Lucky Millinder:	*Apollo Jump (Affinity)*	Miles Davis:	*Live At Carnegie Hall*
Johnny Otis:	*Barrelhouse Stomp (Jukebox Lil)*		*Miles Davis In Europe (CBS)*
Jimmy Reed:	*Big Boss Blues (Charly)*		*My Funny Valentine (CBS)*
Magic Sam:	*West Side Soul (Delmark)*		*Miles Smiles (CBS)*
	Magic Sam Live (Delmark)		*Filles De Kilimanjaro*
Memphis Slim:	*Blues Every Which Way (Verve)*	Bill Dixon:	*Intents And Purposes (RCA)*
Otis Spann:	*Otis Spann Is The Blues (Candid)*	Eric Dolphy:	*Far Cry (Prestige)*
	The Blues Never Die (Ace/Prestige)		*At The Five Spot Vols 1-3 (Prestige)*
Koko Taylor:	*Love You Like A Woman (Chess)*		*Conversations (Douglas)*
Big Mama Thornton:	*Ball and Chain (Arhoolie)*		*Iron Man (Douglas)*
Big Joe Turner:	*Boss of the Blues (Atlantic)*		*Out To Lunch (Blue Note)*
	Jumpin' With Joe (Charly)	Duke Ellington:	*Money Jungle (United Artists/EMI)*
T-Bone Walker:	*Stormy Monday (Charly)*		*And John Coltrane (Impulse)*
Dinah Washington:	*Best of (Mercury)*		*And His Mother Called Him Bill (RCA)*
Muddy Waters:	*Best of (Chess)*	Booker Ervin:	*The Freedom & Space Sessions (Prestige)*
	Live at Newport (Chess)	Bill Evans:	*The Village Vanguard Sessions (Riverside)*
	Mud In Your Ear (Muse)		*At Montreux Vols 1 & 2 (Verve)*
Junior Wells:	*Hoodoo Man Blues (Delmark)*		*Conversations With Myself (Verve)*
Robert Pete Williams:	*Those Prison Blues (Arhoolie)*	Gil Evans:	*Out Of The Cool (Impulse)*
Sonny Boy Williamson:	*King Biscuit Time (Arhoolie)*		*Individualism of Gil Evans (Verve)*
Jimmy Witherspoon:	*Monterey Jazz Festival 1958 (Affinity)*	Stan Getz:	*Jazz Samba (Verve)*
Howlin' Wolf:	*Moanin' In The Moonlight (Chess)*		*Focus (Verve)*
	Real Folk Blues (Chess)		*Getz/Gilberto (Verve)*
			Sweet Rain (Verve)
		Dizzy Gillespie:	*Something Old, Something New (Philips)*
Chapter Eight			*The New Continent (Limelight)*
Cannonball Adderley:	*At The Jazz Workshop (Riverside)*	Dexter Gordon:	*Go (Blue Note)*
	Jazz Workshop Revisited (Riverside/	Milford Graves:	*You Never Heard Such Sounds In Your Life*
	Landmark)		*(ESP)*
Art Ensemble of Chicago:	*A Jackson In Your House (Byg/Affinity)*	Grant Green:	*Idle Moments (Blue Note)*
	Message To Our Folks (Byg/Affinity)	Charlie Haden:	*Liberation Music Orchestra (Impulse)*
Albert Ayler:	*Spiritual Unity (ESP)*	Herbie Hancock:	*Maiden Voyage (Blue Note)*
	Live In Greenwich Village (Impulse)		*Takin' Off (Blue Note)*
	My Name Is Albert Ayler (Debut)	Joe Harriott:	*Free Form (Jazzland)*
Paul Bley:	*With Gary Peacock (ECM)*	Coleman Hawkins:	*Live At The Village Gate (Verve)*
	Barrage (ESP)	Joe Henderson:	*Inner Urge (Blue Note)*
Lester Bowie:	*Numbers 1 & 2 (Nessa)*	Andrew Hill:	*Point of Departure (Blue Note)*
Anthony Braxton:	*Three Compositions (Delmark)*		*Judgement! (Blue Note)*
Marion Brown:	*Three For Shepp (Impulse)*	Joseph Jarman:	*Song For (Delmark)*
Kenny Burrell:	*Guitar Forms (Verve)*		*As If It Were The Sessions (Delmark)*
Gary Burton:	*A Genuine Tong Funeral (RCA)*	Roland Kirk:	*Rip, Rig & Panic (Limelite)*
	Duster (RCA)		*Gifts And Messages (Mercury)*
Don Cherry:	*New York Eye & Ear Control (ESP)*		*Volunteered Slavery (Atlantic)*
Ornette Coleman:	*The Shape Of Jazz To Come (Atlantic)*	Steve Lacy:	*The Straight Horn of (Candid)*
	Change of The Century (Atlantic)	Yusef Lateef:	*The Centaur & The Phoenix (Riverside)*
	This Is Our Music (Atlantic)	Booker Little:	*Out Front (Candid)*
	Free Jazz (Atlantic)	Charles Lloyd:	*Dream Weaver (Atlantic)*
John Coltrane:	*My Favourite Things (Atlantic)*	Bobby Hutcherson:	*Total Eclipse (Blue Note)*
	Impressions (Impulse)	Jackie McLean:	*Let Freedom Ring! (Blue Note)*
	Live At Birdland (Impulse)		*One Step Beyond (Blue Note)*

Herbie Mann:	*At The Village Gate (Atlantic)*
Charles Mingus:	*The Complete Candid Charles Mingus*
	(Mosaic)
	Pre-Bird (Mercury)
	Oh Yeah (Atlantic)
	The Black Saint & Sinner Lady (Impulse)
	Town Hall Concert (JWS/Fantasy)
	Mingus At Monterey (JWS/Fantasy)
Roscoe Mitchell:	*Sound (Delmark)*
Grachan Moncur 111:	*Some Other Stuff (Blue Note)*
	New Africa (Byg/Affinity)
Thelonious Monk:	*Monk Big Band In Concert (CBS)*
	It's Monk's Time (CBS)
	Monk (CBS)
Lee Morgan:	*Search For The New Land (Blue Note)*
	The Sidewinder (Blue Note)
New York Art Quartet:	*New York Art Quartet (ESP)*
Max Roach:	*Freedom Now! Suite (Candid)*
	Percussion Bitter Sweet (Impulse)
	Drums Unlimited (Atlantic)
	The Quartets With Jim Hall (RCA Bluebird)
Sonny Rollins:	*All The Things You Are (RCA Bluebird)*
	Our Man In Jazz (RCA)
	Alfie (Impulse)
	East Broadway Rundown (Impulse)
Roswell Rudd:	*Everywhere (Impulse)*
Pharoah Sanders:	*Tauhid (Impulse)*
	Thembi (Impulse)
Archie Shepp:	*Four For Trane (Impulse)*
	Fire Music (& More Fire Music) (Impulse)
	For Losers (Impulse)
	Kwanza (Impulse)
	Poem For Malcolm (Byg/Affinity)
	Blase (Byg/Affinity)
Wayne Shorter:	*Supernova (Blue Note)*
Sun Ra:	*Heliocentric Worlds of Vols 1 & 2 (ESP)*
	The Magic City (Saturn)
Cecil Taylor:	*Complete Candid Sessions (Mosaic)*
	Into The Hot (Impulse)
	Copenhagen 1962 Sessions (Freedom)
	Unit Structures (Blue Note)
	Conquistador (Blue Note)
	Silent Tongues (Freedom)

Chapter Nine

George Adams:	*Nightingale (Blue Note)*
Air:	*Air Lore (RCA Bluebird)*
Toshiko Akiyoshi:	*Tales Of A Courtesan (RCA)*
Art Ensemble of Chicago:	*Full Force (ECM)*
George Benson:	*Breezin' (WEA)*
Alvin Batiste:	*Musique d'Afrique Nouvelle Orleans (I.N.)*
Carla Bley:	*Escalator Over The Hill (Watt)*
	Live! (Watt)
Arthur Blythe:	*Light Blue (CBS)*
Anthony Braxton:	*In The Tradition Vols 1/2 (Steeplechase)*

Michael Brecker:	*Don't Try This At Home (MCA)*
Stanley Clarke:	*The Collection (Castle)*
Chick Corea:	*Piano Improvisations Vols 1/2 (ECM)*
	Return To Forever (ECM)
	My Spanish Heart (Polydor)
Larry Coryell:	*Toku Do (Muse)*
Miles Davis:	*In A Silent Way (CBS)*
	Bitches Brew (CBS)
	A Tribute To Jack Johnson (CBS)
	Live: Evil (CBS)
	Star People (CBS)
Deodato:	*Prelude (CTI)*
Gil Evans:	*The British Orchestra (Mole)*
Ricky Ford:	*Manhattan Blues (Candid)*
Bill Frisell:	*Strange Meeting (Antilles)*
Jan Garbarek:	*Dis (ECM)*
	Wayfarer (ECM)
	I Took Up The Runes (ECM)
Charlie Haden:	*Ballad of the Fallen (w. Carla Bley) (ECM)*
Scott Hamilton:	*Quintet In Concert (Concord)*
Herbie Hancock:	*Crossings (Warner)*
	Headhunters (CBS)
	VSOP Live (CBS)
	Rockit (CBS)
	Piano (Sony)
Freddie Hubbard:	*First Light (CTI)*
Bobby Hutcherson:	*The View From The Inside (Blue Note)*
	Colour Schemes (Landmark)
Abdullah Ibrahim:	*African Marketplace (WEA)*
	Water From An Ancient Well (Black Saint)
	Ekaya (Black Hawk)
Keith Jarrett:	*Facing You (ECM)*
	Somewhere Before (Vortex/WEA)
	The Koln Concert (ECM)
	Birth (Atlantic)
	Belonging (w. Jan Garbarek) (ECM)
	My Song (ECM)
	Changes (ECM)
Elvin Jones:	*Reunited (w. McCoy Tyner) (Black Hawk)*
Loose Tubes:	*Divine Precipice (Loose Tubes)*
John McLaughlin:	*Inner Mounting Flame (CBS)*
	Between Nothingness & Eternity (CBS)
	Shakti (CBS)
	Johnny McLaughlin, Electric Guitarist (CBS)
Albert Mangelsdorff:	*Trilogue – Live (MPS Jazz)*
Branford Marsalis:	*Royal Garden Blues (CBS)*
Wynton Marsalis:	*Marsalis Standard Time (CBS)*
	Think Of One (CBS)
Charles Mingus:	*Changes 1/2 (Atlantic)*
	Epitaph (as composer) (CBS)
Airto Moreira:	*Fingers (CTI)*
Alphonse Mouzon:	*Best Of (Black Sun)*
David Murray:	*3-D Family (Hat Hut)*
	Ming (Black Saint)
	Sweet Lovely (Black Saint)

bibliography

Hentoff/Shapiro: *Hear Me Talkin' To Ya (Rinehart)*
The New Grove Dictionary of Jazz (ed. Barry Kernfeld)
Carr/Priestley/Fairweather: *Jazz – The Essential Companion (Grafton)*
Gunther Schuller: *Early Jazz (OUP)*
Chris Albertson: *Bessie Smith: A Biography (Barrie & Jenkins)*
Burt Goldblatt: *Newport Jazz Festival (Dial Press)*
John Chilton: *Who's Who Of Jazz (MacMillan)*
Don Marquis: *In Search of Buddy Bolden*
Laurie Wright: *Joe 'King' Oliver (Storyville)*
Blesh/Janis: *They All Played Ragtime (Oak)*
Laurie Wright – *Mr Jelly Lord (Storyville)*
John Hammond: *John Hammond On Record (Ridge/Penguin)*
Eileen Southern – *The Music of Black Americans (Norton)*
Ethel Waters – *His Eye Is On The Sparrow (Jazz Book Club/W.H. Allen)*
Lewis Porter: *Lester Young (MacMillan)*
Louis Armstrong: *My Life In New Orleans (Peter Davies)*
Arnold Shaw: *Honkers And Shouters (Collier)*
LeRoi Jones: *Blues People (MacGibbon & Kee)*
A.B. Spellman – *Four Lives In The BeBop Business (Limelight Editions)*
Ross Russell: *Bird Lives! (Quartet)*
Ramsey & Smith: *Jazzmen (Limelight Editions)*
Sudhalter & Evans: *Bix – Man & Legend (Quartet)*

Ira Gitler: *Jazz Masters of The Forties (Collier)*
Mezz Mezzrow: *Really The Blues (Jazz Book Club/Secker & Warburg)*
Alan Lomax: *Mister Jelly Roll (Jazz Book Club/Cassell)*
Peter Gammond (ed): *Duke Ellington (Jazz Book Club/Phoenix House)*
Ulanov: *A History of Jazz in America (Viking Press)*
Linda Dahl: *Stormy Weather (Quartet)*
James Doran: *Erroll Garner (Scarecrow Press Inc)*
Ian Carr: *Miles Davis (Quartet)*
Brian Priestley: *Mingus – A Critical Biography (Quartet)*
John Chilton: *Sidney Bechet, Wizard of Jazz (MacMillan)*
Paul Oliver: *Screening The Blues (Da Capo)*
Paul Oliver (Ed): *The Blackwell Guide to Blues Records (Blackwell)*
Simosko/Tepperman: *Eric Dolphy – A Musical Biography (Smithsonian)*
Sidney Bechet: *Treat It Gentle (Jazz Book Club/Cassell)*
Maurice Waller: *Fats Waller (Cassell)*
Robert Gordon: *Jazz West Coast (Quartet)*

Thanks are due to Downbeat Magazine for permission to reprint a number of quotations from interviews first published in its pages.

Acknowledgements are also due to Rust, Jepsen and Ruppli in the discographical field, and without whom we'd all be lost.

index

acknowledgements

The Publishers wish to thank all those who loaned photographs for use in this book, in particular Frank Driggs, David Redfern and Val Wilmer.

Front cover photograph by Ed van der Elsken.

The Bettmann Archive: 6(br), 12(t,b), 13, 26/7, 32, 33, 34(l,r), 42(r), 44/5(b), 45(b), 46, 47(t,b), 48(tl,r), 50(b), 51(l), 54(t,bl), 63(r), 74, 82, 84(l), 97, 114(l), 116, 163(l), 164(b);
MGM/The Bettman Archive: 65(b);
UPI/Bettmann: 6(bl), 48(c), 70, 70/1, 75(t), 92/3(b), 106, 111(l), 120, 134;
UPI/Bettmann Newsphotos: 1(r), 36/7, 44/5(t), 49(l), 114(r), 165, 174/5;
Springer/Bettmann film archive: 90(t).
Dat's Jazz Picture Library: 143, 154(r).
Frank Driggs Collection: 14/15, 15(r), 18(t), 21, 26, 30(t,b), 51(c), 56/7, 58, 59, 64(r), 65(t), 66(r), 67, 73, 74/5, 76, 76/7, 83, 88, 89(tr,b), 94(l), 101(l), 116(c,r), 117, 162;
Daguerre Studios/Frank Driggs Collection: 31(b);
Charles Nadell/Frank Driggs Collection: 72(bl), 74/5.
E.M.I.: 81(l).
Nico van der Stam/Fotostock: 101(r), 131(l).
Hulton-Deutsch Collection/Bettmann: 29(l), 45(t), 53, 62, 159(r).
Peter Newark's American Pictures: 1(l), 6(c), 23, 79;
Peter Newark's Western Americana: 15(l), 16/17, 17, 60, 61, 63, 71
Redferns: 7, 103, 104 (all pictures), 119, 121, 124, 128, 129, 130, 133, 137, 139, 142/3, 144, 145(r), 146(t), 147(l,r), 148, 149(r), 150, 151(t,b), 152(l,r), 154(l), 170, 172(t,r), 173;

Beryl Bryden/Redferns: 163(r), 168;
William Gottlieb/Redferns: 20, 35(r), 52, 56(l,r), 68/9, 78, 80(r), 81(r), 96(l), 111(r), 112, 156/7, 158, 159(l), 160, 161(l,r), 164(t);
Tim Hall/Redferns: 7(cr), 155;
Max Jones Files/Redferns: 3, 10/11, 16, 18(b), 19, 22, 27, 28, 31(t), 36(l), 38/9, 41(b), 42(l), 42/3, 43, 55(br), 58(c), 72(tr), 80(l), 105, 113, 118, 164(r), 169;
Bev Baird/MJF/Redferns: 167;
Peter Carr/MJF/Redferns: 64(l);
Jazz Music Books/MJF/Redferns: 30/31;
Howard Lucraft/MJF/Redferns: 85, 100(l);
M.C.A./MJF/Redferns: 50(t);
Melody Maker/MJF/Redferns: 92;
Smalls/MJF/Redferns: 99;
Elliot Landy/Redferns: 137(r);
Andrew Puter/Redferns: 145(l), 149(l);
Charles Stewart/Redferns: 125, 126;
Bob Willoughby/Redferns: 84(r), 86/7, 89, 90(b), 91, 92/3, 95(l), 96(r), 110, 171.
Topham: 6(t), 14, 40, 49, 93, 95(r), 108/9, 166(r);
A.P./Topham: 166(l).
Val Wilmer: 7(cl,b), 24/5, 29(r), 51(r), 58(l), 98, 100, 102, 107(l), 115(l,r), 118(l), 119(b), 121(r), 122/3, 124(l), 127(l,r), 131(r), 132, 132/3, 133(l), 135(l,r), 136, 138(all pictures), 140/41(all pictures), 146(b), 153(t,b), 172(l);
James J. Kriegsmann/Val Wilmer: 102(r);
Marion Post/Val Wilmer 38;
Marion Post/F.S.A/Val Wilmer: 41(t).

The author has used a number of quotations from the following titles in his text: thanks are due to the publishers for permission to publish them.

Jazzmen: Ramsey and Smith (Harcourt Brace Jovanovich Inc., 1939); *Hear Me Talkin' To Ya*: Hentoff/Shapiro Peter Davis Ltd 1955); *My Life in New Orleans*: Louis Armstrong (Simon and Schuster, Inc., 1955); *Mister Jelly Roll*: Alan Lomax (Macmillan Publishing Co. Inc., 1956) *Really The Blues*: Mezz Mezzrow (Martin Secker and Warburg Ltd, 1959); *Duke Ellington:* ed. Peter Gammond (Phoenix House, 1959); *Four Lives in the BeBop Business*: A. B. Spellman (Pantheon Books, 1966); *Jazz Masters of the Forties*: Ira Gitler (Macmillan Publishing Company, 1966); *Bird Lives!*: Ross Russell (Quartet, 1972); *Bix - Man and Legend*: Sudhalter & Evans (Quartet, 1974); *Eric Dolphy - A Musical Biography*: Simosko/Tepperman (Smithsonian Institution Press, 1974); *John Hammond on Record* - John Hammond (Ridge/Penguin, 1977; the estate of John Hammond); *In Search of Buddy Bolden*: Don Marquis (Louisiana State University Press, 1978); *Honkers and Shouters*: Arnold Shaw (Macmillan Publishing Company, 1978); *Miles Davies*: Ian Carr (Quartet, 1982); *Mingus - A Critical Biography*: Brian Priestly (Quartet, 1982); *Lester Young*: Lewis Porter (G. K. Hall & Company, 1985); *Joe 'King' Oliver*: Laurie Wright (Story Ville Publications, 1987); *Sidney Bechet, Wizard of Jazz*: John Chilton (Macmillan, 1987).

Extract from *The Joint is Jumpin'* by Thomas 'Fats' Waller, Andy Razaf and J.C. Johnson is reproduced with the permission of Dorsey Brothers Music Ltd/Redwood Music Ltd, London, England.
Lyrics of *Stones in my Passway* by Robert Johnson - Horoscope MusicPublishing Co.
Lyrics of *I Do Blues* by Robert Wilkins - Wynwood Music Co. Inc.

These acknowlegements were correct to the best of the publisher's knowledge at the time of going to press.